# Guide to
# Tanzania

## 2nd edition

## Philip Briggs

Bradt Publications, UK
The Globe Pequot Press Inc, USA

First published in 1993 by Bradt Publications.
Second edition published in 1996 by
Bradt Publications, 41 Nortoft Road, Chalfont St Peter, Bucks SL9 0LA, England.
Published in the USA by The Globe Pequot Press Inc, 6 Business Park Road,
PO Box 833, Old Saybrook, Connecticut 06475-0833.

**British Library Cataloguing in Publication Data**
A catalogue record for this book is available from the British Library
ISBN 1 898323 36 4

**Library of Congress Cataloging-in-Publication Data**
Briggs, Philip.
    Guide to Tanzania / Philip Briggs. — 2nd ed.
        p. cm. — (Bradt guides)
    ISBN 0-7627-0013-0
    1. Tanzania—Guidebooks.  2. Safaris—Tanzania—Guidebooks.
    3. National parks and reserves—Tanzania—Guidebooks.  I. Title.
    II. Series.
DT437.7.B75    1996
916.7804'4—dc20                                    96-26688
                                                                   CIP

**Cover photographs** *Front:* Lioness and cub (Tom Murphy, Woodfall Wild Images);
*Back:* Elephant (Mike Powles, Woodfall Wild Images).
**Photographs** Philip Briggs (PB), Ariadne van Zandbergen (AVZ),
Catherine Harlow (CH), Nick Garbutt (NG)
**Illustrations** Sarah Elder
**Maps** *Inside covers*: Steve Munns    *Others*: Hans van Well

Typeset from the author's disc by Patti Taylor, London NW10 1JR
Printed and bound in Great Britain by The Guernsey Press Co Ltd

# ACKNOWLEDGEMENTS

For their help in compiling the first edition of this guide, my ongoing gratitude to Laura Grant, Beyers Bezuidenhout, Anthony Briggs, Dr Alan Tye, Charlotte Uhlerbroek, Msafori Allan Shomari, the staff of Hoopoe Adventure Tours, Kelvin Moody, Steven Bell, Howard Geech, Dr Jane Wilson Howarth, David Else, and the countless Tanzanians who helped me out in various small ways.

For their contribution to my research of the second edition, thanks to Terri Rice of Hoopoe Adventure Tours; Godfrey Kiwia, our driver/guide on safari; Jacinta Agbara of Uganda Airways, Isa Shwartz of Interair; Sandy Evans of Abercrombie and Kent; Bill McKinnon of Serengeti Balloon Safaris; Ian Jones of the Sopa Lodge group; Suleiman Madjapa and Leopold Kabendera of TAHI; the management of Lobo and Seronera Wildlife Lodges; Winnie Lawoko Olwe of the Dar es Salaam Sheraton; Mr P J Mshanga of the Ngorongoro Conservation Authority, the Director and Assistant Director of Tanzania National Parks; David Else; Ebbe Nordho; Stig Johanson; Julian Bayliss; Iain Jackson; Dr Peter Stephenson; James Tice; Christopher Jerram; Peter Moore; Siobhan Blaschek; Peter Ede; Nicholas McWilliam; Geert Clauwaert; Steve and Helen Winchester; Simon and Orit Marriot; Peter Gubbins and Dr Bernard Leeman.

On a personal note, thanks and love to Sean and Litziko for giving me a bed and a place to work in London, where I wrote most of this update edition. And boundless love and gratitude to Ariadne, my travelling companion throughout my 1996 trip through Tanzania.

# TANZANIA

## CHAPTERS & RESERVES

## KEY TO PARKS & GAME RESERVES

1. Rubondo Island N.P.
2. Biharamulo G.R.
3. Serengeti N.P.
4. Maswa G.R.
5. Ngorongoro Conservation Area
6. Arusha N.P.
7. Kilimanjaro N.P.
8. Mkomazi G.R.
9. Sadani G.R.
10. Mikumi N.P.
11. Selous G.R.
12. Udzunqwa Mountains N.P.
13. Runqwa G.R.
14. Ruaha N.P.
15. Uwanda G.R.
16. Katavi N.P.
17. Mahale Mountains N.P.
18. Gombe Stream N.P.
19. Ugalla River N.P.
20. Moyowosi G.R.
21. Kigosi G.R.
22. Lake Manyara N.P.
23. Tarangire N.P.

## KEY TO CHAPTERS

5. Dar es Salaam
6. The North Coast and Usambara Mountains
7. Kilimanjaro
8. Northern Safari Circuit
9. Western Tanzania
10. Southern Highlands & Nyasa
11. Tanzam Highway and Southern Reserves
12. The South Coast
15. Zanzibar

# CONTENTS

# Introduction

It would be easy to reduce an introduction to Tanzania to a list of statistics: it contains Africa's highest mountain, most famous national park and largest game reserve, while along its borders lie the three largest lakes on the continent. It would be just as easy to reduce Tanzania to a list of evocative place names: Zanzibar, Kilimanjaro, Serengeti, Dar es Salaam, Ngorongoro Crater, Olduvai Gorge, Gombe Stream, Lake Victoria...

Put simply, Tanzania embodies the Africa you have always dreamed of: vast plains teeming with wild animals, rainforests alive with cackling birds and monkeys, Kilimanjaro's snow-capped peaks rising dramatically above the surrounding flat scrubland, colourful Maasai herding their cattle alongside herds of grazing wildebeest, and perfect palm-lined beaches lapped by the clear warm waters of the Indian Ocean stretching as far as the eye can see. Almost 25% of the country is given over to conservation, protecting an estimated 20% of Africa's large mammals.

You might expect a country that can be described in such superlative terms to be crawling with tourists, but in the 1980s Tanzania attracted a fraction of the tourism of countries like Kenya, South Africa and more recently Zimbabwe. This was for a variety of reasons: an underfunded and underdeveloped tourist infrastructure, a reputation for corruption and bureaucracy, persistent food and fuel shortages, poor roads and inefficient public transport, and a lack of exposure. This is changing, however, and what started off as a trickle of tourism in the late 1980s could soon become a flood. New hotels are being built, main roads have been re-surfaced, trains and ferries run on time, shortages are a thing of the past, and in our experience you couldn't hope to meet more agreeable officials anywhere.

For the average fly-in, fly-out tourist, Kilimanjaro, Zanzibar and the Serengeti are justification enough to visit Tanzania. For the adventurous traveller who is prepared to put up with basic accommodation and slow transport and who is prepared to learn a bit of KiSwahili, the national language, it is one of the most challenging, rewarding and fascinating countries in Africa. Virtually anywhere south of the Dar es Salaam-Mwanza railway line is miles from any beaten tourist track – except for Kigoma and Mbeya, both important junctions for overlanders, we spent two months in this part of Tanzania without seeing another traveller.

When you spend a long time in a country, your feelings towards it are determined as much by the people who live there as by the sights you see. My affection for Tanzania is greater than for any other African country I have visited. It is an oasis of peace and egalitarian values in a continent stoked up with political and tribal tensions, and its social mood embodies all that I respect in African culture. I found Tanzanians to be polite and courteous, yet also warm and genuine, both amongst themselves and in their dealings with foreigners.

Enjoy Tanzania. It's a wonderful country.

# NOTES

## Swahili names
In KiSwahili, a member of a tribal group is given an m- prefix, the tribe itself gets a wa- prefix and the language gets a ki- prefix (for example, an Mgogo person is a member of the wagogo who speak kigogo). The wa- prefix is commonly but erratically used in English books; the m- and ki- prefixes are rarely used, except in the case of KiSwahili. There are no apparent standards; in many books the Swahili are referred to as just the Swahili while non-Swahili tribes get the wa-prefix. I have decided to drop all these prefixes: it seems as illogical to refer to non-Swahili people by their KiSwahili name when you are writing in English as it would be to refer to the French by their English name in a German book. I have, however, referred to the Swahili language as KiSwahili on occasion.

## Lake Nyasa/Malawi
Many readers may not realise that Lake Nyasa and Lake Malawi are one and the same. Nyasa was the colonial name for the lake, just as Nyasaland was the colonial name for what is now the country of Malawi. For historical reasons, the name Nyasa has been retained in Tanzania and it is used both officially and casually; if you ask a Tanzanian about Lake Malawi they will either look at you blankly or tell you to go to Malawi. Despite the initial confusion it may cause, for the purposes of this guide I have referred to the lake as Lake Nyasa.

## Some words you might wonder about...
There are a few terms that crop up occasionally in the text which you might not know. Some are explained elsewhere, but this is as good a place as any to put them all together. *Koppie* (or *kopje*) is an Afrikaans word which in East Africa is used to refer to a small free-standing hill such as those which dot the Serengeti Plains. A *Hoteli* is a local restaurant. *Miombo* and *Acacia* are types of woodland; the first dominated by broad-leaved trees belonging to a variety of families, the second dominated by thorny, thin-leaved trees of the acacia family. The *Cichlids* are a family of colourful fish found in the Rift Valley lakes. A *banda* is a hut.

# Part One

Chapter One

# Background Information

## FACTS AND FIGURES

### Location

The United Republic of Tanzania was formed in 1964 when Tanganyika on the African mainland united with the offshore island state of Zanzibar.

Tanzania lies on the east African coast between 1° and 11°45' south, and 29°20' and 40°35' east. It is bordered by Kenya and Uganda to the north; Rwanda, Burundi and Zaire to the west, and Zambia, Malawi and Mozambique to the south.

### Size

Tanzania covers an area of 945,166km² (364,929 square miles). It is one of the largest countries in sub-Saharan Africa, larger than Kenya and Uganda combined. To put it in a European context, Tanzania is about 4½ times the size of Britain; in an American context, it's about 1½ times the size of Texas.

### Capital

Dodoma is now the official capital of Tanzania, displacing Dar es Salaam.

### Population

The total population of Tanzania is about 28 million (1992 estimate), of which roughly 600,000 live on Zanzibar. Apart from the towns the most densely populated areas tend to be the highlands, especially those around Lake Nyasa and Kilimanjaro.

There are estimated to be 120 linguistic groups in Tanzania. None exceeds 10% of the country's total population. The most numerically significant groups are the Sukoma of Lake Victoria, the Hehe of Iringa, the Gogo of Dodoma, the Chagga of Kilimanjaro and the Nyamwezi of Tabora.

## Government
The ruling party of Tanzania since independence has been Chama Cha Mapinduzi (CCM). Up until 1995, Tanzania was a one-party state, under the presidency of Julius Nyerere and, after his retirement in 1985, Ali Hassan Mwinyi. Tanzania held its first multi-party election in late 1995, when the CCM was returned to power with an overwhelming majority.

## Major towns
Dar es Salaam is far and away the largest town in Tanzania, with a population of around 1.5 million. Other important towns, in rough order of size, are Mwanza, Tanga, Arusha, Mbeya, Dodoma, Zanzibar Town, Mtwara, Moshi, Tabora, Kigoma, Songea, Lindi and Iringa.

## Economy
After independence Tanzania became one of the most staunchly socialist countries in Africa, but since the mid-1980s there has been a swing to free market systems. Tanzania is considered to be one of the five poorest countries in the world, with a per capita GNP of US$150 (1990). Less than 10% of the workforce is in formal employment; most Tanzanians have a subsistence lifestyle. The country's major exports are coffee, cotton, cashew nuts, sisal, tobacco, tea and diamonds. Zanzibar and Pemba are important clove producers. Gold, tin and coal are also mined.

## Languages
KiSwahili and English are the official languages. Little English is spoken outside of the larger towns, but KiSwahili is spoken by most Tanzanians.

## Currency
The unit of currency is the Tanzanian Shilling (pronounced *Shillingi*), which is divided into 100 cents. The rate of exchange in early 1996 was around US$1.00 = Tsh 550.

## Climate
Most of Tanzania has a tropical climate, but there are large regional variations. The coastal belt and the Lake Nyasa and Tanganyika areas are hot and humid, with little relief at night. The rest of the interior is hot and dry, cooling down significantly at night. Highlands such as Kilimanjaro, Ngorongoro and the various mountain ranges of eastern Tanzania are generally warm during the day and cold at night.

Tanzania is too near the equator to experience a recognisable summer and winter. The months between October and April are marginally hotter than May to September. In Dar es Salaam, for instance, the hottest month is March (average maximum 32°C; average minimum 23°C), and the coolest month is July (28°C; 18°C).

Virtually all of Tanzania's rain falls between November and May. The division of this period into short rains (November to December) and long rains (March to May) only applies to coastal areas and the extreme north around Arusha and Lake Victoria, where there is relatively little rainfall in January and February. Available figures suggest that rain falls fairly consistently between mid-November and mid-April in other parts of the country.

## Geography

The bulk of East Africa is made up of a vast, flat plateau rising from a narrow coastal belt to an average height of about 1,500m. This plateau is broken dramatically by the 20 million year old Great Rift Valley, which cuts a trough up to 2,000m deep through the African continent from the Dead Sea to Mozambique.

The main branch of the Rift Valley bisects Tanzania. A western branch of the rift valley forms the Tanzania-Zaire border. Lakes Natron, Manyara, Eyasi and Nyasa-Malawi are all in the main rift, Lake Tanganyika lies in the western branch, and Lake Victoria lies on an elevated plateau between them.

East Africa's highest mountains are volcanic in origin, created by the same forces which caused the Rift Valley. Kilimanjaro is the most recent of these: it started to form about one million years ago, and was still growing as recently as 100,000 years ago. Mount Meru is older. Ngorongoro Crater is the collapsed caldera of a volcano that would once have been as high as Kilimanjaro is today. The only active volcano in Tanzania, Ol Doinyo Lengai, lies a short way north of Ngorongoro.

## HISTORY

Tanzania's rich and fascinating history is also highly elusive. For a non-historian such as myself, unravelling it is a frustrating process. Specialist works often contradict each other to such an extent it is difficult to tell where fact ends and speculation begins, while broader or more popular accounts are riddled with obvious inaccuracies. This is partly because there are huge gaps in the known facts; partly because much of the available information is scattered in out-of-print or difficult-to-find books; partly because once an inaccuracy gets into print it becomes true, and spreads like a virus. For whatever reason, there is not, so far as I am aware, one concise and reliable account of Tanzanian history that is readily available to the layman.

I have tried to make the following account as comprehensive as possible while still keeping it readable. It is, to the best of my knowledge, as accurate as the known facts will allow, but at times I have had to decide for myself the most probable truth amongst a mass of contradictions, and I have speculated freely where speculation seems to be the order of the day. My goals are to stimulate the visitor's interest in Tanzanian history, and to give them easy access to information that would have enhanced our trip greatly.

## Pre-history of the interior

It is widely agreed that the evolution and early history of humanity were played out on the savannahs of East and southern Africa. The hominid (proto-human) evolutionary chain split from that of the pongoid apes (whose modern representatives include chimpanzee and gorilla) about 20 million years ago. Two hominid genera are recognised: *australopithecus* and *homo. Australopithecus* is unlikely to have been a direct ancestor of modern man; it lived contemporaneously with *homo* until about one million years ago.

A 1.75 million year old skull found by Mary Leakey at Olduvai Gorge in Tanzania in 1957 was the first to confirm man's great antiquity and Africa as the probable site of human evolution. Since then further skulls have been found at a number of sites in East Africa. The oldest known hominid skull, found in Namibia in 1991, is about 12 million years old.

The immediate ancestor of modern man, *homo erectus,* first appeared about 1.5 million years ago. *Homo erectus* was the first hominid to surmount the barrier of the Sahara and spread into Europe and Asia, and is credited with the discovery of fire and the first use of stone tools and recognisable speech.

Although modern man, *homo sapiens*, has been around for at least half a million years, only in the last 10,000 years have the African races recognised today more or less taken their modern form. Up until about 1,000BC, East Africa was exclusively populated by hunter-gatherers, similar in physiology, culture and language to the Khoisan (or bushmen) of southern Africa. Rock art accredited to the Khoisan is found throughout East Africa, most notably in the Kondoa-Irangi region of Tanzania near Lake Eyasi, home of the Hadza, the only remaining Tanzanian hunter-gatherers.

The pastoralist and agriculturalist lifestyles which emerged on the Nile Delta in about 5,000BC had spread to various parts of sub-Saharan Africa by 2,000BC, most notably to the Cushitic-speaking people of the Ethiopian highlands and the Bantu-speakers of West Africa. Cushitic-speakers first drifted into Tanzania in about 1,000BC, closely followed by Bantu-speakers. Familiar with iron-age technology, these migrants would have soon dominated the local hunter-gatherers. By

1,000AD, most of Tanzania was populated by Bantu-speakers, with Cushitic-speaking pockets in areas such as the Ngorongoro highlands.

There is no detailed information about the Tanzanian interior prior to 1500, and even after that details are sketchy. Except for the Lake Victoria region, which by then supported large authoritarian kingdoms similar to those in Uganda, much of the Tanzanian interior is too dry to support large concentrations of people. In most of Tanzania, an informal system of *ntemi* chiefs emerged. The *ntemi* system, though structured, seems to have been flexible and benevolent. The chiefs were served by a council and performed a role that was as much advisory as it was authoritarian. By the 19th Century there are estimated to have been more than 200 *ntemi* chiefs in western and central Tanzania, each with about 1,000 subjects.

The *ntemi* system was shattered when southern Tanzania was invaded by Ngoni exiles from what is now the Natal province of South Africa. In Natal, the leader of the small Zulu clan, Chaka, had melded a giant kingdom from the surrounding clans using revolutionary military tactics based on horseshoe formations and a short-stabbing spear. By 1830, his marauding troops had either killed, incorporated or driven away most of the other tribes in the region. The exiled tribes swept northwards, taking with them Chaka's methods, and they in turn wreaked havoc over much of southern Africa, slaughtering existing tribes in order to take their land.

The Ngoni entered southern Tanzania in about 1840. They attacked resident tribes, destroying communities and leaving survivors no option but to turn to banditry. Their tactics were observed and adopted by the more astute *ntemi* chiefs, who needed to protect themselves, but had to forge larger kingdoms to do so. The situation was exacerbated by the growing presence of Arab slave traders. Tribes controlling the areas that caravan routes went through were able to extract taxes from the slavers and to find work with them as porters or organising slave raids. This situation was exploited by several chiefs, most notably Mirambo, who dominated the interior between about 1840 and 1880.

## The coast to 1800

There have been links between the Tanzanian coast and the rest of the world for millennia, but only the barest sketch is possible of events before 1,000AD.

The ancient Egyptians believed their ancestors came from a southerly land called Punt. In about 2,500BC an explorer called Sahare sailed there. He returned laden with ivory, ebony, and myrrh, which suggests he landed somewhere on the East African coast. There is no suggestion that Egypt traded regularly with Punt, but they did visit it again. Interestingly, an engraving of the Queen of Punt, made after an expedition in 1493BC, shows her to have distinctly Khoisan features.

The Phoenicians first explored the coast in about 600BC. According to the 1st-Century *Periplus of the Ancient Sea* they traded with a town called Rhapta. This is thought to have been on the Tanzanian coast, at a major estuary such as that of the Pangani or Rufiji.

Bantu-speakers arrived at the coast about 2,000 years ago. It seems likely they had trade links with the Roman Empire: Rhapta gets a namecheck in Ptolemy's 4th-Century *Geography* and a few 4th-Century Roman coins have been found at the coast. The fact that the Romans knew of Kilimanjaro and the great lakes raises some interesting questions. One suggestion is that the coastal Bantu-speakers were running trade routes into the interior and that these collapsed at the same time as the Roman Empire, presumably because there was no longer anyone with whom they could trade. The idea is attractive and plausible, but the evidence seems rather flimsy. The Romans could simply have gleaned the information from Bantu-speakers who had arrived at the coast recently enough to have some knowledge of the interior.

Historians have a clearer picture of events on the coast from about 1,000AD onwards. By this time, trade between the coast and the Persian Gulf was well established. The earliest known Islamic buildings on the coast, on Manda Island off Kenya, have been dated to the 9th Century AD. Items sold to Arab ships included ivory, ebony and various spices, while a variety of Oriental and Arabic goods were imported for the use of wealthy traders.

The coastal trade was dominated by gold, almost certainly mined in the Great Zimbabwe region. It arrived at the coast at Sofala, in modern-day Mozambique, probably via the Zambezi Valley, and was then transported by local traders to Mogadishu, where it was sold to the Arabs. The common assumption that Swahili language and culture was a direct result of Arab traders mixing with local Bantu speakers is probably inaccurate. KiSwahili is a Bantu language. It spread along the coast in the 11th Century; most of the Arab words which have entered it did so *after* this. The driving force behind a common coastal language and culture was almost certainly internal trade between Sofala and Mogadishu.

More than 30 Swahili city-states were operating between the 13th and 15th Centuries, a large number of which were in modern-day Tanzania. This period is known as the Shirazi Era after the sultans who ruled these city-states, most of whom claimed descent from the Shiraz region of Persia. Each city-state had its own sultan; they rarely interfered in each other's business. The Islamic faith was widespread during this period, and many Arabic influences crept into coastal architecture. Cities were centred around a Great Mosque, normally constructed in rock and coral.

Many Arabs settled on the coast before and during the Shirazi Era. For a long time it has been assumed they controlled the trade, but this has been questioned in recent years. Contemporary descriptions of the city-states suggest they were predominantly populated by Africans. It is possible that African traders claimed Shirazi descent in order to boost their standing, both locally and with Shirazi ships.

In the mid-13th Century, probably due to improvements in Arab navigation and ship construction, the centre of the gold trade moved from Mogadishu to the small island of Kilwa. Kilwa represented the peak of the Shirazi period. It had a population of 10,000 and operated its own mint, the first in sub-Saharan Africa. The multi-domed mosque on Kilwa was the largest and most splendid on all the coast, while another building, now known as *Husuni Kubwa*, was a gargantuan palace, complete with audience courts, several ornate balconies, and even a swimming pool. Kilwa is discussed more fully in *Chapter Twelve.*

Although Kilwa had been superseded in importance by Mombasa by the end of the 15th century, coastal trade was still booming. It came to an abrupt halt in 1505 when Mombasa was captured by the Portuguese and several other coastal towns, Kilwa included, were ransacked. Under Portuguese control the gold trade collapsed and the coast stagnated. In 1698, Fort Jesus, the Portuguese centre in Mombasa, was overthrown by Arabs from Oman. Rivalries between the Omani and the old Shirazi dynasties soon surfaced. In 1728, a group of Shirazi sultans went so far as to conspire with their old oppressors, the Portuguese, to overthrow Fort Jesus, but the Omani re-captured it a year later. For the next 100 years an uneasy peace gripped the coast, nominally under Omani rule but dominated in economic terms by the Shirazi Sultan of Mombasa.

## Slavery and exploration in the 19th century

The 19th century was a period of rapid change in Tanzania, with stronger links established between the coast and the interior as well as between East Africa and Europe.

The decisive figure in the first half of the century was Seyyid Said, the Sultan of Muscat from 1804 to 1854. Britain had signed a treaty with Said's father, and in the wake of the Napoleonic wars did not want to see the coast fall into French hands. In 1827, Said's small but efficient navy captured Mombasa and effectively took control of the coast. It is debatable whether this would have happened without British support.

Said chose Zanzibar as his East African base because of its proximity to Bagamoyo, which had been the terminus of a caravan route to Lake

Tanganyika since 1823. Said's commercial involvement with Zanzibar began in 1827 when he set up clove plantations with scant regard for the land claims of local inhabitants. By 1840, when he moved his capital from Muscat to Zanzibar, commerce on the island was dominated by Said and his fellow Arabs.

The extent of the East African slave trade prior to 1827 is unclear. It certainly existed, but was never as important as the gold or ivory trade. The traditional centre of slave trading was West Africa, but trade there had recently been stopped by the British, leaving the way open for Said and his cronies. By 1839, over 40,000 slaves were being sold from Zanzibar annually. These came from two sources: the central caravan route between Bagamoyo and the Lake Tanganyika region, and a southern route between Kilwa Kivinje and Lake Nyasa.

The effects of the slave trade on the interior were numerous. The Nyamwezi of the Tabora region and the Yua of Nyasa became very powerful by serving as porters along the caravan routes and organising slave raids and ivory hunts. Weaker tribes were devastated. Villages were ransacked; the able-bodied men and women were taken away while the young and old were left to die. Hundreds of thousands of slaves were sold in the mid-19th Century, and no-one knows how many more died of disease or exhaustion between being captured and reaching the coast.

The slave trade was the driving force behind the second great expansion of KiSwahili. This became the *lingua franca* along caravan routes.

Europeans knew little about the African interior in 1850. The first Europeans to see Kilimanjaro (Rebmann, 1846) and Mount Kenya (Krapf, 1849) were ridiculed for their reports of snow on the equator. Arab traders must have had an intimate knowledge of parts of the interior, but no-one seems to have thought to ask them. In 1855, a German missionary, James Erhardt, produced a map of Africa based on third-hand Arab accounts. This showed a large slug-shaped lake in the heart of the continent. Known as the slug map, it fanned interest in a mystery that had tickled geographers since Roman times – the source of the Nile.

The men most responsible for opening up the East African interior to Europeans were Richard Burton, John Speke and David Livingstone, and later Henry Stanley. In 1858, on a quest for the source of the Nile funded by the Royal Geographical Society, Burton and Speke were the first Europeans to see Lake Tanganyika. Later that year, while Burton recovered from fever in Tabora, Speke was the first European to set eyes on Lake Victoria. Speke returned to the northern shore of Victoria in 1863 and concluded that Ripon Falls (near to modern-day

Jinja in Uganda) was the Nile's source. Burton, perhaps the most forceful and intelligent of all the 19th-Century explorers, ridiculed this conclusion. In 1864, on the eve of a public debate on the subject between the two men, Speke died of a self-inflicted gunshot wound. His death was described by the coroner as a shooting accident, but it seems likely he killed himself deliberately.

David Livingstone came from a poor Scots background. He left school at the age of ten, but educated himself to become a missionary. He arrived in the Cape in 1841 to work in the Kuruman Mission, but – overcome by the enormity of the task of converting Africa to Christianity – he decided he would be of greater service opening up the continent so that other missionaries could follow. Livingstone was the first European to cross the Kalahari Desert, the first to cross Africa from west to east and the first to see Victoria Falls. In the same year Speke and Burton saw Lakes Tanganyika and Victoria, Livingstone stumbled across Africa's third great lake, Nyasa.

Like most explorers of his time, Livingstone was obsessed by the Nile issue. Nevertheless, he had ample opportunity to witness the slave caravans at first hand. Sickened by what he saw – the human bondage, the destruction of entire villages, and the corpses abandoned by the traders – he became an outspoken critic of the trade. He believed the only way to curb it was to open up Africa to the three C's: Christianity, Commerce and Civilisation. Though not an imperialist by nature, Livingstone had seen enough of the famine and misery caused by the slavers and the Ngoni in the Nyasa area to believe the only solution was for Britain to colonise East Africa.

In 1867, Livingstone set off from Mikindani to spend the last six years of his life wandering between the great lakes making notes on the slave trade and trying to settle the Nile debate. He believed the source of the Nile to be Lake Benguela (in northern Zambia), from which the mighty Lualaba River flowed. In 1872, he was found at Ujiji by Henry Stanley, an American journalist and explorer. Stanley's alleged greeting, "Dr Livingstone, I presume", comprise probably the most famous words spoken in Africa. Livingstone died near Lake Benguela in 1873. His heart was removed and buried by his porters, who then carried his cured body over 1,500km to Bagamoyo.

Livingstone's quest to end the slave trade met with little success during his lifetime, but his death and highly emotional funeral at Westminster Abbey seem to have acted as a catalyst. Missions were built in his name all over the Nyasa region, while industrialists such as William Mackinnon and the Muir brothers invested in schemes to open Africa to commerce (which Livingstone had always believed was the key to putting the slavers out of business).

In the year Livingstone died, John Kirk was made the British Consul in Zanzibar. Kirk had travelled with Livingstone on his 1856-62 trip to Nyasa. Deeply affected by what he saw, he had since spent years on Zanzibar hoping to find a way to end the slave trade. In 1873, the British navy blockaded the island and Kirk offered Sultan Barghash full protection against foreign powers if he banned the slave trade. Barghash agreed. The slave market was closed and an Anglican Church built over it. The trade continued on the mainland for some years – 12,000 slaves were sold at Kilwa in 1875 – but that too was stopped.

The slave trade continued on a small scale well into the 20th Century and was only fully eradicated in 1918, four years after the British took control of Tanganyika. Within ten years of Livingstone's death, however, the volume was a fraction of what it had been in the 1860s. Caravans reverted to ivory as their principal trade, while many of the coastal traders started up rubber and sugar plantations, which turned out to be just as lucrative as their former trade.

In 1875, Henry Stanley resolved the Nile issue. Lake Benguela was the source of a large river all right, but it was the Congo. Speke had been right all along.

## The partitioning of East Africa

The so-called scramble for Africa was entered into with mixed motives, erratic enthusiasm and an almost total lack of premeditation by the powers involved. Britain already enjoyed a degree of influence on Zanzibar which amounted to informal colonialism and it was quite happy to maintain this mutually agreeable relationship. The government of the time, led by Lord Salisbury, was opposed to the taking of African colonies.

The scramble was initiated by two events. The first, the decision of King Leopold of Belgium to colonise the Congo Basin, had little direct bearing on events in Tanzania. The partitioning of East Africa was a direct result of an about-face by the German Premier, Bismarck, who had previously shown no enthusiasm for acquiring colonies. Germany probably only developed an interest in Africa in the hope of acquiring pawns to use in negotiations with Britain and France.

In 1884, a young German metaphysician called Carl Peters arrived inauspiciously in Zanzibar, then made his way to the mainland to sign a series of treaties with local chiefs. The authenticity of these treaties is questionable, but when Bismarck announced claims to a large area between the Pangani and Rufiji Rivers, it was enough to set the British government into a mild panic. Britain had plans to expand the Sultanate of Zanzibar, its informal colony, to include the fertile lands around Kilimanjaro. Worse, large parts of the area claimed by Germany were already part of the Sultanate. Not only was Britain morally bound to protect these, it also did not want to surrender control of Zanzibar's annual import-export turnover of two million pounds.

Despite pressure put on the British government by John Kirk, angry that his promises to Barghash would not be honoured, there was little option but to negotiate with Germany. A partition was agreed in 1886, identical to the modern border between Kenya and Tanzania. You may read that Kilimanjaro was part of the British territory before Queen Victoria gave it to her cousin, the Kaiser, as a birthday present. This amusing story was possibly dreamed up by a Victorian satirist to reflect the arbitrariness of the scramble. It is a complete fabrication.

In April 1888, the Sultan of Zanzibar unwillingly agreed to lease Germany the coastal strip south of the Umba River. Germany mandated this area to Carl Peters' German East Africa Company (GEAC), which placed agents at most coastal settlements north of Dar es Salaam. These agents demanded heavy taxes from traders and were encouraged to behave high-handedly in their dealings with locals.

The GEAC's honeymoon was short. Emil Zalewski, the Pangani agent, ordered the Sultan's representative, the Wali, to report to him. When the Wali refused, Zalewski had him arrested and sent away on a German warboat. In September 1888, an uprising against the GEAC was led by a sugar plantation owner called Abushiri Ibn Salim. Except at Dar es Salaam and Bagamoyo, both protected by German warboats, GEAC agents were either killed or driven away. A horde of 20,000 men gathered on the coast, including 6,000 Shambaa who refused to relinquish their right to claim tax from caravans passing the Usambara. In November, the mission at Dar es Salaam was attacked. Three priests were killed and the rest captured. The coast was in chaos until April 1889 when the Kaiser's troops invaded Abushiri's camp and forced him to surrender. The German government hanged Abushiri in Pangani; they withdrew the GEAC's mandate and banned Peters from ever setting foot in the area.

The 1886 agreement only created the single line of partition north of Kilimanjaro. By 1890, Germany had claimed an area north of Witu, including Lamu, and there was concern in Britain that they might try to claim the rich agricultural land around Lake Victoria, thereby surrounding Britain's territory. Undeterred by the debacle at Pangani (and with a nod and a wink from Bismarck), Carl Peters decided to force the issue. He slipped through Lamu and in May 1890, after a murderous jaunt across British territory, he signed a treaty with the King of Buganda entitling Germany to most of what is now southern Uganda. This time, however, Peters' plans were frustrated. Bismarck had resigned in March of the same year and his replacement, Von Kaprivi, wanted to maintain good relations with Salisbury's government. In any case, Henry Stanley had signed a similar treaty with the Buganda when he passed through the area in 1888 on his way from rescuing the Emin Pasha in Equatoria.

Germany had its eye on Heligoland, a small but strategic North Sea island that had been seized by Britain from Denmark in 1807. To some extent, German interest in Africa had always been related to the bargaining power it would give them in Europe. In 1890, Salisbury and Von Kaprivi knocked out an agreement which created the borders of Tanzania as they are today (with the exception of modern-day Burundi and Rwanda, German territory until after World War I). In exchange for an island less than 1km² in area, Salisbury was guaranteed protectorateship over Zanzibar and handed the German block north of Witu, and Germany relinquished any claims it might have had to what are today Uganda and Malawi.

## German East Africa

The period of German rule was not a happy one. In 1891, Carl Peters was appointed governor. Peters had already proved himself an unsavoury and unsympathetic character: he boasted freely of enjoying killing Africans and – under the guise of the GEAC – his lack of diplomacy had already instigated one uprising.

The 1890s were plagued by a series of natural disasters. A rinderpest epidemic at the start of the decade was followed by an outbreak of smallpox and a destructive plague of locusts. A series of droughts brought famine and disease in their wake. Many previously settled areas reverted to bush, causing the spread of tsetse fly and sleeping sickness. The population of Tanganyika is thought to have decreased significantly between 1890 and 1914.

It took Peters a decade to gain full control of the colony. The main area of conflict was in the vast central plateau where, led by Mkwawa, the Hehe had become the dominant tribe. In 1891, the Hehe ambushed a German battalion led by Emil Zalewski. They killed or wounded more than half Zalewski's men, and made off with his armoury. Mkwawa fortified his capital near Iringa, but it was razed by the Germans in 1894. Mkwawa was forced to resort to guerrilla tactics, which he used with some success. In 1898, Mkwawa shot himself rather than face capture.

Germany was determined to make the colony self-sufficient. Sugar and rubber were well established on parts of the coast; coffee was planted in the Kilimanjaro region, a major base for settlers; and cotton grew well around Lake Victoria. The colony's leading crop export, sisal, was grown throughout the rest of the country. In 1902, Peters decided that the southeast should be given over to cotton plantations. This was an ill-considered move: the soils were not right for the crop and the scheme was bound to cause great hardship.

The people of the southeast had suffered throughout the 19th Century and distrusted outsiders. They had been terrorised by the notoriously cruel Kilwa slavers and suffered regular raids by the Ngoni; the cotton scheme, which created back-breaking work for little financial return, was the final straw. In 1905, a prophet called Kinjikitile discovered a spring which spouted out magic water. He claimed that bullets fired at anyone who had been sprinkled with this water would have no effect. His messengers carried the water to people throughout the region; by August 1905 the entire southeast was ready to rise against the Germans.

The Maji-Maji (water-water) Rebellion began in Kinjikitile's village in the Mutumbi hills near Kilwa. The house of the German agent in Kibatu was burnt down, as was a nearby Asian trading centre. Troops from the regional headquarters at Kilwa captured and hanged Kinjikitile, but the news of his magic water had already spread. A group of missionaries led by the bishop of Dar es Salaam was speared to death when they passed through the region, several trading posts were burnt along with their occupants, and the entire staff of the Ifakara garrison was killed.

The rebellion's first setback came when 1,000 warriors attacked the Mahenge garrison. The commander had been warned of the attack and a bank of machine guns awaited its arrival. Although many warriors were killed, the garrison was pinned down until troops from Iringa forced the rest to retreat. The Iringa troops then continued to the Ngoni capital of Songea. The Ngoni were extremely dubious about the water's power; when a few Ngoni were shot, the rest fled.

News of the water's ineffectiveness spread; the rebellion had lost much of its momentum by mid-October when Count Gotzen and 200 German troops arrived in the area. Gotzen decided the only way to flush out the ringleaders was to create a famine. Crops were burnt indiscriminately. Within months most of the leaders had been hanged. The ensuing famine virtually depopulated the area: over 250,000 people died of disease or starvation and the densely populated Mutumbi and Ungindo hills were reclaimed by miombo woodland and wild animals. They now form part of the Selous Game Reserve.

The Maji-Maji rebellion was the most important and tragic event during German rule, but it did leave some good effects in its wake. It was the first time a group of disparate tribes had dropped their own disputes and united against European invaders. Many Tanzanians feel the rebellion paved the way for the non-tribal attitude of modern Tanzania and it certainly affected the strategies used against colonial powers throughout Africa. More immediately, the public outcry it caused forced Germany to rethink its approach to its colonies.

Carl Peters was fired from the colonial service in 1906. He believed his African mistress had slept with his manservant, so he had flogged her close to death then hanged them both. His successor introduced a series of laws protecting Africans from mistreatment. To the disgust of the settler community, he created an incentive-based scheme for African farmers. This made it worth their while to grow cash crops and allowed the colony's exports to triple in the period leading up to World War I.

When World War I broke out in Europe, East Africa rapidly became involved. In the early stages of the war, German troops entered southern Kenya to cut off the Uganda Railway. Britain responded with an abortive attempt to capture Tanga. The balance of power was roughly even until Jan Smuts led the Allied forces into German territory in 1916. By January 1918, the Allies had captured most of German East Africa and the German commander, Von Lettow, retreated into Mozambique.

The war disrupted food production, and a serious famine ensued. This was particularly devastating in the Dodoma region. The country was taken over by the League of Nations. Ruanda-Urundi, now Rwanda and Burundi, was mandated to Belgium. The rest of the country was re-named Tanganyika and mandated to Britain.

## Tanganyika

The period of British rule between the wars was largely uneventful. Tanganyika was never heavily settled by Europeans so the indigenous populace had more opportunity for self-reliance than it did in many colonies. Nevertheless, settlers were favoured in the agricultural field, as were Asians in commerce. The Land Ordinance Act of 1923 secured some land rights for Africans; otherwise they were repeatedly forced into grand but misconceived agricultural schemes. The most notorious of these, the Groundnut Scheme of 1947, was an attempt to convert the southeast of the country into a large-scale mechanised groundnut producer. The scheme failed through a complete lack of understanding of local conditions; it caused a great deal of hardship locally and cost British taxpayers millions of pounds.

On a political level, a system of indirect rule based around local government encouraged African leaders to focus on local rivalries rather than national issues. A low-key national movement called the TAA was formed in 1929, but it was as much a cultural as a political organisation.

Although it was not directly involved in World War II, Tanganyika was profoundly affected by it. The country benefited economically. It saw no combat so food production continued as normal, while international food prices rocketed. Tanganyika's trade revenue increased sixfold between 1939 and 1949. World War II was a major force in the rise of African Nationalism. Almost 100,000 Tanganyikans fought for the Allies. The exposure to other countries and cultures made it difficult for them to return home as second-class citizens. They had fought for non-racism and democracy in Europe, yet were victims of racist and non-democratic policies in their own country.

The dominant figure in post-war Tanganyikan/Tanzanian politics is Julius Nyerere. Schooled at a mission near Lake Victoria, he went on to university in Uganda and gained a master's degree in Edinburgh. After returning to Tanzania in 1952, Nyerere became involved in the TAA. This evolved into the more political and nationalist TANU in 1954. Nyerere became the president of TANU at the age of 32. By supporting rural Africans on grass roots issues and advocating self-government as the answer to their grievances, TANU gained a strong national following.

By the mid-1950s Britain and the UN were looking at a way of moving Tanzania towards greater self-government, though over a far longer timescale than TANU envisaged. The British governor, Sir Edward Twining, favoured a system of multi-racialism, which would give equal representation to whites, blacks and Asians. TANU agreed to an election along these lines, albeit with major reservations. Twining created his own "African" party, the UTC.

In the 1958 election there were three seats per constituency, one for each racial group. Electors could vote for all three seats, so in addition to putting forward candidates for the black seats TANU indicated their preferred candidates in the white and Asian seats. Candidates backed by TANU won 67% of the vote; the UTC did not win a single seat. Twining's successor, Sir Richard Turnball, rewarded TANU by scrapping multi-racialism. In the democratic election of 1960, TANU won all but one seat. In May 1961, Tanganyika attained self government and Nyerere was made Prime Minister. Tanganyika attained full independence on 9 December 1961. Not one life had been taken in the process.

Britain granted Zanzibar full independence in December 1963. A month later the Arab government was toppled and in April 1964 the two countries combined to form Tanzania.

## Tanzania

At the very core of Tanzania's post-independence achievements and failures lies the figure of Julius Nyerere, who ruled Tanzania until his retirement in 1985. In his own country, where he remains highly respected, Nyerere is called *Mwalimu* – the teacher. In the west, he is a controversial figure, often portrayed as a dangerous socialist who irreparably damaged his country. This image of Nyerere doesn't bear scrutiny. He made mistakes and was intolerant of criticism – at one point Tanzania is said to have had more political prisoners than South Africa – but he is also one of the few statesmen to have emerged from Africa, and has been a force for positive change both in his own country and in a wider African context.

In 1962, TANU came into power with little policy other than their attained goal of independence. Tanganyika was the poorest and least economically developed country in East Africa, and one of the poorest in the world. Nyerere's first concerns were to better the lot of rural Africans and to prevent the creation of a money-grabbing elite. The country was made a one-party state, but had an election system which, by African standards, was relatively democratic. Tanzania pursued a policy of non-alignment, but the government's socialist policies and Nyerere's outspoken views alienated most western leaders. Close bonds were formed with socialist powers, most significantly China, who built the Tanzam Railway (completed in 1975).

Relations with Britain soured in 1965. Nyerere condemned the British government's tacit acceptance of UDI in Rhodesia. In return, Britain cut off all aid to Tanzania. Nyerere also gave considerable vocal support to disenfranchised Africans in South Africa, Mozambique and Angola. The ANC and Frelimo both operated from Tanzania in the 1960s.

Nyerere's international concerns were not confined to white-suprematism. In 1975, Tanzania pulled out of an OAU conference in Idi Amin's Uganda saying: "The refusal to protest against African crimes against Africans is bad enough...but...by meeting in Kampala...the OAU are giving respectability to one of the most murderous regimes in Africa". Tanzania gave refuge to several Ugandans, including the former president Milton Obote and the current president Yoweri Museveni. Amin occupied part of northwestern Tanzania in October 1978, and bombed Bukoba and Musoma. In 1979, Tanzania retaliated by invading Uganda and toppling Amin. This action was condemned by other African leaders, despite Amin having been the initial aggressor. Ousting Amin drained Tanzania's financial resources, but it received no financial compensation, neither from the west nor from any other African country.

At the time of independence, most rural Tanzanians lived in scattered communities. This made it difficult for the government to provide such amenities as clinics and schools and to organise a productive agricultural scheme. In 1967, Nyerere embarked on a policy he called villagisation. Rural people were encouraged to form *Ujamaa* (familyhood) villages and collective farms. The scheme met with some small-scale success in the mid-70s, so in 1975 Nyerere decided to forcibly re-settle people who had not yet formed villages. By the end of the year 65% of rural Tanzanians lived in *Ujamaa* villages. In many areas, however, water supplies were inadequate to support a village. The resultant mess, exacerbated by one of Tanzania's regular droughts, ended further villagisation. *Ujamaa* is often considered to have been an unmitigated disaster. It did not achieve what it was meant to, but it did help the government improve education and health care. Most reliable sources claim it did little long-term damage to agricultural productivity.

By the late 1970s Tanzania's economy was a mess. There were several contributory factors: drought, *Ujamaa*, rising fuel prices, the border closure with Kenya, lack of foreign aid, bureaucracy and corruption in state-run institutions, and the cost of the Uganda episode. After his re-election in 1980 Nyerere announced he would retire at the end of that five-year term. In 1985 he was succeeded by Ali Hassan Mwinyi. Nyerere remained chairman of the CCM, the party formed when TANU merged with the Zanzibari ASP in 1975, until 1990.

Under President Mwinyi Tanzania has moved away from socialism. In June 1986, in alliance with the IMF, he implemented a three-year Economic Recovery Plan. This included freeing up the exchange rate and encouraging private enterprise. Since then Tanzania has achieved an annual growth rate of around 4% (in real terms). Many locals complain the only result they have seen is greater inflation. In 1990 attempts were made to rout corruption from the civil service, with surprisingly positive results. The first multi-party election took place in October 1995, with the CCM being returned to power with a majority of around 75%. As with independence this transition caused no bloodshed.

Into its fourth decade of independence, most of Africa still suffers from the tribal problems it had at the outset. Nyerere's great achievement is the tremendous sense of national unity he created; by making KiSwahili the national language, by banning tribal leaders, by forcing government officials to work away from the area in which they grew up, and by his own example.

Things look better for Tanzania now than they have at any time since independence. It remains one of the world's 25 least-developed countries, but most sources agree that the economic situation of the average Tanzanian has improved since independence, as have adult literacy rates and health care. Tanzania's remarkable political stability and its increasingly pragmatic economic policies are a positive base for future growth.

Tourism could play a big part in this. Until the closure of the Kenya border in the late 1970s, most of Tanzania's tourism came via Kenya, which profited from it more than Tanzania did. Tourism ground to a standstill during the early 1980s, but Tanzania is now developing a tourist infrastructure independently of an increasingly wobbly-looking Kenya.

When I first visited Tanzania in 1986, it looked to be beyond redemption. Ten years hence it could well be a beacon of hope, stability and relative prosperity in an increasingly turbulent continent.

Chapter Two

# Natural History

## INTRODUCTION

There are plenty of good reasons to visit Tanzania – its beautiful coastline, fascinating history and magnificent scenery – but for most tourists one attraction overwhelms all others. Tanzania is Africa's prime game-viewing country. Its national parks and game reserves, which include the famous Serengeti and Ngorongoro Crater, cover almost 25% of the country and protect an estimated 20% of Africa's large mammals.

All the national parks receive detailed coverage in the main part of the guide, as do any other conservation areas which are reasonably accessible. This chapter provides an overview of Tanzania's conservation areas and natural history, as well as descriptions of the more common large mammals.

## CONSERVATION

The plight of the rhinoceros and elephant has made African conservation a household concern in the west. Despite this, few westerners have any grasp of the issues. What follows is certainly opinionated, and probably simplistic, but does attempt to clarify the root problem as I see it. You may well disagree...

We all romanticise Africa. An incredible amount of drivel was written about it during the colonial era, and this dominates our perception of the continent. The macho blustering of Hemingway and exaggerated accounts of the Great White Hunters vie in our heads with the nostalgic meandering of *Out of Africa*. For the west, Africa represents wildness and space, vast horizons and shimmering red sunsets; powerful images we do not want shattered by the realities of the late 20th Century.

It was, of course, European settlers who destroyed the Africa they mythologised. The vast herds which had existed alongside people for millennia were decimated during the colonial era. By the early 1960s, when most of Africa became independent, these herds were by and large restricted to conservation areas that had been set aside by the colonial governments to preserve something of the Africa they loved. Their vision of unspoilt Africa did not include people: when an area was declared a national park, the people who lived there were moved to the fringes. They had both hunted and conserved the animals for centuries; now hunting was forbidden and they needed new sources of food.

Areas suitable for national parks are not normally densely populated; they tend to be relatively infertile. Even if someone succeeded in growing crops, their efforts could be wiped out by one hungry or angry elephant. This created a circle of poverty around many game reserves, a scenario which worked in the interests of ivory and rhino-horn traders. People living on the verges of reserves would happily kill elephant or rhinoceros for what was a fraction of the market price, but a fortune in local terms.

As you are no doubt aware, rhinoceros are close to extinction in most Africa countries. In Tanzania, there are 20 left in the Ngorongoro Conservation Area and at best a couple of hundred in the Selous. Africa's elephant population is now thought to number about half a million. Tanzania is home to a significant number of these. There are an estimated 30,000 animals in the Selous alone, and at least as many scattered in other reserves.

In the late 1980s the elephant situation seemed hopeless. In some reserves, herds had been poached to within 20% of their size ten years previously. In the Selous, up to 20,000 were killed in a two year period. Most African governments lacked the finance to arrest this process; in some cases they also lacked the will, with strong rumours of corruption and the involvement of government officials. Anti-poaching units armed with old-fashioned rifles were fighting bands of poachers armed with AK47s, and losing. In 1988, I was driven through a part of Kenya's Tsavo East National Park, one of the worst hit reserves, with less than a quarter of its 1972 population of 17,000 animals left. We saw more elephant corpses than we did live animals; those elephant we did see ran off in terror at the approach of a vehicle.

A five-year moratorium on the world ivory trade was implemented in 1989. There is a wide consensus this ban has worked: elephant numbers are on the increase and, without a market, poaching has virtually stopped. Southern African countries want this moratorium to be lifted. Herds in South Africa, Botswana and Zimbabwe are stable and growing, and as elephant are extremely destructive when overpopulated, excess animals are culled. This issue has been greatly misrepresented in Britain at least, where emotive and irresponsible newspaper columns and television programmes have equated culling with murder. Obviously culling is not the ideal solution, but it is difficult to see a practical alternative. (The suggestion most often put forward is that the animals could be moved. To the Cotswolds? Or somewhere where African crops can be trampled?)

It has become evident to many conservationists that a complete change of approach is the only chance for the long term survival of Africa's large animals. Local people must be included in the process. If they benefit from the reserves, they will side with conservationists; if they do not they will side with the poachers. Attempts must be made to ensure that locals benefit from money raised by the reserves, that they are given meat from culled animals, and that wherever possible work is found for them within the reserve. In an increasingly densely populated continent, reserves can only justify their existence if they create local wealth.

Zimbabwe is at the forefront of this more integrated approach to conservation. It is, by western standards, a poor country, and could use the revenue raised by selling elephant tusks which are at present gathering dust. Zimbabwean conservationists argue that they have the right to sell these on a legitimate market; that western countries would not be so keen to impose a moratorium if their commercial interests were at stake; that, ultimately, the west is yet again imposing its will on Africa.

Southern African countries suggest a cartel is created which sells only ivory from countries with stable elephant populations. Countries like Tanzania fear that such a cartel would be difficult to control, and may well lead to renewed poaching in their reserves. There is no simple solution to this conflict of interests. I believe it to be in the interests of most African countries that the moratorium stands for the meantime, but ultimately it should be lifted. Efforts should be made now to rethink conservation policies, so that when it is lifted the same old problems do not recur.

Africa does not belong to the west. I see no reason why Africans should conserve their wildlife for the sake of western aesthetics, unless they perceive it to be in their interest to do so. If some gun-happy soul with a Hemingway fixation is idiot enough to pay enough money to support a village for a year in order that he can hunt an elephant, good. If the meat from an elephant can feed a village for a week, and the money from the sale of the ivory be put back into conservation, good. If we westerners can drop the idealism and allow Africans to both conserve their wildlife *and* feed their bellies, only then is there a chance that our grandchildren will be able to see the Africa we want them to.

Just before going to the printers, I read a glowing review of a new book which addresses many of the issues raised above, called *At the Hand of Man: Peril and Hope for Africa's Wildlife* by Raymond Bonner (Alfred A Knopf 1993).

# CONSERVATION AREAS

There are 12 national parks in Tanzania, and numerous other conservation areas. The most important of these fit broadly into three groups: the northern, southern and western reserves.

## Northern reserves

The northern reserves are the focus of Tanzania's safari industry, which is based in the town of Arusha. The traditional northern safari includes visits to Serengeti National Park, the Ngorongoro Conservation Area and Lake Manyara National Park. With luck, a visit to all three will yield sightings of all the so-called big five (lion, leopard, elephant, buffalo and rhino) and most other large African plains mammals.

The Serengeti is notable for its large migratory herds of wildebeest and zebra. It also harbours large numbers of predators; it is not unusual to see lion, leopard and cheetah in the same day. Although heavily touristed, the Serengeti is vast enough to handle it comfortably.

The centrepiece of the Ngorongoro Conservation Area is the magnificent 600m-deep crater after which it is named, the largest intact caldera in the world. Ngorongoro Crater supports large herds of ungulates and is said to have the world's densest lion population. It is the last place in East Africa where black rhinoceros are reasonably common. Ngorongoro is heavily touristed, and because it is open and its area is limited, this does detract from many people's visit.

Lake Manyara National Park is the least compelling of this triad of reserves. Its once-famous elephant population has suffered badly at the hands of poachers, and its main claim to fame now is the tree-climbing lions which no-one ever seems to see. It is very scenic, however, and there is plenty of other game to be seen.

Many visitors incorporate visits to either Tarangire or Arusha National Park in a northern safari. Tarangire preserves a classic piece of African woodland, studded with plentiful baobabs. It is particularly rich in bird life. A number of localised species such as fringe-eared oryx and gerenuk are present, and elephant are abundant. Arusha National Park is the most low-key of the northern reserves, and considering its proximity to Arusha, it is surprisingly little visited. Despite this, it has a number of attractive features, including Africa's fifth-highest mountain, Meru, and its own mini-Ngorongoro, Ngurdoto Crater.

Kilimanjaro National Park encompasses the peaks and higher slopes of Africa's highest mountain. Thousands of tourists climb it every year. Mount Meru in Arusha National Park is also popular with hikers.

## Southern reserves

Tanzania's southern reserves are less spectacular than those in the north, but they have more of a wilderness atmosphere. The most important reserve in southern Tanzania is the Selous Game Reserve, the largest reserve in Africa. It is bordered by two national parks: Mikumi and the recently proclaimed Udzungwa Mountains. A third national park, Ruaha, lies west of the Tanzam Highway.

With the exception of Udzungwa Mountains, the southern reserves are only really accessible if you go with an organised safari. These are generally more expensive than safaris to the northern reserves. You can, however, see something of Mikumi from the Tanzam Highway, and slow trains between Dar es Salaam and Mbeya pass through the Selous in daylight hours. The Udzungwa can be reached on public transport and once it is developed will be orientated towards hikers.

## Western reserves

The western reserves are very different in character to those in the south and north of the country. They are low-key, have basic accommodation facilities only, and are time-consuming to visit. If you can afford the time, however, all are relatively easy to reach on public transport.

There are four national parks in western Tanzania: Gombe Stream, Mahale Mountains, Rubondo Island and Katavi. The first three are well-forested, noted for their chimpanzees, and can only be reached by boat. Katavi protects a similar habitat to the southern reserves, but is more remote.

# HABITATS AND VEGETATION

The bulk of Tanzania is covered in open grassland, savannah (lightly wooded grassland) and woodland. Most typical African species are at home in all these habitats, but there are exceptions.

The Serengeti Plains are an archetypal African savannah: grassland interspersed with trees of the acacia family. Most acacia are quite short, lightly leaved and thorny. Many have a flat-topped appearance. An atypical acacia, the yellow-fever tree, is one of Africa's most striking trees. It is relatively large, has yellow bark, and is often associated with water. Combretum is another family of trees typical of savannah.

Much of central Tanzania is dry savannah; during the dry season this area is so barren it resembles semi-desert.

Woodland differs from forest in lacking an interlocking canopy. The most extensive woodland in Tanzania is in the miombo belt which stretches from southern and western Tanzania to Zimbabwe. Miombo woodland typically grows on infertile soil, and is dominated by broadleaved *brachystegia* trees. You may come across the term mixed woodland: this refers to woodland with a mix of *brachystegia*, acacia and other species. Many woodlands are characterised by an abundance of baobab trees.

True forests cover less than 1% of Tanzania's surface area, but are its most botanically diverse habitat. The forests of the Usambara, for instance, contain more than 2,000 plant species. Most of the forest in Tanzania is montane. Montane forest is characteristic of a group of mountain ranges known as the Eastern Arc Mountains. These form a broken line from north to south, between 50km and 200km inland, and include the Pare, Usambara, Uluguru, Udzungwa and Poroto ranges. The forests of the Eastern Arc mountains, characterised by a high level of endemism, form one of Tanzania's most ecologically precious habitats. The most accessible montane forest is on the slopes of Kilimanjaro, Meru, the Udzungwa and the Usambara.

The lowland forests found in the extreme west of the country have strong affinities with the rainforests of Zaire. Three national parks contain extensive lowland forests: Gombe Stream, Rubondo Island and Mahale Mountains.

Other interesting but localised vegetation types are mangrove swamps (common along the coast, particularly around Kilwa) and the heath and moorland found on the higher slopes of Kilimanjaro and Meru.

# ANIMALS

## Mammals

Over 80 large mammal species live in Tanzania. On an organised safari your guide will normally be able to identify all the mammals you see. For serious identification purposes or a better understanding of an animal's lifestyle and habits, it is worth investing in a decent field guide or a book on animal behaviour. A number are available; see *Further Reading*. Field guides are best bought before you get to Tanzania.

In the listings below, an animal's KiSwahili name is given in parenthesis after its English name. The KiSwahili for animal is *mnyama* (plural *wanyama*); to find out what animal you are seeing, ask *"mnyama gani?"*

## Predators

**Lion** (*simba*) The largest African cat is the one animal everyone wants to see when they go on safari. Lions are the most sociable of the large cats, living in loosely-structured family groups (prides) which typically consist of between five and 15 animals. Lions normally hunt at night; their favoured prey are medium to large antelopes such as wildebeest, gazelle and impala. Females, working in teams of up to eight animals, are responsible for most hunts. Rivalry between male lions is intense: prides may have more than one dominant male working in collaboration to prevent a takeover and young males are forced out of their home pride at about three years of age. Pride takeovers are often fought to the death; after a successful takeover, it is not unusual for all the male cubs to be killed by the new dominant male. Lions are not active by day: they are most often seen lying in the shade looking the picture of regal indolence. Lions occur in most wooded habitats and are the most numerous large cat in savannah. They are common in all the southern reserves and at Katavi, but are more readily seen in the open savannah of the Serengeti and Ngorongoro Crater.

**Leopard** (*chui*) This is the most common and widespread large cat in Africa, often living in close proximity to humans, but because of its secretive, solitary nature it is rarely seen. Leopards hunt using stealth and power, often getting to within 5m of their intended prey before pouncing, and they habitually store their prey in a tree to keep it from hyenas and lions. They can be distinguished from the superficially similar cheetah by their rosette-shaped spots and powerful build. Leopards are found in all habitats. They are frequently seen in the Seronera Valley of the Serengeti, where they spend their days hiding up in trees.

**Cheetah** (*duma*) Cheetahs hunt using speed instead of stealth; they are the fastest land mammals, capable of running at up to 70km/hour. Their diurnal hunting habits make them vulnerable in areas where there are high tourist concentrations; it's difficult for them to get close to animals when they are surrounded by vehicles. Males are strongly territorial, and in the Serengeti they most commonly defend their territory in pairs or trios. Cheetahs are the least powerful of the large predators: they are chased from a high percentage of their kills and 50% of cubs are killed before they reach three months. Like leopards, cheetahs are heavily spotted and solitary, but their greyhound-like build, distinctive black tear-marks and preference for grassland and savannah preclude confusion. Cheetahs are found in most large reserves and are regularly seen in the Serengeti.

**Caracal** (*sibamangu*) and **serval** (*mondo*) The caracal is a medium-sized lynx-like cat with a uniform reddish-brown coat and tufted ears. The slightly larger serval has a pale spotted coat. Both are widespread, with the serval favouring moister and more densely wooded terrain than the caracal. As both are nocturnal they are rarely seen.

**Civet** (*fungo*) This bulky, long-haired, cat-like creature has been kept in captivity for thousands of years (its anal secretions were used in making perfumes until a synthetic replacement was found) but little is known about its habits in the wild. Civets are primarily carnivorous, feeding on small animals and carrion, but they will also eat fruit. Their grey-white coat is marked with large black spots which merge into stripes towards the head. Civets are widespread and common in most habitats, but they are rarely seen.

**Genet** (*kanu*) The genets are a closely related group of small cat-like creatures with extraordinarily long tails. They are secretive and little-known scientifically, but as they are attracted to human waste they are often seen slinking around campsites after dark. There are ten recognised genet species, but they are difficult to tell apart in the wild. The small-spotted genet is the common genet in Tanzania.

**Ratel** (*nyegere*) Also known as the honey-badger for its habit of raiding bee hives, the ratel has a puppy-like head, black sides and underparts and a greyish-white back. Ratels are adaptable and widespread, and will eat whatever comes their way. They have a symbiotic relationship with a bird called the greater honeyguide: the honeyguide takes the ratel to a bee hive, which the ratel then tears open, allowing the honeyguide to feed on the scraps. According to some sources, the ratel fumigates the bee hive with its anal secretions. Ratels are widespread, but uncommon and rarely seen.

**Spotted hyena** (*fisi*) This is the common hyena in Tanzania and the most abundant large carnivore in the majority of Africa. Although dog-like in appearance, hyenas are more closely related to mongooses and cats than they are to dogs, and despite their image as scavengers, the spotted hyena is an adept hunter capable of killing an animal as large as a wildebeest. In ancient times, the spotted hyena was thought to be hermaphroditic; the female's vagina is blocked by a false but remarkably realistic-looking scrotum; the entrance is via an equally realistic-looking "penis". Most hyena species live in loosely structured clans of around ten animals. Clans are led by females, which are stronger and larger than males. The spotted hyena is bulky with a sloping back, a light brown coat marked with dark brown spots and an exceptionally powerful jaw (used to crack open bones). It is common throughout Tanzania and frequently seen in daylight. The more secretive and uncommon striped hyena is found in some Tanzanian national parks, but is rarely seen. The aardwolf, a hyena which has become so specialised it primarily feeds on one type of termite, is thinly distributed in the drier parts of Tanzania.

**African hunting dog** (*mbwa mwitu*) These endangered animals are always found in packs, normally about ten animals strong, and have cryptically marked black, brown and cream coats. They are ferocious hunters, literally tearing apart their prey as it runs. Although widely distributed and highly successful predators, hunting dogs are threatened with extinction: they are susceptible to canine disease and their highly social behaviour has made them vulnerable to epidemics. They are present in most national parks, but are thinly distributed.

**Jackal** (*mbweha*) Jackals are small dogs, not much bigger than a fox. They are adaptable and versatile hunters and scavengers, and are found throughout Tanzania. The common species is the black-backed jackal, which can be distinguished by a black and gold saddle. The uncommon golden and side-striped jackals are found in small numbers in the Serengeti. The bat-eared fox, which can be distinguished from any other small canine by its large ears and black eye-mask, is common in the Serengeti.

## Primates

**Chimpanzee** (*sokwe-mtu*) This distinctive black-coated ape is closely related to man. Chimpanzees live in the lowland forests of western Tanzania. They are found naturally in two national parks – Gombe Stream and Mahale Mountains – and have been introduced to Rubondo Island. Chimpanzees live in large family groups and have complex social behaviour, which has been extensively studied by Jane Goodall at Gombe Stream and Japanese researchers at Mahale.

**Baboon** (*nyani*) Baboons are heavily built greyish primates, superficially similar to monkeys but larger than any monkey species found in East Africa. Baboons live in large troops, and spend most of their time on the ground. Troops have a complex and rigid social structure, held together by matriarchal lineages. Males frequently move between troops in their search for social dominance. Baboons are omnivorous and highly adaptable, and are the most common and widespread primate in Africa. Several subspecies are recognised: the olive baboon is found in northern Tanzania, while the smaller yellow baboon is found in the southern reserves.

**Vervet monkey** (*tumbili*) This light grey monkey has a black face and the male has distinctive blue genitals. The vervet is associated with a wide variety of habitats and is the only monkey you are likely to see outside of forests. Vervet monkeys are common in most Tanzanian national parks.

**Black-and-white colobus** (*mbega mweupe*) In Tanzania, this most distinctive of monkey species is restricted to montane forests such as those on Kilimanjaro, Meru, Mahale, and most of the Eastern Arc ranges. It is a beautifully marked animal with a primarily black body and long white tail. Black-and-white colobus live in small groups and are exclusively arboreal. They are capable of jumping up to 30m, a spectacular sight with their white tail streaming behind. A good place to see black-and-white colobus is on the Ngurdoto Crater rim in Arusha National Park.

**Blue monkey** (*kima*) The most widespread forest-dwelling monkey is the blue (or samango) monkey, which is a uniform dark blue-grey colour except for its white throat and chest patch; the black face mask of the vervet precludes confusion between the two. The blue monkey is found in virtually all Tanzanian forests, from the fig forest of Lake Manyara to the montane forest of Mount Meru, Kilimanjaro and Ngorongoro Crater rim.

Several more localised monkey species are found in Tanzania. These include red colobus (*chondi*), redtailed (*nkunge*) and patas (*ngedere*) monkeys. The best national parks for keen monkey-watchers are Mahale Mountains, Gombe Stream, Rubondo Island and Udzungwa.

**Bushbaby** (*komba*) This small nocturnal primate is common throughout Tanzania. Its piercing cry is one of the distinctive sounds of the African night – I have even heard a bushbaby in Dar es Salaam. If you want to see one, trace the cry to a tree, then shine a torch into it – you should easily pick out the bushbaby's large round eyes.

## Antelope
### Large antelope
All the antelope described below have an average shoulder height of above 120cm (4ft), roughly the same height as a zebra.

**Common wildebeest** or **gnu** (*nyumbu*) This bizarre and ungainly antelope is the most common large mammal in Tanzania. Wildebeest are widespread and usually found in large herds. In the Serengeti, the annual migration of over a million animals forms one of Africa's great spectacles. Five subspecies are recognised, of which three can be seen in Tanzania: the western white-bearded race lives in the Serengeti, the eastern white-bearded race is found east of the Rift Valley and north of the Rufiji River, and the Nyasa race occurs south of the Rufiji.

**Hartebeest** Hartebeest are also rather ungainly looking. They have large shoulders, a sloping back and relatively small horns. Most hartebeest species are brownish in colour and live in small family groups. Liechtenstein's hartebeest (*kongoni*) is a dull yellow-brown animal found in southern Tanzania. The similar-looking Kongoni (*kongoni*) is largely restricted to the Serengeti Plains, as is the dark red-brown Topi (*nyamera*).

**Waterbuck** (*kuro*) This shaggy-looking animal has a grey-brown coat and distinctive white ring around its rump. Waterbuck are common in small numbers throughout Tanzania and are normally seen in small family groups grazing near water.

**Eland** (*pofu*) Africa's largest antelope has a bovine appearance. It is fawn-brown in colour, has a large dewlap and short spiralled horns, and sometimes has light white stripes on its side. Eland are widespread, but are thinly distributed and often skittish. They are most normally seen in open or lightly wooded grassland.

**Kudu** (*tandala*) This very large antelope favours woodland habitats. It is grey-brown with thin white stripes. The male has a small dewlap and large spiralling horns. Greater Kudu (*tandala mkubwa*) are found in most parts of southern Tanzania, but are nowhere common. They are replaced by the rare and smaller lesser kudu (*tandala ndogo*) in northern Tanzania. Both species are present in Ruaha National Park, where they can be told apart by their size and the number of stripes on their torso (greater kudu have between six and ten stripes; lesser kudu have eleven or more).

**Roan antelope** (*korongo*) The roan is a handsome animal with a light reddish-brown coat, short backward-curving horns and a small mane on the back of the neck. It could be mistaken for a female sable, but is paler and lacks the sable's well-defined white rump and belly. Roan are associated with miombo woodland. They are present in small numbers in the Serengeti, but are more common in the southern reserves and Katavi National Park.

**Sable antelope** (*pala hala*) This striking antelope has a black (male) or chestnut-brown (female) coat, white underbelly and rump, and long backward-curving horns. Sable are associated with miombo woodland and are present in most southern Tanzanian reserves, where they are widespread but thinly distributed.

**Fringe-eared oryx** (*choroa*) These regal-looking antelope are ash-grey in colour and have distinctive scimitar-shaped horns. Oryx are found in dry habitats and are present in much of northern Tanzania. They are common in Tarangire National Park.

## Medium-sized antelope
All the antelope listed below have a shoulder height of between 75 and 90cm. The male sitatunga has a shoulder height of around 110cm.

**Gazelle** (*swala*) Gazelle are lightly built antelope found in open grassland. Three species are found in Tanzania: Grant's gazelle (*swala granti*) and Thomson's gazelle (*swala tomi*) are both common on the Serengeti plains. Grant's gazelle is larger than Thomson's, and lacks the Thomson's black side-stripe. The distinctive gerenuk (*swala twiga*) is a red-brown gazelle with an extraordinarily long neck (hence its Swahili name, which literally means gazelle-giraffe). Gerenuk are adapted to semi-desert conditions and are occasionally seen in Tarangire National Park, Mkomazi Game Reserve and along the Arusha-Nairobi road.

**Impala** (*swala pala*) These slender, handsome antelope are superficially similar to gazelle, but in fact belong to a separate family. Impala can be distinguished from any gazelle by their chestnut colouring, sleek appearance, and the male's distinctive lyre-shaped horns. They can jump up to 3m high and have been known to broad-jump over 10m. Impala live in herds of between 20 and a few hundred animals. They favour well-wooded savannah and woodland fringes, and are often abundant in such habitats.

**Bushbuck** (*pongo*) Bushbuck are normally found in forests and riverine woodland. The male has a dark chestnut coat marked with white spots and stripes. The female is lighter in colour; it is similar in appearance to a duiker but larger. Bushbuck are secretive, but common in suitable habitats.

**Sitatunga** This semi-aquatic buck is similar in appearance to the bushbuck, but the male is larger and has a shaggier coat. Both sexes are striped. Sitatunga live in papyrus swamps and are found on Rubondo Island, where they are thought to interbreed with bushbuck, and at Biharimulo Game Reserve.

**Puku** This golden-brown antelope, closely related to the Uganda Kob, lacks distinctive markings. It lives in marshy areas and on flood plains. In Tanzania it is known from the Rukwa area.

**Reedbuck** (*tohe*) Reedbuck are grey-brown antelope with small crescent-shaped horns. They are usually seen in pairs near water and are found in most Tanzanian national parks. In northern Tanzania they are replaced by the darker mountain reedbuck (*tohe mlima*).

## Small antelope

The antelope listed below all have a shoulder height of between 30 and 50cm, except for oribi and klipspringer which are slightly larger (55-60cm).

**Klipspringer** (*mbuze mawe*) Klipspringer have dark, bristly coats which give them a speckled appearance. As their KiSwahili name suggests, they have goat-like habits: they are invariably found in the vicinity of koppies or cliffs. Their name means rock-jumper in Afrikaans. They live in pairs in suitable habitats throughout Tanzania.

**Kirk's dik-dik** (*digidigi*) This is the most commonly seen small antelope in Tanzania. It is uniform greyish-brown with a distinctive white ring around its eye. Dik-dik are usually seen singly or in pairs in tall grass or thick undergrowth.

**Steenbok** (*tondoro*) This nondescript rusty-brown antelope is common in some southern reserves. It favours open country.

**Oribi** (*taya*) Oribi are similar to steenbok but larger. They are found mainly in tall grassland and are most likely to be seen in the northern Serengeti.

**Duiker** Duiker are a group of tiny forest-dwelling buck. Several species are present in Tanzania's forests, but they are elusive and seldom seen clearly enough to identify. Abbot's duiker (*minde*) is chestnut brown and has a tuft of red hair on its forehead. It is endemic to Tanzania and can be found in the forests of Kilimanjaro. Common duiker (*nsya*) are grey-brown and have a vaguely speckled appearance. They are widespread and less habitat-specific than other duikers. Red duiker (*pofu*) are very small and are light chestnut-brown in colour. Blue duiker (*kima*), the smallest African antelope, are greyish-blue. Blue and red duiker are both reasonably widespread. Ader's duiker is found only in two forests: Jozani on Zanzibar and the Sokoke in Kenya.

## Other herbivores

**Elephant** (*tembe*) The world's largest land animal is also one of the most intelligent and entertaining to watch. A fully grown elephant is about 3½m high and weighs around 6,000kg. Female elephants live in closely knit clans in which the eldest female takes a matriarchal role over her sisters, daughters and granddaughters. Mother-daughter bonds are strong and, because elephants live to a similar age to humans, they may exist for up to 50 years. Males generally leave the family group at around 12 years, after which they either roam around on their own or form bachelor herds. Under normal circumstances, elephants range widely in search of food and water, but when concentrated populations are forced to live in conservation areas, their habit of uprooting trees can cause serious environmental damage. Despite heavy poaching, Tanzania still has an awesome elephant population. They are extremely adaptable animals, so are common in most large game reserves and national parks, particularly the Selous, Ruaha, Tarangire and Katavi. They are less common in the Serengeti.

**Black rhinoceros** (*faru*) These imposing creatures have been poached close to extinction in Tanzania, but are still likely to be seen in Ngorongoro Crater. There is said to be a significant population in the Selous, but they are probably extinct in all the national parks. The closely related white rhinoceros is not found in Tanzania.

**Hippopotamus** (*kiboko*) These lumbering aquatic animals are found in most stretches of water within reserves. Hippos spend most of the day submerged in water, but they emerge from the water at night in order to graze. They are strongly territorial, with herds of ten or more animals being presided over by a dominant male. Hippo are abundant on the Rufiji River in the Selous Game Reserve. The best places to see them in northern Tanzania are the hippo pool in Lake Manyara National Park and the picnic site in Ngorongoro Crater. Hippo are still quite common outside of reserves, where they are responsible for killing more people than any other African mammal.

**Buffalo** (*nyati*) The African buffalo is an adaptable and widespread animal. It lives in large herds on the savannah and smaller herds in forested areas. Herds are mixed-sex and normally comprise several loosely related family clans and bachelor groups. Buffalo are found in virtually all Tanzania's national parks and game reserves.

**Giraffe** (*twiga*) The world's tallest animal (up to 5.5m) is distinctive. Giraffe live in loosely structured mixed-sex herds numbering between five and 15 animals. As herd members may be dispersed over 1km or so, they are frequently seen singly or in smaller groups. Giraffes' long necks give them a slightly ungainly appearance when they amble; they look decidedly absurd when they adopt a semi-crouching position in order to drink. Giraffe are common throughout Tanzania, though they are not found in the Ngorongoro crater or in the Selous south of the

Rufiji River. Only one subspecies, the Maasai giraffe, is found in Tanzania.

**Burchell's zebra** (*punda milia*) Zebra are striped members of the horse family, common and widespread throughout Tanzania. They are often seen in large herds, but their basic social unit is the small, relatively stable family group, which typically consists of a male, up to five females, and their collective offspring. Zebra are often seen in the company of wildebeest. Two other species of zebra are found in Africa, but neither is present in Tanzania.

**Pigs** The only pig you are likely to see is the warthog (*ngiri*), which is widespread and common in savannah and woodland. Warthogs are a uniform grey colour, and both sexes have impressive tusks. They are normally seen in family groups, trotting away briskly in the opposite direction with their tails raised stiffly and a determinedly nonchalant air. The bulkier and hairier bushpig (*nguruwe mwitu*) is found mainly in thickets and dense woodland; although widespread and reasonably common, it is not often seen due to its nocturnal habits and favoured habitat. The giant forest hog (*nguruwe*), the largest African pig, is an animal of true forest. It lives in suitable habitat throughout Tanzania but is rarely seen.

**Elephant shrews** (*sange*) These bizarre rodents look like miniature kangaroos with absurdly elongated noses. A number of species are present in Tanzania, but they are secretive and nocturnal, so rarely seen. The giant elephant shrew of the Usambara is about the size of a duiker.

**Hyraxes** (*pimbi*) These guinea-pig-like animals look like rodents but are more closely related to elephant (though you are unlikely to have any difficulty telling them apart). Three types of hyrax are generally recognised, all of them found in Tanzania. Rock hyrax and bush hyrax both dwell on cliffs and koppies, and often live alongside each other. Both species are brown, but the rock hyrax is larger than the bush hyrax and has coarser fur with a yellowish tinge. Bush and rock hyrax are tame and common at Lobo and Seronera Lodges in the Serengeti. The tree hyrax is a nocturnal creature generally found in montane forests; though seldom seen, its shrieking call is unforgettable if heard.

# Birds

Tanzania is a bird-watcher's dream, with over 1,000 species recorded. Casual visitors will be stunned at the abundance of bird life: the brilliantly coloured lilac-breasted rollers and superb starlings, the numerous birds of prey, the giant ostrich, the faintly comic hornbills, the magnificent crowned crane – the list could go on forever.

For serious birders, virtually anywhere in Tanzania offers good birding; in many areas a reasonably competent observer could hope to see between 50 and 100 species in a day. Any of the northern reserves are recommended: Arusha and Lake Manyara National Park are both good for forest and water birds; the Serengeti and Tarangire are good for raptors and acacia and grassland species.

Forest is an especially important birding habitat. The forests of the Eastern Arc Mountains hold numerous endemics. Amani and the Udzungwa National Park are the most accessible places for seeing some of these. Miombo-associated species can be seen in the southern reserves: the Selous, with the advantage of the many birds which live along the Rufiji River, is particularly recommended. Western reserves such as Gombe Stream and Rubondo Island offer a combination of water and forest habitats, with the possibility of glimpsing one or two West African specials. If you visit Mwanza, don't bypass Saa Nane Island – in an hour there I saw five species I've not seen elsewhere in Tanzania.

Of special interest to birders visiting Tanzania are the 20 species thought to be endemic to the country. Details of these birds and where they are most likely to be seen follow.

The **Udzungwa partridge** (*Xenoperdix udzungwensis*) is the sort of bird that gets twitchers frothing: it was discovered in 1991 in Udzungwa National Park, and has been placed in its own genus. It is presumably restricted to forest interiors in the Udzungwa Range. The **rufous-winged sunbird** (*Nectarinia rufipennis*) is another Udzungwa special, a bird of forest undergrowth which was only discovered in 1981. **Lagden's bush shrike** (*Molaconotus lagdeni*) and the **Iringa akalat** (*Sheppardia lowei*) are both restricted to montane forests in the Udzungwa area.

The **Pemba green pigeon** (*Treron pembaensis*) is an attractive species, closely related to the green pigeon found on the mainland, but restricted to Pemba Island. Also unique to this island is the **Pemba scops owl** (*Otus pembaensis*), which has not been heard or seen in recent times and may well be extinct.

The stunningly beautiful **Fischer's lovebird** (*Agopornis fischeri*) is common in the Serengeti. Arguably, it is no longer a true endemic, as a feral population is found in Naivasha, Kenya, where it regularly interbreeds with the **yellow-collared lovebird** (*Agopornis personata*), another Tanzanian endemic that has gone feral in Kenya. Within its natural range, the yellow-collared lovebird is commonly seen in Terengere National Park.

Also common in the Serengeti are the **grey-breasted spurfowl** (*Francolinus afer*), a game bird that lives in grassland scattered with trees, and the **rufous-tailed weaver** (*Histurgops ruficauda*), an atypical member of the weaver family, which looks and behaves much like a babbler. The rufous-tailed weaver is also common in Terengere National Park, where you can be certain of seeing the **ashy starling** (*Cosmopsarus unicolor*), a rather drab member of this normally colourful group of birds.

Several species are restricted to the montane forests of northeastern Tanzania, among them three varieties of sunbird. The **banded green sunbird** (*Anthreptes longuemarei*) is a bird of forest fringes, while **Loveridge's sunbird** (*Nectarinia loveredgei*) is generally observed in forest undergrowth and **Moreau's sunbird** (*Nectarinia moreaui*) in forest interiors. Birds with a similar habitat preference and distribution are **Nicoll's weaver** (*Ploceus nicolli*) and **Mrs Moreau's warbler** (*Bathmoceros winifredae*).

The final four Tanzania endemics are the **Kungwe apalis** (*Apalis argentea*), found in forest and bamboo east of Lake Tanganyika; the **Uhehe fiscal** (*Lanius marwitzi*) a bird of open country in the Iringa area; the **Tanzanian masked weaver** (*Ploceus reichardi*), which lives in swampy areas in southwestern Tanzania; and the **Kilombera weaver** (*Ploceus burnieri*), which inhabits riverside swamp in south-eastern Tanzania.

Field guides are discussed under *Further Reading*.

# Reptiles

The world's largest reptile, the Nile crocodile (*mamba*), is common in most large rivers and lakes, except where it has been hunted out. On the Rufiji River, in Selous Game Reserve, we saw some of the largest crocodiles we have seen anywhere in Africa. Crocodile feed on a variety of fish and mammals; the latter they drag into the water, submerge till drowned, then store underwater for a period of time until suitably decomposed.

Hundreds of different snakes and lizards are found in Tanzania. Perhaps fortunately, snakes are generally shy and are very seldom seen. You can expect to see lizards everywhere, even in hotel rooms. Saa Nane Island near Mwanza is a prime spot for reptile enthusiasts, with colourful rock agama in abundance, a healthy population of water monitor (Africa's largest lizard which grows up to about 2m long), and a chance of seeing crocodile. Several species of chameleon are found in Tanzania, but even though they are common, even in towns, they are difficult to find unless you know where to look. You're most likely to see a chameleon by luck; when you are on safari you could ask your guide to try to find one for you. Don't expect your chameleon to change its skin colour to match its background. This is a myth. Colour change is triggered by emotion.

# Cichlids

Lakes Nyasa, Tanganyika and Victoria vie with each other for the distinction of harbouring the most fish species of any lake in the world (though, since the introduction of the Nile perch, many of Lake Victoria's endemics have become extinct; see Chapter Nine). The majority of these fish are cichlids, a group of colourful fish well-known to anyone who keeps a tropical aquarium (particularly the *mbuna* cichlids of Lake Nyasa). Many cichlid species are mouth-brooders: the eggs are fertilised and left to hatch in the female's mouth, after which the young are released into secluded rocky crevices where they are safe from predators. If you have a mask and snorkel, the best place to look for cichlids is near rocky stretches of shore on Lakes Nyasa and Tanganyika (see *Matema Beach*, Chapter Ten). You should be aware of the fact that areas favoured by cichlids may also attract crocodiles.

# HIKING

In the 1980s, the only recognised hiking areas in Tanzania were Mount Kilimanjaro and more recently Mount Meru. Travellers who attempted to hike off the beaten track frequently met with suspicion, and if they did not have the required permits they risked being arrested. This no longer appears to be the case: while few travellers explore the hiking possibilities in Tanzania, the reports I have heard suggest there are few obstacles preventing them from doing so.

## New hiking areas

It is not only Kilimanjaro and Arusha National Parks (Mount Meru) that allow walking. In the west of the country, Rubondo Island and Mahale Mountains (both described in Chapter Nine) can only be explored by foot, while the new and more accessible Udzungwa Mountains National Park (Chapter Eleven) is likely to have a couple of hiking trails open within the next two years. It is possible to hike in the Ngorongoro Conservation Area (Chapter Eight) with the permission of the Conservation Authority in Arusha. Hiking in national parks is relatively expensive as an entrance fee of $15 per 24 hours is charged along with a camping fee of $10 per night. You may only hike if you are accompanied by an armed ranger, which costs $10 per day.

Outside of the national parks, the most accessible areas for hiking are the Usambara Mountains (Chapter Six), the Mbeya Range and the Poroto Mountains (both described in Chapter Ten). As yet, none of these areas is explored by travellers with any frequency, but they are beginning to open up and it is relatively easy to get up-to-date information about them.

Right now there is probably no country in east and southern Africa with Tanzania's potential for truly off-the-beaten-track hiking. Meru and Kilimanjaro excluded, even the places mentioned above are seldom visited by travellers, and they are only the tip of the iceberg. For keen hikers with a sense of adventure, some of the more intriguing possibilities follow (chapter number given where there is further information in the main part of the guide): the Pare Mountains near Same, the Livingstone Range east of Lake Nyasa (Chapter Ten), Mahenge Mountain south of Ifakara, the Kitulo Plateau east of the Poroto (Chapter Ten), Mount Hanang west of Babati, the Mbizi Mountains between Sumbawanga and Lake Rukwa (Chapter Nine), the Uluguru Mountains near Morogoro (Chapter Eleven) and Ukerewe, Maisome and Kome Islands in Lake Victoria (Chapter Nine).

With so little information available on most of these areas, I'd be delighted to hear from anyone who does visit some of them.

## Maps and equipment

In the national parks you may only walk when accompanied by a guide, so maps are probably not necessary. In the Poroto, Usambara and Mbeya mountains there are day hiking possibilities which would not require you to have detailed maps or specialist equipment. If you plan to undertake other hikes in these areas or to explore elsewhere, you will need good maps and equipment, and should ideally have some previous experience of wilderness hiking.

Essential equipment includes a compass, a tent, a sleeping bag and mat, warm clothing for areas at altitudes above about 1,500m, a stove and food, water bottles and, if you are hiking in the wet season, waterproof clothing. Unless you have a fair grip on the language already, a KiSwahili dictionary or phrase book will be more than useful.

You should be able to buy 1:50,000 survey maps of the area you plan to visit from the Department of Lands and Surveys in Dar es Salaam. This is a straightforward procedure and maps cost no more than $2 apiece. You must decide where you want to hike before you leave Dar es Salaam. You will not be able to get hold of maps elsewhere in the country.

## Permits

As I understand it, provided you stick to roads and footpaths no special permission is needed to hike anywhere in Tanzania. This is not as limiting as it may sound. The roads that pass through the type of place listed above are unlikely to see more than a vehicle or two daily – if that.

I have heard too few reports from hikers to say with total confidence that you will not hit bureaucratic problems hiking in remote areas, but it seems unlikely. The attitude to tourists has changed greatly in recent years, especially since the ANC was unbanned in South Africa. We went to several remote areas in the course of researching this book and experienced nothing that suggests there is any great suspicion of travellers in places where people are not used to them.

Having said that, at the time of writing many of the places mentioned above have not seen hikers for years. You will be charting unknown territory; before you do this it would be wise to make enquiries, if only to let someone in authority know your plans and to check there are no temporary restrictions on the area you plan to visit. The district or regional headquarters is the best place to enquire. If an area falls in a forest reserve the local Forestry Department office would be more appropriate. If the area is too remote for there to be either, ask at the police station. It would be worth trying to get something in writing with an official stamp on it, just in case you are questioned at some point.

If you pass through villages when hiking, it is polite to exchange greetings with the village chairman. You are also less likely to arouse suspicion if you do this. Be discreet with your camera. Never photograph villagers without asking first and don't photograph anything in the vicinity of bridges, railway lines, radio masts or any other government property.

It is forbidden to hike in national parks without a ranger or without paying the entrance fee. If you do the latter you could be arrested.

Chapter Three

# Practical Information

## TOURIST INFORMATION AND SERVICES

The main office of the Tanzania Tourist Corporation (TTC) is in Dar es Salaam, on Maktaba Street opposite the New Africa Hotel. The staff do their best, but their information is often out of date. The TTC is only worth visiting for information about Zanzibar or Dar es Salaam. The address is PO Box 2485, Dar es Salaam. Tel: (051) 27671/2/3/4/5.

There are TTC offices in London, New York, Stockholm, Milan and Frankfurt, and these may supply you with an information pack on the country.

**UK** Tanzania Tourist Office, 78-80 Borough High St, London SE1. Tel: 0171 407 0566.
**US** Tanzania Tourist Office, 210 E 42 Street, New York, NY 10017. Tel: 986 7124.

## WHEN TO VISIT

Tanzania's rainy season is between November and April. These months are warmer than May to October, but in most parts of the country by only a couple of degrees. Along the coast and in parts of northern Tanzania there are two rainy seasons: the short rains in November and December and the long rains from March to May.

Tanzania can be visited at any time of year. If you want to see the Serengeti at its best, don't come during the dry season – most of the animals will have migrated to the Maasai Mara across the border in Kenya. If you plan to explore the south coast or other remote areas, bear in mind that many roads become impassable during the rainy season. The rainy months are best avoided if you plan to hike.

## PUBLIC HOLIDAYS

| | |
|---|---|
| 1 January | New Year's Day |
| 12 January | Zanzibar Revolution Day |

| 26 April | Union Day |
| 1 May | International Workers' Day |
| 7 July | Public Holiday |
| 8 August | Peasants' Day |
| 9 December | Independence Day |
| 25 December | Christmas Day |

Other public holidays are Good Friday, Easter Monday, Idd-ul-Fitr, Islamic New Year and the Prophet's Birthday. These fall on different dates every year.

# RED TAPE

## Visas

Visas are required by all except citizens of Commonwealth and Scandinavian countries and the Republic of Ireland. They must be obtained in advance from a Tanzanian Embassy. Since early 1996, British nationals require a visa to enter Tanzania, at a cost of £38 (US$50). A visa extension currently costs US$300 for British nationals.

A visitor's pass, required by all visitors, is normally issued for free and without any fuss when you enter the country. You can obtain a visitor's pass in advance at any Tanzanian Embassy, but it will cost around $40. Your visitor's pass will probably be valid for up to one month. It can be extended at any Immigration Office with a minimum of fuss. This is best done in a small town; in Dar es Salaam or Arusha you will face a long queue.

## Embassies abroad

There are Tanzanian embassies or high commissions in Angola, Belgium, Britain, Burundi, Canada, China, CIS, Egypt, Ethiopia, France, Germany, Guinea, India, Japan, Kenya, Mozambique, Namibia, Netherlands, Nigeria, Rwanda, Sudan, Sweden, Uganda, USA, Zaire, Zambia and Zimbabwe. Below are addresses of those you are most likely to need.

**Germany** Botschaft der Vereinigte Republik von Tansania, Theaterplatz 26, 5300 Bonn, Germany. Tel: 0228 358051-4; Fax: 0228 358226.
**UK** High Commission of the United Republic of Tanzania, 43 Hertford St, London, England W1Y 8DB. Tel: 0171-499 8951; Fax: 0171-491 9321.
**US** Embassy of the United Republic of Tanzania, 2139 R Street NW, Washington DC 2000, USA. Tel: 202 9396129.

## Immigration and customs

The official requirements for entering Tanzania are an onward ticket and sufficient funds. This is only likely to be enforced if you arrive by air. If you are not carrying much money (less than US$1,000) try to bring a credit card; this is normally considered sufficient funds.

An onward ticket is a ticket out of Tanzania. A ticket leaving from another African country is just as good. You obviously won't have an onward ticket if you fly into Tanzania to start extended African travels and only plan to buy a ticket home at a later stage. Again, a credit card will help get you through.

One possibility is an MCO (Miscellaneous Charge Order). This is a blank air ticket, charged to the value of your choice and exchangeable worldwide for a variety of travel services. MCOs are normally refundable, but the terms should be checked with the individual airline.

If you think you might have problems with immigration (you don't have an onward ticket or credit card, don't want to buy an MCO and are short of cash) it is worth having a visa or visitor's pass for a neighbouring country stamped in your passport before you fly into Tanzania. This will help back up your claim that you plan to become another country's problem within a reasonable time span.

Having said all this, I met plenty of travellers who flew into Tanzania without an onward ticket, and none had a problem.

You no longer need to complete a currency declaration form when you enter Tanzania. Restrictions on South Africans and people who have a South African stamp in their passport have been lifted.

## Bribery

Bribery is not much of an issue. There is said to be plenty of corruption in Tanzanian business circles, but it is unlikely to affect tourists. I have never been in a situation where I felt a bribe was being hinted at, nor have I heard of one from another traveller.

## Bureaucracy

In the 1980s you often heard stories about travellers clashing with Tanzanian officials. Most incidents were camera-related: it was illegal to take photographs outside tourist areas, largely because of the number of ANC training centres in Tanzania at that time. It may have been paranoid to suspect every backpacker with a camera of being a spy, but as South Africa had used European passport holders disguised as backpackers to bomb an alleged ANC office in Zimbabwe, it was understandable. Things have relaxed greatly since South Africa unbanned the ANC. In our time in Tanzania we experienced nothing more sinister than mild abruptness; in general, Tanzanian officials will go out of their way to accommodate foreigners.

Some travellers behave as if they expect to be allowed to do what they like in African countries, as if they are above the law because they have a white skin and a foreign passport. This attitude is on the decline, but it still persists amongst some budget travellers. So, for the sake of clarity: if, for instance, you climb Kilimanjaro via an illegal route to avoid paying park entrance fees and are arrested, the person who arrests you is not being officious or bureaucratic, he is merely doing his job.

In remote parts of the country you may from time to time be approached by an immigration or police officer who wants to look over your passport. This happened to us a few times and in every instance it was handled in a relaxed, friendly manner. If it happens to you, expect to be asked where you have come from, where you are going, what you are doing in Tanzania etc. Don't read too much into this; it is the typical stuff of KiSwahili small talk. The officer concerned is as likely to be savouring an opportunity to practise his English as he is to have any professional interest in the trivia of your holiday. If you are in a rush, it can be a bit irritating to be cornered like this. There is no point in letting your irritation show. Smile, keep your answers simple, and you will soon be on your way.

# GETTING TO TANZANIA

## By air

The following airlines fly to Tanzania from Europe or the United Kingdom: Aeroflot, Air Tanzania, British Airways, Gulf Air, KLM, Lufthansa and Swissair. African airlines which fly to Tanzania from elsewhere in Africa include Air Botswana, Air Tanzania, Air Zimbabwe, EgyptAir, Ethiopian Airlines, Kenya Airways, Royal Swazi, South African Airways and Zambia Airways.

There are plenty of flights from Europe to Dar es Salaam. It is often cheaper to fly with an airline that uses a less direct route, such as Aeroflot or EgyptAir. Most African airlines fly to London and they are often cheaper than European airlines. London is the best place to pick up a cheap ticket; many continental travellers buy their tickets there.

Most people fly into Tanzania at Dar es Salaam, but there are also international flights to Kilimanjaro Airport (between Arusha and Moshi), and to Zanzibar. It is relatively straightforward to visit northern Tanzania from Nairobi (buses between Nairobi and Arusha take eight hours). It is generally cheaper to fly to Nairobi than Dar es Salaam; on the other hand a high percentage of travellers get ripped off in their first few days in Nairobi, so it is not the greatest introduction to the continent. Nairobi is the best place to pick up cheap tickets out of East Africa. For short stays in East Africa, some of the best deals are charter flights to Mombasa (Kenya), a day's bus ride from Tanga or an overnight train ride from Nairobi.

Two London travel agents specialise in Africa: African Travel

Systems (Glen House, Stag Place, London SE1E 5AG, tel: 0171 630 5434, fax: 0171 630 5470) and Africa Travel Shop (4 Medway Court, Leigh Street, London WC1H 9OX, tel: 0171 387 1211, fax: 0171 383 7512).

Trailfinders (42-48 Earls Court Road, London W8 6EJ, tel: 0171 938 3366) and STA (Priory House, 6 Wrights Lane, London W8 6TA, tel: 0171 361 6262, fax: 0171 937 9570) are both respected agents who do cheap flights worldwide, and are particularly worth speaking to for round-the-world type tickets. There are STA branches worldwide.

When you fly out of Tanzania, a $20 airport tax must be paid in hard currency. Travellers cheques are *not* accepted.

## Overland

Both overland routes between Europe and East Africa appear to be difficult at present. Southern Sudan is closed to tourists, so if you want to use the Nile route you must fly from Khartoum to Nairobi. From what I hear, several overland truck companies have stopped using the Sahara route due to banditry. Possibly people are still getting through, but in six months in East Africa, I didn't meet anyone who had come overland from the north.

Since South Africa has moved away from apartheid, the Cape to Nairobi route has become an overlander's standard. Some people start this trip in East Africa, others start in South Africa – there's not a lot in it. The advantage of starting in the south is that you can adapt to African conditions in the more organised environment of South Africa and Zimbabwe before you hit the relative chaos of East Africa; the disadvantage is that you will have to put up with the most trying travel conditions of the trip towards the end, after the novelty of being in Africa has worn off. These days Johannesburg is almost as good as Nairobi for cheap air tickets, so that is not a factor.

A proliferation of overland truck companies run regular trips between southern Africa (normally Johannesburg or Harare) and East Africa. The advantages of travelling on an overland truck are that it will visit remote areas which you would be unlikely to reach otherwise, and that you will see far more than you would by travelling independently for the same period of time; the disadvantages are that you will be in the company of the same 10 to 20 other people for the duration of the trip, and that the truck will cut you off from everyday African life.

Most of the people I've spoken to say their main reason for travelling on a truck is safety. It's worth saying, therefore, that this is by-and-large a safe and well-travelled region and that you will meet plenty of other single travellers. If you feel you would prefer to travel independently, don't let fear swing you in the opposite direction.

# Border crossings

Tanzania borders eight countries. A brief outline of frequently used border crossings follows:

## To/from Kenya

The most popular crossing is between Nairobi and Arusha via the Namanga border post. Several shuttle bus services run in both directions between Arusha and Nairobi daily. These take about four hours and cost $15 to $25 per person. They are advertised all over Arusha and Nairobi.

You can also do the trip between Nairobi and Arusha in stages, by catching a minibus between Nairobi and Namanga (these leave Nairobi from Ronald Ngala Road), crossing the border on foot, and then catching a shared taxi to Arusha. Expect this to take around six hours and cost $7 total in fares.

Provided your papers are in order, Namanga is a very straightforward border crossing. There is a bank where you can change money during normal banking hours. At other times, you'll have to change money with private individuals – don't change more than you need to as there are several con artists about.

An increasingly popular route between Kenya and Tanzania is from Mombasa to Tanga or Dar es Salaam. Again, this is straightforward enough, and a couple of buses do the run every day. However, you are strongly advised against taking the bus all the way to Dar es Salaam – it arrives at around midnight, when you would run a high risk of being mugged. Get off at Tanga and continue the next day.

A third route connects Moshi to Voi (on the Nairobi-Mombasa road) via Taveta. By road, this is a fairly slow route, involving a change of vehicles at Taveta, but you should get through in a day. In early 1996, a train service was resumed between Moshi and Voi, part of a weekly service that connects Dar es Salaam to Mombasa and Nairobi (see *Rail*).

A final route is between Kisumu and Mwanza on Lake Victoria. There are several buses daily along this route, leaving in the early morning and taking around 12 hours. Since early 1996, there is also a weekly ferry service between the two towns (see *Chapter Nine*).

## To/from Uganda

The simplest option is the weekly ferry between Port Bell and Mwanza (see *Chapter Nine*). The other route is via Masaka and Bukoba. Regular minibuses run from Masaka to Kyotera, where the odd pick-up truck leaves for the Mutukulu border. At Mutukulu you can pick up a Landrover to Bukoba. There are overnight ferries between Bukoba and Mwanza (see *Chapter Nine*).

## To/from Rwanda

The only route between Kigali and Mwanza is by road. This has never been a very popular route, even before Rwanda erupted into genocidal civil war in 1994. In 1992, you could get public transport between Kigali and the border at Rusumu, where there was a friendly but basic guesthouse on the Tanzanian side. From Rusumu, it was easy to get a truck through to Geita, where there are plenty of guesthouses and also buses through to Mwanza. I've not heard of anybody using this route in the last couple of years, but as recent reports suggest there are no major obstacles to travelling in Rwanda, it is presumably safe – nevertheless, you are advised to keep your ear to the ground.

## To/from Burundi

The straightforward option is the Lake Tanganyika ferry (see *Chapter Nine*). The trip can also be done in steps. Minibuses go from Bujumbura to the immigration office at Nyanza Lac and on to the border. At Kagunga, a 20-minute walk past the border, lake taxis run to Gombe Stream and Kalalangabo, 3km from Kigoma.

## To/from Zaire

Cargo boats between Kigoma and Kalemie might sometimes carry passengers, but don't rely on this. Most people go via Burundi.

## To/from Zambia

Zambia, the main gateway between East and southern Africa, can be reached by boat or rail. Tazara trains run twice-weekly from Dar es Salaam to Kapiri Mposhi, and are met by a bus to Lusaka. From western Tanzania, the easiest way to get to Zambia is on the Lake Tanganyika ferry (see Chapter Nine).

## To/from Malawi

The turn-off to the Malawi border is 5km from Kyela, on the Mbeya road. From there you can either take a bicycle taxi to the border or wait for a lift. In Malawi, a bus to Karonga arrives at the border at 7.00pm and leaves at 6.00am. It is forbidden to stay overnight at the border so the bus is of no use to travellers. However, provided that you arrive at the border before late afternoon, you should have no difficulty picking up a ride on a pick-up truck to Karonga.

# WHAT TO BRING

This depends largely on how you plan to travel. The following suggestions are mainly aimed at independent travellers.

## Backpacking and camping gear

A backpack is the only practical way to carry your luggage on public transport. An internal frame is more flexible than an external one. Ensure your pack is durable, that the seams and zips are properly sewn, and that it has several pockets. It is useful to carry a day pack.

Normally I wouldn't dream of travelling in Africa without a tent, but there are very few campsites in Tanzania. Nevertheless, it is advisable to carry a tent if you plan to travel or hike in remote areas. If you are going to camp, bring a sleeping bag and mat. Many parts of Tanzania are cold at night.

## Clothes

If you are travelling with everything on your back, keep your clothes to a minimum. A sweater is essential; more than one if you are heading into the mountains. Bring a pair of trousers for walking and to wear in the evening. Light cotton trousers are cooler and more practical than jeans. A track suit will double as thermal underwear if you intend to do high-altitude hiking. A hat and sunglasses are recommended.

Whatever else you bring should be light, flexible, comfortable, and made of cotton. A few T-shirts, a pair of shorts and/or a skirt, and a few pairs of underpants and socks is adequate.

What shoes you should bring depends on the sort of travelling you will be doing. The normal combination is a pair of trainers or hiking boots and either sandals, flip-flops or light slip-on shoes. I don't like flip-flops or sandals as they offer little protection against thorns, biting insects or potholed pavements, but I seem to be in a minority.

Tanzania's large Muslim population finds it offensive for a woman to expose her knees or shoulders. Women who do so can expect to meet with a certain amount of hostility. It is difficult to make hard and fast rules about what to wear, but some generalisations may help. Shorts are out, except at beach resorts, in game reserves, and possibly in Dar es Salaam or Arusha where people are used to tourists. For women, trousers are frowned upon in some quarters but they are just about acceptable. The ideal thing to wear is a skirt which covers your knees. A shoulderless t-shirt which exposes your bra – or worse – is unlikely to go down well (you laugh: I met someone dressed like this who couldn't figure out why she was hissed at wherever she went).

Men, too, should be conscious of what they wear. Shorts seem to be acceptable, but few Tanzanian men wear them and it is considered more respectable to wear trousers. Walking around in a public place without a shirt is totally unacceptable.

Many Tanzanians think it is insulting for westerners to wear scruffy or dirty clothes. Quite accurately, they feel you wouldn't dress like that at home. It is difficult to explain that at home you also wouldn't spend three successive days in crowded buses on dusty roads with a limited amount of clothing crumpled up in a backpack. If you are travelling rough, you are bound to look a mess at times, but it is worth trying to look as spruce as possible.

## Other odds and ends

This is a random series of observations on what is and isn't available in Tanzania.

Don't come without a torch, a towel, a day pack, and, if you are camping, pots and other cooking equipment. You cannot buy Camping Gaz in Tanzania.

If you wear contact lenses, bring all the fluids you need. They are not available in Tanzania. It is not necessary to carry a spare pair of glasses unless you already have one; they are cheap (around $10) and can be made up quickly in most Tanzanian towns. Bring your prescription though.

Locally manufactured insect repellent is a joke. The stuff we used left a trail of insects glued to our arms. Bring some with you, preferably roll-on.

Loo paper is widely available and cheap, but most toilets don't have any (this includes communal toilets in upper-range hotels). Always carry a spare roll with you.

Sanitary towels are manufactured locally. They are available in most large towns, but it is advisable to carry some spares. Tampons are imported and available in large towns only.

Many older hotels have baths but no bath plugs. You might want to consider carrying your own bath plug (though bear in mind that it's unusual for budget and moderate hotels to have hot water; a splash is often preferable to a wallow anyway).

Some cheap guesthouses don't supply you with a padlock. Bring your own just in case.

A collapsible umbrella offers useful protection against both sun and rain.

A travel alarm clock will be useful for all those 5.00am bus departures.

Books of any description are difficult to get hold of in Tanzania. Bring whatever field guides etc you want with you.

## Binoculars

It's worth bringing binoculars. They will add greatly to your enjoyment of a safari by allowing you to look at birds and distant animals. If you are buying binoculars especially for the trip, the newer compact variety generally have a crisper image than traditional binoculars, and they will certainly add less weight to your luggage; on the other hand, compact binoculars are considerably more expensive than the traditional variety, and they have a smaller field of vision. If you are spending an extended period of time in Tanzania, bear in mind that dust, rain and bad roads will all take their toll; you have less to lose if you buy a cheapish (or even secondhand) pair. For most uses, 8x32 compact or 7x35 traditional binoculars are good enough; if you are interested in birds and have reasonably steady hands, I recommend 10x40 or 10x50.

## MONEY

The unit of currency is the Tanzanian shilling. This is divided into 100 cents. At the time of writing the exchange rate is in the region of US$1 = Tsh300 to 600 with better rates offered at private Bureaux de Change than at banks. Throughout this guide prices are given in US dollars, calculated at the Bureau de Change rate.

Notes are printed in Tsh 1,000, 500, and 200/- denominations. There are also Tsh 10, 20 and 50/- coins. There are rumoured to be cent coins, but you are unlikely ever to see them (or find a use for them if you do).

### Foreign exchange

Foreign money can be changed into Tanzanian shillings at any bank or Bureau de Change (known locally as forex bureaux). Banking hours are from 08.30 to 12.30 on weekdays, and 08.30 to 11.30 on Saturdays. In larger towns, some banks stay open in the afternoon. Most forex bureaux stay open until 15.00 or 16.00.

Tanzania's currency was freed in early 1992 and since then a number of forex bureaux have opened, offering far more favourable rates than the banks. There are government-run forex bureaux at the main branch of the National Bank of Commerce in Arusha, Dar es Salaam, Mwanza and Namanga, and privately run forex bureaux in Arusha, Dar es Salaam, Mwanza, Mbeya and Dodoma. By the time you read this there should also be forex bureaux in Tanga and Kigoma. You can change money at any time of day at Dar es Salaam airport.

Privately run bureaux give the best rates. In Dar es Salaam there can be a variation of up to 10% in the rate offered by various forex bureaux. It is worth shopping around. Before you change a large amount of money, check the forex bureau has Tsh 500 or 1,000 banknotes.

Forex bureaux have killed the black market which previously thrived in Tanzania. Private individuals may give you a slightly better rate, but the official rate is so favourable it seems unfair to exploit this. In Dar es Salaam or Arusha you will be offered exceptionally good rates on the street. If you are stupid or greedy enough to accept these, expect to be ripped off.

There are plenty of forged $100 bills floating around Tanzania. Assume that anyone who suggests a deal involving a $100 bill is trying to unload a forgery.

At most overland borders there is nowhere to change money legally. You will have to change money with individuals. This is illegal, but as there is no option it is usually fairly open. If you can, get hold of some Tanzanian money in advance (ask travellers coming from Tanzania if they have some to swap).

On overland crossings I always carry a small surplus of the currency of the country I am leaving (about $10 worth), and try to change this into the currency I need. I feel safer swapping African currencies than changing US dollars.

Most hard currencies are accepted in Tanzania, but it is simplest to carry US dollars. There is a big difference in the exchange rates offered for cash and travellers cheques (cash gets you about 10% more). It is worth having some cash, but bring the bulk of your money in travellers cheques as they can be replaced if they are stolen. Many places will refuse to exchange $100 bills, due to the number of forgeries in circulation.

Some travel guides which include coverage of Tanzania claim that you are unlikely to use much local currency. Except at the very top of the range, this is rubbish and always has been. Most safari companies insist on being paid in hard currency, but the only other things that must be paid for in dollars are aeroplane fares, national park fees, airport and port taxes, and rooms at tourist hotels. Road, rail and ferry transport, meals, drinks, goods in shops and markets, and almost all moderate and budget accommodation can be paid for in local currency.

It is essential that you bring about US$200 in $5 and $10 bills for small payments that must be made in cash.

## Credit cards

There are several advantages in carrying a credit card: it will help you through immigration, will reduce the amount of cash you need to carry, and would be useful if all your money was pinched. Having said that, except in Dar es Salaam and Arusha, there are few places in Tanzania where credit cards are accepted. On balance I think it is worth carrying a credit card, but only to use in emergencies.

## Budgeting

Tanzania can be a very cheap country to travel in, though it is now considerably more expensive than countries such as Malawi and Ethiopia. Prices have risen by roughly 100% in the last few years, and most recognised tourist activities are relatively expensive.

Day-to-day costs in Tanzania are cheaper than they would be in most westernised countries. A soft drink will cost you around $0.50 and a beer slightly over $1 in a local bar, but considerably more in a tourist hotel. A meal in a local restaurant costs around $2, while a meal in a better restaurant might cost anything from $5 to $10. Basic local guesthouses typically cost around $3-4, though you can expect to pay double this in towns which see a lot of tourist traffic. Self-contained rooms in moderate hotels start at around $10, while you might pay anything up to $200 for a double room in a game lodge.

To give budget conscious travellers a broad idea of what to expect, you can get by in most parts of Tanzania on around $15 per day for one person or $20 per day for two. Double this amount, and within reason you can eat and stay where you like. You should expect to spend around $100 per day for the duration of activities such as a camping safari or Kilimanjaro climb.

## Notes on prices
All prices are in US dollars, calculated at the rate of US$1 = Tsh 500. The Tanzanian shilling has declined in value in the last few years, and if it continues to do so a price quoted in dollars is more likely to mean something in two years' time than one in Tanzanian shillings. Having said that, the currency has stabilised since it was floated. If it remains stable while internal inflation increases, prices may increase for tourists.

All these prices were in early 1996. Where HC appears after a price it must be paid in hard currency.

## GETTING AROUND
### By air
Air Tanzania flies between Dar es Salaam and several other Tanzanian towns. It has a poor reputation for reliability on more obscure routes, but flights between Dar es Salaam, Arusha and Zanzibar are more regular and reasonably reliable. Fares are around $50 return to Zanzibar and $125 return to Kilimanjaro International Airport (for Arusha or Moshi).

A private company called Precision Air (PO Box 1636, Arusha, tel: (057) 6903 or 2836 or 7319) flies between Arusha, Seronera (in the Serengeti), Mwanza, Bukoba, Dar es Salaam, Zanzibar and Mombasa (in Kenya). Their fares are cheaper and the flights are reputedly more reliable.

### By rail
There are three main railway lines in Tanzania. The northern line connects Dar es Salaam, and Moshi. The central line connects Dar es Salaam, Kigoma, Mwanza and Mpanda. The Tazara line connects Dar

es Salaam, Mbeya and Kapiri Mposhi (Zambia).

Trains are the most reliable and comfortable way of getting around. I used Tanzanian trains about ten times and only once did a train leave more than a few minutes late. That said, there has been little maintenance on trains in the last decade. The compartments are very run down and they have a pervasive smell of sweat and urine.

There are three classes. First class consists of two-berth compartments and second class consists of six-berth compartments. Men and women may not share a first or second class compartment unless they book the whole thing. Compartments vary in condition from acceptable to very tired-looking. Third class consists of seated carriages, but there are always more passengers than seats; it's only worth thinking about if you value neither your comfort nor your possessions.

Theft from train windows at night is not unusual. I have heard of someone whose rucksack was taken this way. Close the windows securely when you turn the light off. A block of wood is provided for this purpose; if you cannot find one in your compartment speak to the steward. Don't leave loose objects lying around the compartment; keep your luggage under the bunks. If you leave the compartment take all valuables with you.

All trains have dining cars. Meals are good and reasonably priced. Beers and sodas are normally available.

If you travel first class and do not want to leave your cabin empty, the steward can bring meals to you. In second class I would have no hesitation about going to the dining car provided other passengers remained in the compartment. At many stations vendors sell snacks and meals through the window.

It is advisable to book train tickets three days to a week in advance. It is easier to get last minute bookings on trains heading towards Dar es Salaam than on trains leaving it.

You may read elsewhere that ticket officers sometimes refuse to issue a ticket without a bribe. The story is that you go to the booking office on the morning of departure, and are told there are no tickets. You offer a bribe and are told to come back later, when a ticket magically appears. This has happened to me on a few occasions, but minus the bribe. It turns out a number of tickets are automatically held for institutions such as the army, police, and hospitals until a few hours before departure. If they are not taken, they become available to the public. I've not heard or seen anything that supports the bribe story.

## Central line

The central line runs from Dar es Salaam to Mwanza and Kigoma, stopping at Morogoro, Dodoma and Tabora. The train splits at Tabora: one half goes to Mwanza, the other to Kigoma. A third branch from

Tabora to Mpanda is run as a separate service.

Trains leave Dar es Salaam on Tuesday, Wednesday, Friday and Sunday at 18.00. Trains in the opposite direction leave on Tuesday, Thursday, Friday and Sunday. They leave Mwanza at 19.00 and Kigoma at 16.00. The full journey takes about 40 hours. Tickets can only be booked in advance at Dar es Salaam, Kigoma, Tabora and Mwanza. Elsewhere you will have to get on the train and hope for the best.

There is no direct service between Kigoma and Mwanza. You will have to take a train to Tabora, where you can make an onward booking. Extra carriages are added at Tabora, so most people have no problem getting through.

Trains to Mpanda leave Tabora on Monday, Wednesday and Friday. Trains to Tabora leave Mpanda on Tuesday, Thursday and Friday. In both directions, they leave at 22.45 and take 12 hours.

## Tazara line

Two trains run every week between Dar es Salaam and Kapiri Mposhi (Zambia). These leave Dar es Salaam on Tuesday and Friday at 16.55, and take 36 hours. Three additional slow trains run every week as far as Tunduma. These leave Dar es Salaam on Monday, Thursday and Saturday at 11.00. All trains stop at Ifakara, Mbeya and Tunduma. Slow trains pass through the Selous Game Reserve during daylight hours. There is usually plenty of game to be seen.

## Northern line

The northern line used to connect Dar es Salaam, Moshi and Tanga three times a week, but presumably due to the recent upgrading of roads in this part of Tanzania, the service has been cut back to twice a week, and there are no longer any passenger trains to Tanga. Trains from Moshi to Dar es Salaam leave at 16.00 on Monday and Saturday, while trains from Dar es Salaam leave at 16.00 on Friday and Sunday.

## Fares

Fares can be paid in local currency. Sample fares from Dar es Salaam to various destinations (in US dollars) follow:

|  | 1st | 2nd |
| --- | --- | --- |
| Mbeya | 45 | 25 |
| Kapiri Mposhi | 80 | 55 |
| Kigoma | 36 | 25 |
| Mwanza | 35 | 25 |
| Moshi | 23 | 17 |

In Dar es Salaam a 50% discount on the Tazara line is given to anyone with a student card. This takes a couple of hours. You must collect an application form from the Tazara station. You must then go to the Department of Education on Kivukoni Front where the form will be stamped. Finally you must return to the station to buy a ticket.

## Lake and ocean

There are several useful ferry services in Tanzania. A few boats go daily between Dar es Salaam and Zanzibar. A weekly service connects Dar es Salaam, Mtwara and Mafia, and another connecting Dar es Salaam, Zanzibar, Tanga, Pemba and Mombasa started operating in early 1993. In Dar es Salaam, details of all ferries can be obtained from the booking offices near the port on Kivukoni Front. See Chapters Twelve and Thirteen for further details.

There are ferry services on all three great lakes, run by the Tanzania Railway Corporation. For details see Chapter Nine (Victoria and Tanganyika) and Ten (Nyasa).

## Road

Bus services in Tanzania used to be amongst the worst in Africa, with old and poorly maintained vehicles trundling along dramatically potholed roads in a country where spares were practically non-existent. In 1986, I took an "express" bus between Nairobi and Dar es Salaam – 24 hours of bumping, grinding hell. Since the mid-1980s, there has been a gradual improvement in Tanzania's major roads and also in the vehicles used. The trip that took 24 hours in 1986 might take half that time now. For the nostalgic and masochistic, it's still perfectly possible to capture the flavour of public transport in the 1980s by bussing through more remote areas.

There are now speedy reliable express buses connecting Arusha, Moshi, Lushoto, Tanga and Dar es Salaam. Along these routes, you can expect to cover around 60km per hour, including a few breaks for drinks and meals. Bus services along the main south road connecting Dar es Salaam to Morogoro, Iringa and Mbeya are also reasonably quick and reliable, as are services between Mbeya and Kyela, and Dar es Salaam and Dodoma.

Elsewhere in Tanzania, buses are only worth considering where no rail or lake transport exists. The roads are generally in poor shape, vehicles are old and usually very crowded, and they tend to stop every couple of kilometres to pick up more passengers. A travelling time of around 20km per hour is not unusual, which means that a 250km trip can take around 12 hours. In the southern coastal region, you're pretty much stuck with bus transport, but in the west, you are strongly advised to use trains and ferries. Routes which should be avoided include the road between Dodoma and Arusha, and the Singida route between Mwanza and Arusha, which can take up to three days.

On some routes there is no formal public transport. You will generally find such routes are covered by *matatus* – a generic name for practically any vehicle that isn't a bus, most commonly an overcrowded and overpriced pick-up truck.

When you check out bus times, be very conscious of the difference between western time and Swahili time. Many Tanzanians will translate the Swahili time to English without making the six hour conversion – in other words, you'll be told a bus leaves at 11.00 when it actually leaves at 05.00. This fools a high proportion of travellers over their first few days in Tanzania. The best way to get around this area of potential misunderstanding is to confirm the time you are quoted in Swahili – for instance ask *"saa moja?"* if you are told a bus leaves at 13.00. See the appendix on Swahili Time for more details.

## Fares

It is impossible to document the price of every possible route in the country. To give you an idea of what to expect, here are some fairly typical rides, the distance covered and mode of transport, and approximate times and prices in US dollars. All road transport can be paid for in local currency. Prices quoted were collected in 1992, but there was only a negligible increase on routes I travelled again in 1996.

| | | Distance (km) | Hours | Price |
|---|---|---|---|---|
| Arusha/Dar es Salaam | bus | 647 | 12-15 | 10.00 |
| Arusha/Dar es Salaam | express bus | 647 | 10-12 | 12.50 |
| Arusha/Moshi | bus | 85 | 2 | 1.50 |
| Tanga/Lushoto | bus | 154 | 6+ | 2.00 |
| Mwanza/Arusha | bus via Serengeti | 692 | 12-18 | *65.00 |
| Mwanza/Arusha | bus via Singada | 855 | 36+ | 12.50 |
| Tanga/Dar es Salaam | express bus | 354 | 8 | 5.00 |
| Mtwara/Dar es Salaam | bus | 555 | 15+ | 6.00 |
| Dar es Salaam/Morogoro | bus | 196 | 4 | 2.00 |
| Dar es Salaam/Iringa | bus | 501 | 12 | 5.00 |
| Morogoro/Iringa | minibus | 305 | 7 | 3.50 |
| Dar es Salaam/Mbeya | bus | 851 | 15+ | 8.50 |
| Dodoma/Iringa | bus | 251 | 10+ | 2.50 |
| Dodoma/Arusha | bus | 687 | 20+ | 7.50 |
| Mbeya/Kyela | bus | 141 | 4 | 2.50 |
| Mbamba Bay/Mbinga | pick-up truck | 61 | 3+ | 3.00 |
| Mbinga/Songea | bus | 103 | 3 | 1.50 |
| Songea/Njombe | bus | 237 | 5 | 2.50 |
| Mbeya/Sumbawanga | bus | 322 | 8+ | 3.50 |
| Sumbawanga/Mpanda | lift with truck | 235 | 8+ | 5.00 |
| Mpanda/Ikola | lift with truck | 126 | 4+ | 4.00 |
| Rusumu/Mwanza | lift with truck | 400 | 18-48 | 10.00 |

*includes $40.00 in national park fees

## Bookings

On busy routes, buses leave when they are full. There is no need to book. On long hauls and quiet routes, there is normally a fixed departure time, so it is advisable to book the day before you leave. We were often given wildly inaccurate information about bus schedules. Ask a few people; don't take the word of the first person you speak to. In the main part of the guide I have given the current situation regarding frequency of buses and whether booking is necessary. Things change, however; you should make your own enquiries.

## Theft on buses

Wherever I have travelled in East Africa, I have handed my luggage to the conductor and let him get on with it. My bags have never been tampered with. Three months into this trip, I met a girl whose rucksack was broken into on Tanzanian buses four times in two weeks. I could not believe this was just a matter of luck, so in order to establish a pattern, I quizzed everyone I met about their experiences.

• The roof is the worst place for your luggage. Some conductors insist on putting it there (there is often no real option) but if possible try to get it into the body of the bus. If it does not fit on the racks, put it up near the driver.

• Avoid overnight buses. Almost all the theft stories I have heard relate to them. The Arusha-Dodoma and Dar es Salaam-Mbeya routes are particularly bad.

• Be wary of strangers who offer you food. I have heard of travellers being given drugged food and having their possessions taken while they are asleep (one incident each on the two routes mentioned above).

• Be vigilant when the bus is stationary. The snatch-and-grab experts who hang round most bus stations are not above grabbing something through the window. If anyone is hanging around, catch their eye so they know you are aware of them.

• Don't leave valuables on your lap. It sounds obvious; I met someone whose money belt was snatched from his lap while he was fiddling in his day pack.

## Hitching

There is little scope for hitching in Tanzania. On routes where there is no public transport you may have to hitch, but generally this will be on the back of a truck and you will have to pay. Hitching is an option on the Arusha-Dar es Salaam-Mbeya road.

## Car hire

Self-drive car hire isn't a popular or particularly attractive option in Tanzania, as it is generally more straightforward to visit game reserves on an organised safari. Until recently, there were also no reliable car rental companies in the country. Avis is now represented in Dar es Salaam (tel: 30505/34562, fax: 37426/37442), with an office off Maktaba Street, right behind the YWCA. Their rates start at $50/day for a saloon car and $80/day for a 4x4, with unlimited kilometres if you take a vehicle for three days or more.

# ACCOMMODATION

Most Tanzanian towns have a variety of moderately priced and budget hotels. Even the smallest villages usually have somewhere you can stay for a dollar or so. Except in major tourist centres, there is little in the way of luxury accommodation.

I have divided accommodation into four categories: camping, budget, moderate and upper range. These categories are based more on feel than on price, but except in Dar es Salaam and Arusha, prices are reasonably consistent: budget is under $3, moderate from $3 to $10, and upper range anything above that. In Dar es Salaam and Arusha, budget is under $10, moderate up to $30, and upper range anything above that.

Remember that in KiSwahili, *hoteli* means restaurant; if you ask people for a hotel, you will get a *hoteli* (see *Swahili* appendix).

## Camping

There are few campsites in Tanzania, and those that exist tend to be in national parks, where camping costs $20 per person. There are private campsites in the Arusha-Kilimanjaro area. If you ask at moderate hotels in out of the way places, you may be allowed to camp in their grounds for a fee.

If you are hiking in areas off the beaten track, a tent will be a distinct asset. You should, however, be discreet; either set up well away from villages or else ask permission from the village headperson before you pitch a tent. I've not met many people who have camped rough in Tanzania, but it's hard to imagine there would be a significant risk attached to camping in rural areas, provided you didn't flaunt your presence or leave your tent unguarded for a lengthy period.

## Budget

Most budget accommodation in Tanzania consists of guesthouses. These are almost exclusively used by locals, and are remarkably uniform in design and price. The typical guesthouse is made up of cell-like rooms forming three walls around a central courtyard, with a reception area or restaurant at the front. Toilets are more often than not long-drops. Washing facilities usually amount to a lockable room and a bucket of cold water, though some have showers. There are perhaps five guesthouses in the whole of Tanzania which have running hot water. Quite a few will supply you with a basin of hot water on request.

Tanzanian guesthouses may be basic, but the majority are reasonably clean and pleasant, and are good value when compared to similar establishments in neighbouring countries. You will rarely pay more than $5 for a room in a Tanzanian guesthouse. We found that guesthouses run by women or with a strong female presence were generally cleaner and more hospitable than those run by men. There is a strong town-to-town variation in guesthouse quality: in some towns a clean, freshly-painted room with mosquito nets and a fan is standard; in others – Iringa and Bukoba leap to mind – three-quarters of the places we looked at were totally unappealing.

In most medium-sized towns there are a couple of dozen guesthouses, usually clustered around the bus station and often with little to choose between them. In such cases I have avoided making individual recommendations.

There are a handful of church-run guest houses and hostels in Tanzania. These are normally included under budget accommodation.

## Moderate

This category covers everything that isn't a guesthouse or a so-called tourist hotel, and defies generalisations. Typically, a moderate hotel has self-contained rooms with cold running water, and can be paid for in local currency. Most moderate hotels include a continental breakfast in the price of a room, but this rarely amounts to more than dry bread and coffee.

## Upper range

These are official tourist hotels, and must be paid for in hard currency. Prices vary wildly, but typically you will be looking at around $60 to $120 for a double room, double that for lodge accommodation in national parks. This invariably includes breakfast. Tourist hotels are concentrated in Dar es Salaam, Zanzibar, Tanga and the Kilimanjaro-Arusha-Serengeti area. There are only a handful in the south and west of the country. Most hotels in this range have a lower rate for Tanzanian residents. This difference can be as much as 60% less, especially in hotels run by the TTC. All TTC hotels offer a 50% discount between the day after Easter Monday and 30 June.

## Staying with Tanzanians

Unless you travel off the beaten track or have addresses of friends, you are unlikely to stay with Tanzanians much. If you stay with expats, be sensitive to their way of life. People living in the sticks are often delighted to have fresh company, but not always. If people evidently have a busy lifestyle, try not to get in the way: play with their children (if they have any) and help around the house.

In the past travellers have taken it to be their right to stay with aid workers or at missions. This goes back to the days when comparatively few backpackers travelled in Africa and those who did received a level of hospitality which reflected their novelty. Those days are long gone, but the on-the-cheap attitude still persists in some quarters. Many expats have suffered from travellers overstaying their welcome; don't necessarily expect people to welcome you with open arms.

# EATING AND DRINKING

## Eating

If you are not too fussy and don't mind a lack of variety, you can eat well and cheaply almost anywhere in Tanzania. In most towns numerous local restaurants, called *hotelis*, serve unimaginative but filling meals for around $2. *Hotelis* vary greatly in quality: I have had some very tasty meals in them, but as often as not gristle and sludge would be an appropriate description of what you are served.

Most *hoteli* food is based around a stew eaten with one of four staples: rice, *chapati*, *ugali* or *batoke*. *Ugali* is a stiff maize porridge eaten throughout sub-Saharan Africa. *Batoke* or *matoke* is cooked plantain, served boiled or in a mushy heap. In the Lake Victoria region, *batoke* replaces *ugali* as the staple food. The most common stews are chicken, beef, goat and beans. In coastal towns and around the great lakes, whole fried fish is a welcome change.

*Mandazi*, the local equivalent of doughnuts, are tasty when freshly cooked. They are served at *hotelis* and sold at markets. You can eat cheaply at stalls around markets and bus station. Goat kebabs, fried chicken, grilled groundnuts and potato chips are often freshly-cooked and sold in these places.

Cheap it may be, but for most travellers *hoteli*-fare soon palls. In most larger towns, there are what could be termed proper restaurants. These are normally within the reach of any budget, and would typically serve a variety of meat, steak and chicken dishes with potato chips or rice, and cost around $5 for a main course. There is considerably more culinary variety in Dar es Salaam and Arusha, where for around $8-10 you can eat very well.

At one time, walking around a Tanzanian market you would see little but onions and bananas. This has improved, and in most towns a reasonable variety of fruits, vegetables, pulses and beans can be bought, depending on the season. The most common fruits are mangoes, oranges, bananas, pineapples, papaya and coconuts. Fresh fruit is dirt cheap in Tanzania.

**Note**: KiSwahili names for various foods are given in the KiSwahili appendix.

## Drinks

The most widely drunk beverage is *chai*, a sweet tea where all ingredients are boiled together in a pot. Along the coast *chai* is often flavoured with spices such as ginger. In some places *chai* is served *ya rangi* or black; in others *mazewa* or milky. Sodas such as Coke, Pepsi, Sprite and Fanta are widely available, and cost about $0.25. In large towns you can often get fresh fruit juice.

The two main alcoholic drinks are beer and *konyagi. Konyagi* is a spirit made from sugar cane. It tastes a bit strange on its own, but mixes well and is very cheap. The local beers, Safari, Pilsner and Guinness, come in 500ml bottles and cost around $1.50. Pilsner is OK, Guinness is unlikely to tempt any Irishmen to emigrate, and Safari, the most widely available beer, is never better than drinkable. Kenyan beers are better, and are widely available north of Dar es Salaam. Around Mbeya, try Carlsberg Green, an excellent Malawian beer. Around Lake Tanganyika, another excellent beer, Zairean *Primus*, comes in 750ml bottles and costs about $1. In Dar es Salaam, a variety of Kenyan, South African and European beers are available, but they are quite expensive.

A variety of imported spirits is available in larger towns, often at ridiculously cheap prices.

## SHOPPING

Until a few years ago it was difficult to buy anything much in Tanzania. One of my most vivid memories of Dar es Salaam in 1986 was walking into a general store where a lone shelf of teaspoons was the only stock. Things have improved greatly since then. In Dar es Salaam and most other large towns a fair range of imported goods is available, though prices are often inflated. If you have any very specific needs – unusual medications or slide film for instance – bring them with you.

Toilet roll, soap, toothpaste, pens, batteries and locally-produced food are widely available. *Dukas*, the stalls you see around markets or lining roads, are cheaper than proper shops and are open seven days a week. Even in Dar es Salaam, we were rarely overcharged because we were tourists.

Shopping hours are normally between 08.30 and 16.30, with a lunch break between 13.00 and 14.00.

## Curios

A variety of items specifically aimed at tourists is available: Makonde carvings, batiks, musical instruments, wooden spoons, and various soapstone and malachite knick-knacks. The curio shops near the clock tower in Arusha are the best place to shop for curios. Prices are competitive and the quality is good. Prices in shops are fixed, but you may be able to negotiate a discount. At curio stalls, haggling is necessary. Unless you are good at this, expect to pay more than you would in a shop.

If you have an interest in African music, a good range of tapes is available at stalls in Dar es Salaam city centre. Most are of Zairean groups which are popular in East Africa: Loketa, Kanda Bongoman, Bossi Bossiana and the like.

The colourful *Vitenge* (the singular of this is *Kitenge*) worn by most Tanzanian women can be picked up cheaply at any market in the country. I've been told Mwanza is a particularly good place to shop for these and other cloths.

## Bargaining

It is commonly asserted that nothing in Africa has a fixed price. To an extent this is true; nevertheless, you need a certain amount of sensitivity to know when haggling is appropriate. Many travellers arrive in Africa expecting everyone to overcharge them and so they enter into all transactions with paranoid aggression; this is understandable but unnecessary.

There are no hard and fast rules as to when you should and shouldn't bargain. You must be responsive to each situation and judge it on its own merits. My own feeling is that the issue of bargaining has been misrepresented by travel guides in the past; it's worth discussing in some detail.

Anyone who regularly deals with tourists will be open to negotiation. This includes taxi drivers, safari operators and stall owners in Dar es Salaam and Arusha, and curio stalls anywhere. Where haggling is the norm, it is best viewed as something that can add an enjoyable new dimension to your holiday. With experienced hagglers you must appear to be firm. This doesn't mean you need to be ungracious; except in extreme situations, yelling and throwing tantrums is simply loutish.

In non-tourist areas, you will seldom be overcharged. Some travellers challenge every price as a matter of course, often accompanied with accusations of dishonesty. Try, instead, to establish the going rate in advance: find out what locals pay (it helps if you can count in Swahili) or visit a few stalls before you buy (an inflated price will drop the moment you walk away). If someone is unwilling to barter, the probability is that they asked a fair price in the first place.

You should be wary of rigid advice; for instance, that you will normally be asked double the price the person will eventually settle for. In Kenya, I was once asked Ksh 200/- for a batik; I didn't want it so said Ksh 20/- as a joke. I got it for Ksh 30/-. At the other end of the scale, on about half the occasions when we used taxis in Dar es Salaam (where I would expect to be overcharged) we were asked the going rate straight off.

Do not assume that things will cost the same from one town to the next. As an example, in three successive villages we passed through on a bus, oranges cost Tsh 5/-, 10/- and 20/- (the price they were asking locals, not us). You'll often find large price differences from town to town for such commodities as beer, sodas and fruit – and even accommodation.

Above all, don't lose your sense of proportion. No matter how poor you may feel, it is your choice to travel on a tight budget. Most Tanzanians are much poorer than you will ever be and they do not have the luxury of choice. If you find yourself quibbling with an old lady selling a few piles of fruit on the roadside, stand back and look at the bigger picture. There is nothing wrong, occasionally, with erring on the side of generosity.

## PHOTOGRAPHY

Tanzania's abundant wildlife, varied scenery and colourfully dressed people are a photographer's dream. Low speed 64 ASA and 100 ASA films are ideal, but for close-up shots of animals faster speeds such as 400 ASA may be better. Except in Dar es Salaam and Arusha, film is difficult to get hold of. If you use slide film, bring what you need with you.

If you are buying a camera especially for the trip, bear in mind that the simpler the camera is, the less there is to go wrong. Complex electronic gadgetry is highly sensitive to rain and dust. The most solid and reliable camera for African conditions is the Pentax K1000; a good second-hand one shouldn't cost more than £100 in London. For animal photography, a zoom lens is essential (200 magnification is adequate). Don't forget to bring a couple of spare lens caps and, if your camera uses one, a spare battery.

Until recently, photographing something outside of a game reserve could land you in trouble. This has relaxed in the last few years, but it remains illegal to photograph military installations or government buildings (bridges, stations etc). If in doubt, ask.

It is rude to photograph someone without permission. Most people will let you take their photo, but always ask first. If someone refuses or demands a fee, that is their prerogative.

# MEDIA AND COMMUNICATIONS

## Newspapers

The English language *Daily News* is available in Dar es Salaam and other major towns. It doesn't have much international news, but the local news can make interesting reading. The Kenyan *Daily Nation*, available in Dar es Salaam, Arusha and Mwanza, is better.

Stalls in Uhuru Avenue, Dar es Salaam, sell *Time* and *Newsweek*, as well as a variety of European, British and American papers. You can sometimes buy foreign newspapers at the bookstall in the New Arusha Hotel in Arusha.

The weekly *East African*, an English language newspaper published in Kenya, gives good regional coverage.

## Post

Post from Tanzania is cheap and reliable. Incoming post arrives surprisingly quickly, and the Poste Restante service in Dar es Salaam is amongst the best in Africa. There is a nominal charge for collecting letters. Mail should be addressed as follows:

BRIGGS, Philip
Poste Restante
Main GPO
Dar es Salaam
Tanzania

Suggest when people write to you they underline your surname, so that the letter doesn't get misfiled. It is advisable to check under both names when you visit the post office.

## Phone calls

If you want to make an international phone call or fax, there is a TCC Extelcomms centre in most large towns. The staff are normally helpful and calls are cheap by international standards. Some Extelcomms centres will receive as well as send faxes. Phone calls and faxes to Europe cost around $16 per minute or page.

# PLANNING AN ITINERARY

Tanzania's main tourist circuit centres around Zanzibar, Dar es Salaam, Kilimanjaro and the northern game reserves. If you only have two or three weeks in the country and plan on visiting Zanzibar, climbing Kilimanjaro and going on safari, you are unlikely to be able to fit much else in. If you have a few extra days, however, or don't want to climb Kilimanjaro, you could include just about anywhere covered in Chapter Six in your itinerary, or could think about climbing Mount Meru or visiting Pemba Island.

The itinerary below is fairly typical, and includes a five-day safari and three nights on Zanzibar. You would need an extra five or six days to climb Kilimanjaro.

| Day 1 | Dar es Salaam |
|---|---|
| Day 2 | Catch a bus to Arusha |
| Day 3-4 | Organise safari from Arusha, book train for day 10 |
| Day 5-9 | Safari; sleep night 9 in Arusha |
| Day 10 | Overnight train to Dar es Salaam |
| Day 11-13 | Zanzibar |
| Day 14 | Return to Dar es Salaam |
| Day 15 | Fly home |

Beyond this, it is difficult to recommend any particular itinerary. Tanzania is a large, diverse country, transport there is slow, and people's tastes and interests differ. Unless you have a lot of time – six weeks at least – you are unlikely to be able to do more than concentrate on a couple of particular areas. Whatever you do, allocate your time reasonably generously; if you don't you are likely to spend most of your trip on public transport.

To give you some idea, if you wanted to visit Rubondo Island, you would be looking at a 10 to 14 day round trip from Dar es Salaam, and even Gombe Stream would be a week's round trip. The south coast could be explored comfortably over seven to ten days, the Udzungwa Mountains would be a good four to five day trip, the southern highlands and Lake Nyasa would be good for anything over a week, and the Selous is normally visited on a four to five day safari.

Visitors who have a longer period of time could do one of a few loops: you could, for instance, catch a train to Mbeya, spend a few days exploring around Tukuyu, cross to Mtwara via Lake Nyasa and Songea and then work your way up the south coast. Another possibility from Mbeya is to work your way up to Mwanza via Lake Tanganyika taking in some of the western national parks on the way, then catch a bus across the Serengeti to Arusha and return to Dar es Salaam from there. For either of these trips, you would want around a month.

When it comes to really off-the-beaten-track hiking, the only limitation is your imagination. Even a small-scale map of Tanzania throws up plenty of alluring possibilities, some of which are mentioned under *Hiking* in *Chapter Two*.

Chapter Four

# Health and Safety

*Written in collaboration with Dr Jane Wilson Howarth*

Tanzania boasts an array of tropical diseases but, although most travellers who spend a while in the country will become ill at some point in their trip, the cause is most likely to be simple travellers' diarrhoea or a cold. Provided that you receive the necessary immunisations before travelling to Tanzania, the only major causes for concern once you are in the country are malaria and bilharzia. These can be largely avoided by taking sensible precautions (subjects which are covered more fully below).

## PREPARATIONS

### Travel insurance

Don't think about visiting Tanzania without a comprehensive medical travel insurance: one that will fly you home in an emergency. The ISIS policy, available in Britain through STA (tel: 0171 361 6262), is inexpensive and has a good reputation.

Pack a good insect repellent, at least one long-sleeved cotton shirt and one pair of long trousers, a hat and sunscreen; these are also important insurance measures.

### Immunisations

British readers are advised to visit one of the 36 British Airways Travel Clinics (tel: 0171 831 5333 for the nearest location) before they visit Tanzania. These clinics are amongst many which now have daily-updated computer links with centres for tropical medicine. It is thus easy to ascertain what you risk in a particular season and region. It is advisable to make such enquiries several weeks before you depart, as some immunisations involve more than one shot over a course of two or three weeks. They also stock a range of products useful to travellers, including bed nets, repellents, etc.

You will need a yellow fever immunisation, and may be required to show an international immunisation certificate as proof of this. It is wise to be immunised against meningitis, polio and tetanus. Hepatitis

A immunisation with the Havrix vaccine, launched in the UK in 1992, is also recommended. The immunisation, which can be given by your GP or any travel clinic, is more expensive than most (£40). Don't let this dissuade you from having it. Havrix gives you ten years' protection against a disease which could effectively end your travels and leave you ill for several months; local doctors say that visitors to Tanzania commonly catch hepatitis A. If you intend travelling far from medical facilities, consider typhoid and rabies immunisation. Rabies is cheapest if arranged through a travel clinic since one ampoule can be used for eight patients; your GP is unlikely to have that number of applicants unless you are travelling as a group.

## Medical kit

Take a small medical kit with you. This should contain malaria tablets and a thermometer, soluble aspirin or paracetamol (good for gargling when you have a sore throat and for reducing fever and pains), plasters (Band-aids), potassium permanganate crystals or another favoured drying antiseptic, iodine for sterilising water and cleaning wounds, syringe and needles, sunblock, and condoms or femidoms. Some travel clinics in Britain will try to persuade you to buy a variety of antibiotics. This is not necessary: most antibiotics are widely available in Tanzania, and you should be hesitant about taking them without medical advice. Depending on your travel plans, it is a good idea to carry a course of treatment for malaria – the combination of Fansidar and quinine tablets is currently recommended. As food in Tanzania tends to be based around meat and carbohydrates some people may like to carry vitamin pills.

## DISEASES

### Diarrhoea and related illnesses

Diarrhoea affects at least half of those who travel in the tropics. The best solution is to rest up for a day, and to stop eating heavy greasy foods, avoid alcohol, and take only clear fluids. Stick to a very light plain diet – lots of fluids plus dry biscuits or boiled potatoes or rice. The bacteria which are responsible for most diarrhoea and related symptoms (such as the abdominal pains caused by the stomach trying to expel bad food) will normally die within 36 hours if they are deprived of food.

Blockers such as Imodium, Lomotil and Codeine Phosphate should only be taken if you have no access to sanitation, for instance if you *have* to travel by bus. Blockers keep the poisons in your system, and so make you feel bad for longer. They are sometimes useful if bowel cramps persist for more than 48 hours, as can be the case with salmonella food poisoning. On the other hand, it is dangerous to take blockers when you have dysentery (evidenced by blood, slime or fever with the diarrhoea). Really, if diarrhoea or stomach problems persist beyond 36 hours, the sensible thing to do is consult a doctor or pharmacist. The chances are you have nothing serious, but you may have something treatable.

When you have diarrhoea, it is important to drink a lot. Paediatric rehydration fluids such as Dioralyte and Rehidrat are excellent, or you can make your own salt and sugar rehydration fluid (see box below). If you are vomiting you can still absorb sipped fluids, and combinations of sugar, salt and water or commercial rehydration solutions are absorbed best. Sip the drink slowly and avoid anything that is very hot or cold. Try to drink a glass of rehydration fluid every time your bowels open. If you are not eating, you need to drink around three litres of fluid daily in a temperate climate, more if it is hot, you are at a high altitude, or you have fever or diarrhoea. If you are vomiting, do not worry about the quantity you produce – it is never as much as it looks. Dehydration is the only serious complication of diarrhoea and vomiting; provided you keep sipping slowly you will replace sufficient lost fluids, even if you have cholera.

Stomach problems associated with severe flatulence, abdominal distension, stomach cramps and sulphurous belching may well be caused by giardia. Giardia is not a serious illness, but it is unpleasant enough that you will want treatment as quickly as possible. Giardia is cured with a course of Flagyl (Metronidozole), 2g daily for three days, and this is readily available in Tanzania. You shouldn't touch alcohol while taking treatment for giardia.

If you have diarrhoea with blood, or you have a fever, see a doctor for a stool test. Provided that you are taking plenty of fluids, you need not be in a great rush about this, but nor is there any point in delaying: chronic diarrhoea will make it practically impossible to travel anywhere, and if nothing else seeing a doctor will ease your mind.

## How to avoid diarrhoea and other food-and-water-borne diseases

There are a great many myths about how diarrhoea is acquired, but most travellers become sick from contaminated food. Salads, especially lettuce, are always a likely source of diarrhoea. Food which is freshly cooked or thoroughly reheated should be safe, and sizzling hot street foods are invariably safer than those served at buffets at expensive hotels. Ice-cream is an ideal medium for bacterial cultures and it is often not kept adequately frozen due to power cuts. Ice may be made with unboiled water, and it could have been deposited by the roadside on its journey from the ice factory.

The best way to purify water is by boiling it: simply bringing it to the boil kills 99% of bugs, and keeping it on the boil for a further minute kills everything at any altitude you are likely to ascend to. Boiling water is more effective than using iodine, which is in turn more effective than any chlorine-based water purification tablet.

## Malaria

Malaria kills about a million Africans every year. Of the travellers who return to Britain with malaria, 92% have caught it in Africa. You are 100 times more likely to catch malaria in Africa than you are in Asia.

The risk of contracting malaria in Tanzania should not be underestimated. Malaria is present in most parts of tropical Africa below 1,800m, and the *Anopheles* mosquito which transmits the malaria parasite is most abundant near the marshes and still water in which it breeds. In other words, malaria is most prevalent in low-lying wet areas, especially after rain.

In Tanzania, malaria can be contracted anywhere that lies below an altitude of 1,800m, which includes almost all of the country. In medium altitude areas, malaria is only a serious cause for concern during the rainy season and cases are comparatively rare during the drier months. The risk is greatest at lower altitudes, notably the coast and Lake Nyasa, Tanganyka and Victoria areas. In such places malaria is a major risk at any time of the year, but especially bad during the rainy season.

The first step in preventing malaria is to take prophylactic drugs.

---

## HOW TO MAKE ORAL REHYDRATION FLUID

People with diarrhoea or who are vomiting regularly need to take in more fluids or they will become dehydrated. When the intestine is upset absorption of fluids is less efficient. All solids, especially if they are greasy, are poorly tolerated and may cause colic. The ideal solution is a mixture of two heaped teaspoons of glucose and a three-finger pinch (less than a quarter of a teaspoon) of salt in a glass of cooled boiled water. Drink a glass of this at least every time your bowels open; more often if you want. If you feel nauseous or are actually vomiting, sip the drink very slowly. If glucose is unavailable, sugar, palm syrup or honey are good substitutes. If none of these, or boiled water, are available put a pinch of salt in any flattened sweet soda such as cola.

Any clear solution is OK to drink: from sweet black tea, a staple in Eritrea, to drinks made from Marmite and Bovril and clear thin soup. The secret is to drink a combination of salt and sugar, so add a little salt to sweet drinks, or sugar to salty drinks. The solution should taste no more salty than tears. Quantity is more important than constituents.

You can ignore any stories you hear on the travellers' grapevine about it being better to acquire resistance than to take tablets. It is not possible to build up any real effective resistance to malaria and travellers risk death by not taking precautions. It is foolhardy not to take malaria tablets.

The malaria tablet currently recommended for visitors spending less than a year in East Africa is Larium (Mefloquine). Larium is generally effective in preventing malaria, and surveys on returning travellers have shown less side effects than with the combination of Chloroquine and Paludrine (the other option). Side effects probably are less common with Larium, but they are also more dramatic when they do occur. Many people who use Larium experience sleeplessness or disturbing nightmares, and in extreme cases (generally only in curative doses) the drug can lead to serious psychological problems. Larium should definitely not be taken by someone with a history of psychological problems or severe depression. If you don't fall into this category, and you are a non-pregnant adult, Larium is the recommended drug. You can exclude side effects by taking it for two to three weeks prior to departure; if it starts affecting your moods or sleep patterns, you might want to switch to the Chloroquine and Paludrine combination. If you are spending more than a year in the region or are planning a pregnancy (when you should take special advice), you should probably take Chloroquine (two weekly) and Paludrine (two daily) from the start, as Larium is a new drug and doctors are uncertain about how long it is safe to take it for.

Malaria resistance patterns change, and so thus does the effectiveness of any given drug. Your GP may not be aware of new developments, or have specialist knowledge regarding potential side effects and contra-indications; you are advised to consult a travel clinic for current advice, or to phone 0171 636 7921 for recorded information.

Equally as important as taking malaria pills is making every reasonable effort not to be bitten by mosquitoes between dusk and dawn. Many travellers assume that simply taking pills gives then full protection against malaria. It doesn't. It stuns me how many travellers wander around at night in shorts and flip-flops in parts of Africa where malaria is prolific. Resistance to prophylactics is widespread in Africa, and the most certain way not to catch malaria is to not be bitten by mosquitoes. This doesn't mean that avoiding bites is an alternative to taking pills – nobody will be able to prevent every potential bite – but you should do both. Measures for preventing bites are discussed later in this chapter under the heading *Insects*.

Even if you take your malaria tablets meticulously and take care to avoid being bitten, you might still contract a resistant strain of malaria. If you experience headaches and pains, or even a general sense of

# BILHARZIA OR SCHISTOSOMIASIS

*Dr Jane Wilson Howarth*

Bilharzia or schistosomiasis is a common debilitating disease afflicting perhaps 200 million people worldwide, but those most affected are the rural poor of the tropics who repeatedly acquire more and more of these nasty little worm-lodgers. Fortunately travellers and expatriates generally suffer fewer problems if they acquire bilharzia because they pick up relatively few parasites and so their burden of worms is less; they are also likely to realise they have bilharzia early and get it treated promptly.

When someone with bilharzia excretes into freshwater, bilharzia eggs hatch and swim off to find a suitable freshwater snail to infest. Once inside the snail, they develop, change and emerge as torpedo-shaped cercariae; these are only just visible to the naked eye, and can digest their way through human or animal skin. This is the stage that attacks people as they wade, bathe or even shower in infested water, and unfortunately many lakes, including Lake Nyasa, and also rivers and irrigation canals in Africa carry a risk of bilharzia.

The pond snails which harbour bilharzia are a centimetre or more long; they like well-oxygenated, still or slowly moving freshwater, with plenty of vegetation (water-weed, reeds, etc) for them to eat. The most risky shores will be close to places where infected people use water, where they wash clothes. Winds disperse the cercariae though, so that they can be blown some distance, perhaps 200m, from where they entered the water. Scuba diving off a boat into deep off-shore water, then, should be a low risk activity, but showering in lake water or paddling along a reedy lake shore near a village carries a high risk of acquiring bilharzia.

Water which has been filtered or stored snail-free for two days, or water which has been boiled, treated with Cresol or Dettol is also safe. Covering your skin with an oily insect repellent like DEET before swimming or paddling is also protective.

Cercariae live for up to 30 hours after they have been shed by snails, but the older they are, the less vigorous they are and the less capable of penetrating the skin. Cercariae are shed in the greatest numbers between 11am and 3pm. If water to be used for bathing is pumped early in the morning, from deep in the lake (cercariae are sun-loving) or from a site far from where people urinate, there will be less risk of infestation. And

disorientation or flu-like aches and pains, you may have malaria. It is vital you seek medical advice immediately. Local doctors see malaria all the time; they will know it in all its guises and know the best treatment for local strains. Untreated malaria can be fatal, but even resistant strains normally respond well to treatment, provided that you do not leave it too late.

If you are unable to reach a doctor you may well be forced to diagnose afternoon swims will be a much higher risk than an early morning plunge. Since cercariae take perhaps 10-15 minutes to penetrate, a quick shower, or a splash across a river, followed by thorough drying with a towel, should be safe. Even if you are in risky water longer it is worth vigorously towelling off after bathing: this will kill any cercariae which are still in the process of penetrating your skin.

Only a proportion of cercariae which successfully penetrate will survive and cause disease. Although absence of early symptoms does not necessarily mean there is no infection, infected people usually notice symptoms two or more weeks after penetration. Travellers and expatriates will probably experience a fever and often a wheezy cough; local residents do not usually have symptoms. There is now a very good blood test which, if done six weeks or more after likely exposure, will determine whether or not parasites are going to cause problems and then the infection can be treated. While treatment generally remains effective, there are treatment failures and retreatment is often necessary; the reasons for treatment failures are not yet fully understood, but there now may be some drug resistance. Since bilharzia can be a nasty illness, avoidance is better than waiting to be cured and it is wise to avoid bathing in high risk areas.

## Summary points

If you are bathing, swimming, paddling or wading in freshwater which you think may carry a bilharzia risk, try to get out of the water within ten minutes.

• Dry off thoroughly with a towel.

• Avoid bathing or paddling on shores within 200m of villages or places where people use the water a great deal, especially reedy shores or where there is plenty of water weed.

• Ideally cover yourself with DEET insect repellent before swimming.

• If your bathing water comes from a risky source, try to ensure that the water is taken from the lake in the early morning and stored snail-free, otherwise it should be filtered or Dettol or Cresol added.

*Thanks to Dr Vaughan Southgate of the Natural History Museum, London, and to Dr G B Wyatt of the Liverpool School of Tropical Medicine for up to date information on bilharzia in Lake Nyasa.*

and treat yourself. For this reason, it is advisable to carry a cure in your medical kit. Expert opinion is that the most safe and effective cure available at present is the combination of Fansidar and quinine. This cure needs to be used in conjunction with a thermometer, so carry one of these as well. The correct procedure is to take two quinine tablets every eight hours until the fever subsides, for a maximum of three days. When the fever subsides, or if it hasn't subsided after three days, take a single dose of three Fansidar tablets. Provided you follow this procedure before the symptoms have become severe, it is practically 100% effective. Be warned, however, that you must try to drink a lot of water after you take Fansidar.

The quinine/Fansidar combination is a slow cure, for which reason many people will advise you to skip the quinine altogether and to take the Fansidar straight away. There is certainly an argument for going straight on to Fansidar (I've spoken to several people who've been up and walking within 24 hours of taking it), but the problem with this approach is that, on its own, it is not always completely effective. It could easily be that the best cure for malaria changes during the lifespan of this edition, so seek current advice from a travel clinic or another reliable source before you leave for Tanzania.

Malaria typically takes one to two weeks to incubate but it can take as long as a year. This means that you may only display symptoms after you leave Tanzania, for which reason you are advised to continue with prophylactics for four weeks after returning home. It is all too easy to forget your pills once you are in the everyday routine of life at home, but you should make every effort to remember. If you display symptoms which could possibly be malarial, even if this happens a year after you return home, get to a doctor and, in order that they don't overlook the possibility, ensure that they are aware you have been exposed to malaria.

Finally, if you have a fever and the malaria test is negative (though this does not exclude malaria), you may have typhoid, which should also receive immediate treatment. Where typhoid-testing is unavailable, a routine blood test can give a strong indication of this disease.

## Sleeping sickness

This is carried by tsetse flies, which look like oversized houseflies, and have a painful bite. Tsetse flies commonly occur in low-lying game reserves throughout tropical Africa. Sleeping sickness has a patchy distribution. It is much less widespread than the distribution of tsetse and occurs within a small proportion of their range: it cannot be considered a real threat to travellers and it's a treatable ailment. In Tanzania, tsetse flies are common in several game reserves. Tsetse flies bite during the day and are attracted to blue.

## AIDS and venereal disease

HIV and other venereal diseases are widespread in Tanzania. The risks involved in having unprotected casual sex barely need stating. Condoms and femidoms offer a high level of protection against HIV and other venereal diseases, and the additional use of spermicides and pessaries also reduces the risk of transmission.

Hospital workers in Tanzania deal with AIDS victims on a regular basis. Contrary to western prejudices, health professionals do realise the danger involved in using unsterilised needles, and you are unlikely to be confronted with one in a town hospital or clinic. If, however, you need treatment in a really remote area, where supplies might be a problem, you might be glad to be carrying a few needles and hypodermic syringes in your medical kit.

## Meningitis

This is a particularly nasty disease as it can kill within hours of the first symptoms appearing. The telltale symptom is a combination of a blinding headache and usually high fever. Immunisation protects against the common and serious bacterial form in Africa, but not against all kinds of meningitis. Local papers normally report local outbreaks. If you show symptoms, get to a doctor immediately.

## Rabies and animal bites

Rabies can be carried by any mammal. The domestic dog most often passes it to man, commonly after a bite from an infected animal; a scratch or a lick on an open wound can also be dangerous.

The immunisation against rabies is highly effective and the vaccine is innocuous. Once symptoms show, though, rabies is incurable, and the way that you die is so horrible that all doctors advise a post-exposure boost. If you are not immunised and there is any possibility that you have been exposed to a rabid animal, get to a doctor as soon as you can. This should be done promptly, but since the incubation period can be a month if, for instance, you are bitten on the hand, it's not too late to get this done weeks after exposure. As the incubation period for rabies is determined by the distance between the point of infection and the brain, as well as the severity of the bite-wound, people who are bitten on the face (as is common with children) have ten days at most and must get help immediately. The message, then, is to be fully immunised against rabies, especially if you intend visiting remote places or handling wild animals. Any wild animals that seem unusually tame should be assumed to be rabid: do not handle them.

All animal bites should be cleaned as protection against infection. *Scrub* the wound with soap under running water for five minutes (time it with a watch), then liberally apply povidone iodine or 40% alcohol – gin or whisky will do – or aqueous iodine. Cleaning the wound won't necessarily protect you from rabies. Nor will it automatically prevent tetanus infection, a far more immediate concern.

If you haven't had a tetanus shot in ten years or you are unsure, get a tetanus toxoid injection *and* a tetanus booster as quickly as possible.

## Tetanus
Tetanus is caught through deep, dirty wounds, so ensure that any wounds are thoroughly cleaned. Immunisation gives good protection for ten years, provided you do not have an overwhelming number of tetanus bacteria on board. Keep immunised and be sensible about first aid.

## Ticks and tick-bite fever
There are several unpleasant illnesses which can follow a tick bite in Africa, including Lyme Disease, but the good news is that even if a tick is carrying disease organisms, it will not inevitably infect you. You are less likely to be infected if you get the tick off promptly and do not damage the tick.

Remove any tick as soon as you notice it on you – it will most likely be firmly attached to somewhere you would rather it was not – grasp the tick as close to your skin as possible and pull steadily and firmly away, at right angles to your skin. The tick will come away complete as long as you do not jerk or twist. If possible then douse the wound with alcohol (gin, whisky, rum or local spirit) or iodine.

Spreading redness around the bite and/or fever and/or aching joints after a tick bite imply you have an infection requiring antibiotic treatment, so seek advice.

## INSECTS

Even if you are taking malaria tablets, you should take steps to avoid being bitten by insects, and by mosquitoes in particular, especially between dusk and dawn. Whatever pills you take, there remains a significant risk of being infected by malaria in areas below 1,800m. Of much less concern, but still a risk, are several other mosquito-borne viral fevers which either are, or else might be, present in low and medium altitude parts of Tanzania. Dengue, the only one of these diseases that is anything close to being common, is very nasty with symptoms that include severe muscle cramps, high fever and sometimes a measles-like rash; fatalities are exceptional but medical help should be sought. The other diseases in this category are too rare to be a cause for serious concern. Nevertheless, they are difficult to treat, and some of them are potentially fatal. And it is not only mosquitoes that might carry nasty diseases. Leishmania, another difficult to treat disease, is spread by sandfly bites. Before you panic, it should be stressed that all these diseases other than malaria are most unlikely to be caught by travellers. I mention them mainly to illustrate that malaria pills on their own do not guarantee your safety against serious insect-borne diseases.

The *Anopheles* mosquito which spreads malaria emerges at dusk, as do sandflies and most other disease-carrying, biting flies. You will thus greatly reduce your chances of being bitten and contracting insect-borne diseases if you wear long trousers and socks in the evening and cover exposed parts of your body with insect repellent, preferably a DEET-based preparation such as Jungle Jell. Sprays or roll-ons of this sort are not available in Tanzania; bring one with you.

The *Anopheles* mosquito hunts mostly at ground level and it can bite through thin socks, so it is worth putting repellent on your ankles, even if they are covered. When walking in scrub and forest areas, you should wear long clothes, tuck trousers into socks and apply repellent by day as well; the *Aedes* mosquito which spreads dengue and yellow fever is a day-biter – and these precautions will keep ticks off too. Solid shoes, socks and trousers will, in any case, protect you against snakes, sharp thorns, and harmless but irritating biters like midges.

Like many insects, mosquitoes are drawn to direct light. If you are camping, never put a lamp near the opening of your tent, or you will have a swarm of mosquitoes and other insects waiting to join you when you retire. In hotel rooms, be aware that the longer you leave on your light, the greater the number of insects with which you are likely to share your accommodation.

Once you are in bed, the most effective form of protection against mosquitoes is a net. Mosquito coils, widely available in Tanzania, will reduce the biting rate, and, even though strains of mosquito have evolved that are skilled at flying in turbulent air, so will a fan. Far better, though, is to carry your own permethrin-impregnated net, which will protect you against everything. Both nets and impregnation kits are available from MASTA at the London School of Tropical Medicine and Hygiene and from British Airways Travel Clinics.

To balance the warnings, it should be stressed that the overwhelming majority of insects don't bite people, and of those that do, the vast majority are entirely harmless. Mattresses quite often contain bedbugs and fleas, but they are both essentially harmless.

## MEDICAL FACILITIES

There are private clinics and hospitals in most large towns, and doctors generally speak fluent English. Consultation fees and laboratory tests are remarkably inexpensive when compared to most western countries, so if you do fall sick it would be absurd to let financial considerations dissuade you from seeking medical help.

In larger towns pharmacies are well stocked with medicines and toiletries. You shouldn't have any difficulty locating widely used drugs such as general purpose antibiotics and malaria prophylactics.

Fansidar is sold cheaply at pharmacies. Quinine tablets are generally only available in the large towns.

# OUTDOOR HEALTH

## Sun and heat

The equatorial sun is vicious. Although it is impossible to avoid some exposure to the sun, it would be foolish to do so needlessly. Tanning ages your skin and it can cause skin cancer. If you are coming to Tanzania from a less harsh climate, let your body get used to the sunlight gradually or you will end up with sunburn. Take things too far, and sunstroke – a potentially fatal condition – may be the result. Wear sunscreen and build up your exposure gradually, starting with no more than 20 minutes a day. Avoid exposing yourself for more than two hours in any day, and stay out of the sun between noon and 3pm. Be particularly careful of sunburn when swimming or snorkelling. A shirt will protect your shoulders and a pair of shorts will protect the back of your thighs.

In hot parts of Tanzania, you may sweat more than usual. To counter the resultant loss of water and salt, you should drink more than normal and eat extra salt if you develop a taste for it (salt tablets are useless). Prickly heat, a rash caused by sweat trapped under the skin, is harmless, but highly uncomfortable and a common problem when you first enter a hot area. It will help if you wear 100% cotton clothing and splash yourself regularly with water, but avoid excessive use of soap.

Always wear clothes made from natural fabrics such as cotton. These help prevent fungal infections and other rashes. Athlete's foot is prevalent, so wear thongs in communal showers.

Small cuts are inclined to go septic in the tropics. Clean any lesion with a dilute solution of potassium permanganate two to three times daily. Antiseptic creams are not suitable for the tropics; wounds must be kept dry and covered.

# SAFETY

## Theft

As in any country, there are parts of Tanzania where theft is a real risk. That said, it is considerably safer than many African countries, and I have heard of few instances of the kind of theft that would spoil a holiday. With a bit of care, I think you would be unlucky to experience any serious problems in this direction.

### Mugging

Muggings are comparatively unusual in Tanzania. In all the time I spent in the country I heard of only one incident and even that was third-hand. Dar es Salaam and the roads connecting the beach resorts north of it are the main risk area, and Bagamoyo has a bad reputation. Never walk between the beach resorts except possibly in large groups. In Dar es Salaam, avoid back streets after dark. I always felt safe in the area immediately around Maktaba Street, but if crossing from, say, the New Africa Hotel to the Jumbo Inn after dark, I would play safe and get a taxi (this costs about $2; think of it as supplementary travel insurance). If you are mugged, the personal threat is minimal provided you hand over what is asked for.

## Casual theft

The bulk of theft in Tanzania is casual snatching or pickpocketing. This is not particularly aimed at tourists (and as a consequence not limited to tourist areas) but you are fair game. The key to not being pickpocketed is not having anything of value in your pocket; the key to avoiding having things snatched is to avoid having valuables in a place where they are snatchable. Most of the following points will be obvious to experienced travellers, but they are worth making:

• Most casual thieves hang around bus stations and markets. Keep a close watch on your belongings in these places and avoid having loose valuables in your pocket or day pack.

• Keep all your valuables – passport, travellers cheques etc – in a money belt. One you can hide under your clothes has obvious advantages over one of the currently fashionable codpieces which are worn externally.

• Don't carry your spending money in your money belt. A normal wallet is fine provided it only contains a moderate sum of money. Better still is a wallet you can hang around your neck. If I plan to visit a high risk area such as a busy market, I sometimes wear shorts under my trousers and keep my cash in the shorts pocket.

• Distribute your money throughout your luggage. I always keep the bulk of my foreign currency in my money belt, but I like to keep some cash and travellers cheques hidden in various parts of my pack and day-pack.

• Many people prefer to carry their valuables on their person. I think it is better to leave them in your hotel room. In all my African travels I have only once heard of a hotel room being broken into (that was in Nairobi, about the only place in East Africa where paranoia is apt), whereas I have met countless people who have been pickpocketed, mugged, or had possessions snatched from them.

• If you have jewellery that is of high personal or financial value, leave it at home.

• If you can afford it, when you first arrive in a large town catch a taxi to your hotel, especially if you arrive after dark.

• Avoid overnight buses. They have a bad reputation for theft. In Zanzibar and on overnight buses I have heard of people being given drugged food and robbed (more details about theft on buses are given under *Transport* in *Chapter Three*).

## Con tricks
Dar es Salaam is not Nairobi as far as conmen are concerned. There are a few dodgy characters who hang around the New Africa Hotel trying to change money, but they are pretty transparent. You may encounter similar characters in Arusha, but you would have to be very gullible to get involved with them.

## Documentation
The best insurance against complete disaster is to keep things well-documented. If you carry a photocopy of the main page of your passport, you will be issued a new one more promptly. In addition, keep details of your bank, credit card (if you have one), travel insurance policy and camera equipment (including serial numbers).

Keep copies of your travellers cheque numbers and *a record of which ones you have cashed*, as well as the international refund assistance telephone number and local agent. If all this information fits on one piece of paper, you can keep photocopies on you and with a friend at home.

You will have to report the theft of any item you wish to claim insurance against to the police.

## One last thought
If you are robbed, the temptation is to chase the thief. If the items stolen are not of great value, you might want to think before you do this. Street justice is harsh: an identified thief is likely to be descended on by a mob, beaten, and quite possibly killed. I have met a few travellers who have found themselves in the bizarre position of having to save someone who has just ripped them off.

# CREATURES GREAT AND SMALL

Some people arrive in Africa with images of man-eating lions, rampaging elephants and venomous snakes lurking around every corner. This idea can quickly be dispelled. Most animals avoid contact with people and the chance of being attacked is remote. Having said that, any animal large enough to kill a person might do so under the right circumstances. Wild animals should always be treated with caution and respect, and deliberately feeding or provoking them is highly irresponsible. Never assume that an animal isn't dangerous because it appears to be tame: the most dangerous animals are often those that have been hand-reared, or that have come to depend on the presence of humans for food or as security from predators.

Except for carnivores, which might attack for food, animals are only likely to attack humans if they feel threatened, and they are especially dangerous if they panic. The animals most likely to charge are hippo, elephant, buffalo and rhino, but even an antelope will attack in some circumstances, especially if it has young or is cornered. Many animals have what could be termed a fleeing and attacking circle: the closer you are when it first becomes aware of your presence, the more likely it is to choose confrontation over escape. If you see a large animal in the distance and want to approach it, use your common sense. If the animal is aware of your presence and you approach it reasonably openly and slowly, it is far less likely to panic than if it is initially unaware of your presence and you attempt to sneak up to it. If the animal becomes edgy or aggressive, remove the threat: back away slowly and calmly. Unless you are experienced or armed, it is foolhardy to approach an elephant or buffalo on foot; on the other hand, you would have to get very close to a giraffe or zebra before there was a remote chance of it attacking you. Never approach an animal in such a way that it might feel cornered (by a koppie or a lake, for instance); even a bushbuck will charge if it has no escape route. Be very cautious approaching a thicket or patch of woodland where, for instance, a buffalo or leopard might be hiding.

Most animals rely strongly on smell; whether you are trying to avoid an animal or approach it, the prevailing wind is an important consideration. If you want to get around an animal, it is far less likely to notice you if you stay upwind of it. If you want to approach the animal, you will get closer by staying upwind, but you are also more likely to startle it.

Before discussing specific animals, I should stress that the likelihood of an animal attacking you whilst you are in Tanzania is extremely small, certainly far less than the risk of being killed by malaria or in a road accident. The dangers associated with wild animals were greatly exaggerated by the so-called Great White Hunters, and many of the myths they created have stuck in the popular image. Nevertheless, in their haste to debunk the myths, many travel guides have gone to the other extreme and underplayed the potential risks. There are dangers associated with walking or camping where wild animals are present, and no matter how slight they may be, tourists should be aware of them.

## Crocodiles

These are responsible for more deaths than any other African animal (apart from the mosquito!). They attack animals that are in or next to water and they are responsible for many deaths in river or lakeside villages where people have no option but to take their chances. If you keep a few metres between yourself and crocodile-infested water, the risk is small. Crocodiles are fast on land, so if they are out of the water don't sneak up too close. If you intend fishing or swimming, ask local advice; in many places all crocodiles large enough to attack an adult human have been hunted out.

## Hippo

Hippo pose a very real threat to tourists. The danger is coming between a hippo and water. Their instinct when threatened is to head straight for water; they will mow down anything in their way. Always be alert when walking near a lake or river where hippo are present, especially at times when they are likely to be out of the water grazing (at night, in the early morning and late afternoon, and in overcast weather) and avoid walking in reed beds. If you are on foot and see hippo, it may be tempting to get as close as you can but it is more sensible to give them a wide berth. Hippo are not normally dangerous if they are in the water and you are on land, but be cautious.

## Predators

Most large predators avoid contact with people and attacks are very unusual. You are safe in a vehicle, but be aware that most predators perceive a vehicle as a unit; if you are very close to a lion or leopard and do something that breaks the vehicle's outline, you may startle the animal and it could lunge at you. A tent offers good protection provided it is closed up properly and there is no meat in it. Never sleep with your head poking out of a tent. If you have no tent, a head poking out from a sleeping bag may provoke curiosity in a lion or hyena. Sleep with your head against a tree or a wall, or towards a campfire. On foot, most predators will give you a wide berth. If one does take an interest in you, never run away – it is much faster than you are. Your best bet is to climb a tree. If there is no tree around, stand your ground and yell at it aggressively in the hope you will convince it that it has far more reason to be scared than you have.

## Buffalo and rhino

In real terms, buffalo are the most dangerous land animal: they are common in many of the forests where people walk, and are less inclined to mock charge than, for instance, elephant. Solitary buffalo pose the greatest threat. If you encounter buffalo on foot, never try to approach them and don't run away unless you are actually charged. If they appear not to have seen you, walk away slowly and discreetly. If they have seen you, stand your ground or back off slowly and they will probably move on. If you are charged, try to get up a tree or an anthill; if none is available, run like hell. Rhino are as unpredictable as buffalo, if not more so, but their scarcity in East Africa makes it highly improbable you would ever encounter one on foot.

## Elephant

Elephant can be very unpredictable and aggressive, especially lone bulls and mothers with young. There are few places in Tanzania where an unguided tourist on foot would be likely to encounter an elephant, but it could happen. In the vast majority of instances, the elephant will simply move on or ignore you, but never try to approach it.

It is impossible to give hard and fast advice about what to do if you are on foot and an elephant becomes aggressive: no two situations are the same and you will have to use your judgement as to what its intentions are. Elephant are highly intelligent when compared to buffalo or rhino, and they are more likely to react in an individual way. If an elephant charges you in earnest and without warning, there is probably little you can do but try to climb a tree or run away. Normally, however, an elephant will warn you off by trumpeting and/or mock charging.

When an elephant trumpets a warning, the odds are that it just wants you to clear off. Unless it is particularly bad-tempered, it is unlikely to charge unless you provoke it further. The most common advice is either to walk or back off calmly and quickly (but don't run), thereby removing the threat to the elephant, or else to stand your ground and try to frighten the elephant off by waving things at it and yelling aggressively. If one doesn't work, try the other, all the time looking for cover should it decide to charge.

If an elephant charges, climb a tall tree or, as elephants do not like steep inclines, make for a sharp rise or gulley. If there is no cover, you must gamble. If it is a mock charge, you are best standing your ground (but may still be all right if you run away); if it charges in earnest, the only chance you have is to run. On balance, you are probably better running than standing your ground, but I've heard differing opinions.

Provided you are sensible, elephants pose little risk in campsites. They are unlikely to walk in if they are concerned about your presence and, unless there is fruit inside, they will almost always walk around a tent. It would be stupid to tease or feed an elephant, and if it hasn't seen you, don't attempt to sneak up on it. If elephants come into your campsite at night, don't take photos; a flashlight might startle them.

Elephants sometimes attack vehicles. Always approach them cautiously; if they show signs of aggression or edginess, back off gently and wait for them to pass. If they are at the side of the road and show no signs of aggression, make your way past them before you stop and watch. If you don't do this and another car comes up behind you, you will have no escape route should the worst happen. It's a question of judgement, but I would never switch off my engine in close proximity to an elephant.

## Primates

Most primates are shy of people. At some campsites, however, baboons and vervet monkeys have become used to people. Vervet monkeys are unlikely to progress beyond being a nuisance, but baboons should be considered dangerous. I'm only aware of one place in Tanzania where baboons are a problem (Gombe Stream) but they are rampant in some Zimbabwean and Kenyan campsites. As tourism to Tanzania increases so will the number of places where baboons are a problem.

Baboons have sharp teeth and are very powerful and aggressive. They are capable of severely wounding an adult and have often been known to kill children. If baboon are present, don't leave food lying around or in your tent. Have a pile of stones next to you when you cook. If you have children, keep a close watch on them and never let them tease or play with baboons or monkeys.

When a baboon approaches you aggressively, it is largely bluff. Unlike the other animals discussed here, a baboon will not be after you but after your food. Once it has what it wants it will be off like a shot. Throw stones and yell aggressively to scare it off, but if this doesn't work don't try to call its bluff: should you provoke a confrontation you are bound to come off second best.

I've not encountered this in Tanzania, but in some parts of Africa troops of baboons or monkeys wait for tourists to feed them by the roadside. If a baboon or monkey is very tame or leaps on to your car, close the windows. If it gets into the vehicle it will panic and could seriously injure someone. When baboons and monkeys become too bold they often have to be shot; deliberately feeding one not only creates problems for other tourists, it may well sign the animal's death warrant.

Chimpanzees are capable of killing a person and could easily do so if they felt sufficiently threatened. Unhabituated chimps are too shy and localised to be a cause for concern, but it would be an error to assume that habituated chimps are tame. Chimp viewing at Gombe Stream and Mahale Mountains is well organised. There is no danger provided you obey your guide.

## Snakebite

Although poisonous snakes are present throughout Tanzania, they pose little real threat to humans (in South Africa, where there are just as many poisonous snakes, they kill fewer than ten people every year – less than the number of people killed by lightning!). The reason for this is that most snakes are very shy and secretive, and will move off at the slightest sign of human activity. In three years of African travel, I have seen snakes no more than half-a-dozen times, and in all but one instance they slithered off harmlessly.

The one place where you should be conscious of the possible presence of snakes is on rocky slopes and cliffs, particularly where you are scrambling up or down using your hands. This is because snakes respond to seismic vibrations – in most habitats they will sense your footsteps and slither away long before you get near them, but they may not on a rocky slope. You also have a greater danger of cornering a snake, or being unable to get away yourself, in a steep rocky habitat. Finally, rocky areas are the favoured dwelling place of Africa's most dangerous snake, the puff adder. Although this is not a particularly venomous species, it is capable of inflicting a fatal bite. The danger with puff adders is that they are unusually slothful, and the one species of venomous snake that doesn't generally move off in response to human foot treads.

As a general rule, you should wear trousers, socks and solid boots when you walk in the bush. Good boots will protect against the 50% of snake bites that occur below the ankle; trousers will help to deflect bites higher up on the leg. If you see a snake, wait to let it pass. If it rises to strike, the common advice is to stand dead still, as snakes strike in response to movement. All well and good, but on the one occasion where a snake reared at me, and twice when I've been with someone who this happened to, instinct won over logic and the person concerned beetled off as quickly as possible in the opposite direction. This tactic worked perfectly well.

If the worst should happen, don't panic. Most snakes are non-venomous, venom is dispensed only in about 50% of bites by venomous snakes, and it is quite uncommon for a bite to contain enough venom to kill an adult. The chances are that you will not come to any harm. Keep the victim still and calm; wash the wound with soap then wipe it gently with a clean cloth to remove any venom from the skin surface. Remove rings, bangles or watches in anticipation of swelling. If possible, splint the bitten limb as movement quickens the rate of venom absorption, or if you have a crepe bandage apply this firmly from the end of the bitten extremity towards and over the site of the bite. Keep the bitten part *below* heart height. The victim should then be taken to a doctor or hospital. There they should be kept under observation and antivenin will be administered by a trained health person if and when signs of envenomation occur. Do not attempt to catch the snake unless you are sure there is no risk of someone else being bitten and remember that even a decapitated head can envenomate; having a positive identification of the snake will help effective treatment, however.

Finally, note that after a snake bite many "traditional" first aid measures do more harm than good:

DO NOT give alcohol or aspirin; paracetamol is safe.
DO NOT cut, incise or suck the wound; suction devices do not work.
DO NOT apply a tourniquet.
DO NOT apply potassium permanganate or ice.
DON'T panic – you are unlikely to have been envenomed.

# Part Two

Chapter Five

# Dar es Salaam

## INTRODUCTION

Dar es Salaam is Tanzania's largest city and most important port. Although it is no longer the capital of Tanzania (Dodoma is now the official capital), it seems likely to remain the commercial and social heart of the country for the foreseeable future. The city draws extreme reactions from travellers, most of whom either love it or hate it. It is my favourite East African city, with all the hustle and bustle of Nairobi, yet none of that city's underlying aggression.

Dar es Salaam's distinctive character comes from the cultural mix of its people and buildings, and the sloth-inducing coastal humidity which permeates every aspect of day-to-day life. German, British, Asian and Arab influences are all evident, but it is fundamentally a Swahili city. Dar es Salaam is a friendly place. People are willing to pass away the time with idle chat and will readily help out strangers, yet you are rarely hassled, except around the New Africa Hotel where money-changers froth into action every time a tourist walks past.

I first visited Dar es Salaam in 1986. Then it looked decidedly down at heel. The streets were acneous with potholes and the pavements were lifeless, shops had given up the pretence of having anything to sell, water ran for about an hour every day and, except for the odd overland traveller crossing between Kenya and southern Africa, tourists were something of a novelty. In 1988, when I next passed through, things were still pretty torpid, but there were definite signs of recovery.

It was extremely heartening to return in 1992 and find a lively, bustling city, comparable in many ways to Nairobi. Most of Dar es Salaam's buildings could still do with a scrub and whitewash, but the streets have been resurfaced, the pavements are alive with peddlers and colourful impromptu markets, the shops are well-stocked, water runs more often than not – and tourists are flocking back.

## History

By coastal standards, Dar es Salaam is a modern town. Until 1862, when Sultan Majid of Zanzibar first visited the area, it was the site of an insignificant fishing village called Mzizima. Majid was so impressed by the natural harbour and surrounding scenery he decided to establish a trading centre. A coral palace called Dar es Salaam (haven of peace) was built in 1866 and a small Arab settlement was established. In 1870, after Majid died, his successor Barghash abandoned all plans for further development.

In 1877 Dar es Salaam was proposed as the starting point for the construction of a road by the anti-slaver Sir William Mackinnon. He hoped the road would encourage legitimate trade between the coast and Lake Nyasa. Known as Mackinnon's Road, the project never took off and was abandoned after 112km had been completed.

Dar es Salaam acquired real significance under German rule. In 1887 a camp was established; four years later the fledgling city was the capital of German East Africa. Between 1893 and 1899 several departments of the colonial government were established there and in 1898 a Roman Catholic Cathedral was built. The construction of the central railway consolidated Dar es Salaam's position; by 1914, when the line was completed, Dar es Salaam was the country's most significant harbour and trading centre.

Dar es Salaam was captured by a British ship soon after the outbreak of World War I. When German East Africa became Tanganyika, Dar es Salaam remained the capital, and its importance has never been challenged, although the capital is now Dodoma. Dar es Salaam remains the country's economic hub, with a population of around 1.5 million.

## GETTING THERE AND AWAY

Dar es Salaam has good local and international links. Details of transport to other parts of the country are given throughout this guide, under the relevant town or area. A brief overview follows:

## By air

There are air links between Dar es Salaam and many African and European cities, and domestic flights to most large Tanzanian towns. Further details are under *Air* in Chapter Three.

The airport is 13km from the city centre. A shuttle bus to the airport, run by Air Tanzania, leaves from in front of the New Africa Hotel every other hour between 08.00 and 16.00, and returns every other hour between 09.00 and 17.00. An up-to-date timetable is posted at the New Africa. You can also get to the airport on a 67 bus. There is a taxi rank at the airport.

## Airlines

| | Address | Tel |
|---|---|---|
| Aeroflot | Eminaz Mansion, Samora Avenue | 46005 |
| Air France | Peugeot House, cnr Upanga/UWT | 46653/4 |
| Air India | cnr Upanga/UWT | 46803 |
| Air Tanzania | ATC Building, Ohio Street | 46643 |
| Air Zaire | IPS Building, cnr Samora/Maktaba | 20836 |
| British Airways | Sheraton Hotel, Ohio Street (PO Box 791) | 44651/4 |
| EgyptAir | Matsalamat Building, Samora Avenue | 46806 |
| Ethiopian Airlines | TDFL Building, Ohio Street | 20868 |
| Kenya Airways | Tanganyika Motors Building,Upanga Rd | 46875-7 |
| KLMT | DFL Building, Ohio Street | 46497 |
| Lufthansa | Peugeot House, cnr Upanga/UWT | 46813-5 |
| Pakistan Airlines | IPS Building, cnr Samora/Maktaba | 46820/1 |
| Sabena | Mbwana Salum, Ugweno Street | 50476 |
| Swissair | Luther House, Sokoine Drive | 46816 |
| Uganda Airlines | IPS Building, cnr Samora/Maktaba | 46818/9 |
| Zambia Airways | IPS Building, cnr Samora/Maktaba | 46662 |

Mozambique, Royal Swazi, Somali and Saudi Arabian Airlines are represented by Holiday Africa in the TDFL Building on Ohio Road (Tel: 30395). A number of other airlines which only do occasional flights are represented by Air Tanzania.

## By boat

There are several boats between Dar es Salaam and Zanzibar every day, and reasonably regular services to Pemba, Mtwara, Tanga, and Mombasa (Kenya). Boats to Mafia, Lindi and Kilwa are rare. All the commercial boat operators have kiosks near the harbour on Sokoine Drive. If you are heading for a place where there is no regular service and have no joy at the harbour, try the Tanzanian Coastal Shipping Line (Tel: 26192).

## By rail

Trains to northern and western destinations such as Moshi, Mwanza and Kigoma leave from the central station on Sokoine Drive. Bookings to these destinations should also be made at this station. Trains to southern destinations such as Ifakara and Mbeya leave from the Tazara Station 5km from the city centre. The booking office for southbound trains is at Tazara Station. Buses there leave from the Post Office (Posta).

Details of all train services are under *Rail* in Chapter Three.

# By bus

There are buses between Dar es Salaam and virtually every town in Tanzania. There is no central bus station in Dar es Salaam; buses leave from all over the city centre. There is a semblance of a pattern, but it should not be viewed too rigidly.

Buses to Arusha and Moshi leave from the large bus station on the corner of Morogoro Road and Libya Street, as do most buses to coastal destinations south of Kilwa. Most buses to Tanga, Iringa, Mbeya and Songea leave from Mnazi Mmoja on UWT Street. Buses to Bagamoyo, Morogoro and Kilwa generally leave from the backstreets around Kariakoo Market. Most buses to western destinations such as Dodoma, Tabora and Mwanza leave from Msimbazi Street, a few blocks from the market.

If in doubt, the best place to make enquiries is the Morogoro Road/ Libya Street bus station. It is the biggest and the most central bus station, and people seem to have a helpful attitude to travellers.

There is a simple way to navigate through the chaos. Taxi drivers are familiar with the bus system, often speak good English, and, in my experience, are very helpful. Enlisting some knowledgeable support is well worth the price of a taxi-fare (about $1.50 within the city centre). If you want to leave immediately, a taxi driver is far better equipped than you to cut through the bullshit, find the next bus to leave, and make sure you get a seat.

For long distance trips, it is worth booking a ticket the day in advance, is this not only guarantees you a seat, but allows you to choose which one you want.

# WHERE TO STAY

Although there are plenty of hotels in the city centre, budget hotels tend to fill up early in the day. If you arrive late in the afternoon it may be easier to settle for something more expensive and look for a cheap room the next morning.

Although things have improved recently, there are still regular water and electricity cuts in Dar es Salaam. Electricity cuts are generally localised and only last a couple of hours, but water only runs for about half the day in most parts of town. If there is running water when you get a room, shower while the going is good.

## *Upper range*

The **Dar es Salaam Sheraton** (Ohio Street, PO Box 791, tel: 44111, fax: 44847) opened in October 1995, since when it has usurped the Kilimanjaro's reputation as the top hotel in Dar es Salaam. The attractively decorated rooms have en suite bathrooms, air conditioning, mini-bars and television, and they suffer from none of the shabbiness which characterises other upmarket hotels in Dar es Salaam. The level of service is also a pleasing contrast to the shambling disorganisation you come to expect in other hotels in the capital. There is a 24-hour business centre, and several meeting and business rooms. Other facilities include two restaurants, a shopping arcade, and a gymnasium, sauna and outdoor swimming pool. Ordinary rooms cost $192/202 HC single/double exclusive of breakfast, and suites are available ranging in price from $320 to $1500.

The **Kilimanjaro Hotel** (PO Box 9574, tel: 46528) is the most attractively situated hotel in the city centre, with views from sea-facing rooms over the harbour. Rooms are adequately furnished, if a bit worn at the edges, and the en suite bathrooms have a reliable supply of hot water. Other attractions include a large swimming pool (open to non hotel residents for a $2 fee) and an excellent restaurant on the top floor. $90/100 HC single/double.

The **Motel Agip** (PO Box 529, tel: 23511, fax: 39833) has been refurbished in recent years, and it is now regarded by many tour operators to be the best value for money in Dar es Salaam in its price range. Rooms cost $90/95 HC single/double or $50/60 for residents.

The **Embassy Hotel** (PO Box 3152, tel: 68062) looks rather shabby these days when compared to the competition. Facilities include a swimming pool. $70/80 HC single/double, or $40/60 for residents.

The **New Africa Hotel** (PO Box 9314, tel: 46546), built on the site of the Kaiserhof, the first hotel in Dar es Salaam, was closed for renovations in early 1996 and is due to re-open by the end of that year, when prices will probably be a bit higher than at the Kilimanjaro. The outdoor bar at the New Africa has traditionally been a popular meeting point in Dar es Salaam, reminiscent of the New Stanley in Nairobi. No doubt it will resume this role once it re-opens.

Less central, the **Oyster Bay Hotel** (PO Box 2261, tel: 68062, fax: 68631) is on a beach 6km out of town. It has a good restaurant and bar, and is in many respects superior to the majority of hotels in the town centre. All rooms are air-conditioned and sea-facing. $120/150 HC single/double.

## *Moderate*
The **Peacock Hotel** (UWT Street, tel: 35075, fax: 44215) is a popular and convenient place to stay, and the rooms are reasonably priced at $45/50 single/double.

The **Starlight Hotel** next door (PO Box 3199, tel: 37185, fax: 37182) is also recommended: self-contained rooms with air-conditioning and fans cost $36/40. Both hotels have a good restaurant.

A bit more run-down, but otherwise very similar in standard, the **Mawenzi**

## KEY TO WEST CENTRAL DAR ES SALAAM

| | |
|---|---|
| 1 PALM BEACH HOTEL | 17 IMRAM RESTAURANT |
| 2 NYUMBA YA SANAA GALLERY | 18 NEW DAR GUEST HOUSE |
| | 19 TRAFFIC LIGHT MOTEL |
| 3 ALITALIA, KENYA AIRWAYS and AMERICAN AIRWAYS | 20 HOLIDAY HOTEL |
| 4 RICKSHAW TRAVEL | 21 RENDESVOUS RESTAURANT |
| 5 COASTAL TRAVELS | 22 MNAZI MMOJA BUS STATION |
| 6 HOTEL MAWENZI | 23 DELUXE INN |
| 7 NIGHTS OF ISTANBUL | 24 CLOCK TOWER |
| 8 CEDARS RESTAURANT | 25 CITY HALL |
| 9 AMGRAPALI RESTAURANT | 26 OLD BOMA |
| 10 SECOND-HAND BOOKSHOP | 27 FERRY OFFICES |
| 11 MOTEL AFRIQUE | 28 HOTEL TAMARINE |
| 12 KARIAKOO MARKET | 29 HOTEL INTERNATIONALE |
| 13 PEACOCK HOTEL | 30 HOTEL CONTINENTAL |
| 14 SAFARI INN | 31 KIBODYA HOTEL |
| 15 STARLIGHT HOTEL | 32 CANTON RESTAURANT |
| 16 JAMBO INN | 33 SUPREME RESTAURANT |

**Hotel** (PO Box 322, tel: 27761, fax: 46561) has large air-conditioned rooms for $35/40 single/double.

Further out of town – about 20 minutes' walk along the Bagamoyo Road – the **Palm Beach Hotel** is a rambling and rather atmospheric place known as much as anything for its evening barbecues. Rooms are a touch run-down, but air-conditioned, and cost between $30 and $40 for residents and $16 and $35 for non-residents.

The **Motel Afrique** (PO Box 9482, tel: 46557/8) is conveniently central and has comfortable self-contained doubles for $29, as well as rooms using communal facilities for $10/17 single/double.

The **Hotel Continental** is a little tatty, but about the cheapest place in this range, and conveniently situated near the railway station. Double rooms cost $20 with a fan and $27 with air conditioning.

### Budget

Two places where you should normally have no difficulty finding a room are the **YMCA** (PO Box 767, tel: 26726) and **YWCA** (PO Box 2086, tel: 2243), which lie a block apart on Maktaba Street.

A few years ago, the YMCA seemed very overpriced, and it also suffered from a reputed security problem. However, as room prices at the YMCA have remained constant while those elsewhere have risen, and I've not heard of a security complaint for years, it is now a viable option. The rooms are small and clean, have mosquito netting but not fans, and seem fair value at $10/ double.

The YWCA has long been a favourite with couples and single women, though these days it seems to be no more than acceptable value for money. The rooms are clean, have fans and mosquito nets, and cost $8 (single), $12 (double for two women sharing) and $10 (compartmentalised double for a couple). The canteen serves inexpensive, unexciting meals.

Another perennially popular place to stay is **Luther House** (PO Box 389, tel 32154), which is tucked away in a building behind the main Lutheran Church on the waterfront. It used to be practically impossible to get a room here without booking days in advance, but last time I checked there were plenty of vacancies – perhaps due to a quadrupling of prices since 1992, with double rooms at $15 and self-contained singles at $20.

The main cluster of budget hotels is around the Morogoro Road bus station. The nicest places here are the **Jambo Inn** (PO Box 5588, tel: 35359/35531) and the **Safari Hotel**, both of which have self-contained rooms with a reasonably reliable water supply for $10/16 single/double, as well as air-conditioned rooms for $20/double. The rooms strike me as a bit shabby at the price, but otherwise they are fine, and the hotels are very secure.
The **New Dar Guest House**, **Holiday Hotel** and **Traffic Light Motel** are all very run-down and generally fully booked. If you find a vacant room at one of these hotels, expect to pay around $6 to $8.

Another cluster of budget hotels can be found near the clock tower. Generally, it's much easier to find a vacant room here than around the bus station. The one place that *is* often full, rated by many as the best budget accommodation in Dar, is the **Tamarine Hotel**, which has good self-contained doubles for $8.

The nearby **International Hotel** and **Deluxe Hotel** both have ordinary doubles for $8 and the Deluxe also has self-contained doubles for $11.

The **Kobodya Hotel** is much smarter; the clean self-contained doubles with hot water, fan and netting are good value at $16.

## WHERE TO EAT

Dar es Salaam has restaurants to suit all tastes and budgets, and more had opened every time we visited the city. Typical opening hours are lunch between 12.00 and 15.00 and dinner between 19.00 and 22.00. Generally food is of a high standard and good value for money. It would be impossible to list every restaurant and *hoteli* in Dar es Salaam; you might well want to adventure beyond the following recommendations.

## Upper range

We found the best value to be at upper range hotels rather than specialist restaurants. The open-air restaurant on the top floor of the **Kilimanjaro Hotel** has a great view over the harbour, and the food and service are excellent. Main courses cost around $7, three-course set menus cost $8.

The restaurant in the **Motel Agip** lacks the view of the Kilimanjaro, but is similar in price and standard, and has a more varied menu. The Agip's buffet breakfast has also been recommended – it costs $5 including a newspaper. You could also try the grill on the second floor of the **Embassy Hotel**; it serves the best steaks in town.

**The Alcove** is a well-established Indian restaurant. It was popular with budget travellers in the mid-1980s and although there is more competition these days, it is still the place to head for if you feel like a good Indian or Chinese meal. A main course with rice costs around $10.

The **Nights of Istanbul** specialises in Indian and Turkish dishes. It is highly rated but the prices are steep for Tanzania: around $10 for a main course.

**The Bushtrekker** is similar in standard and price to the restaurants in the Kilimanjaro and Agip. Getting there at night involves walking down a long stretch of unlit road. Take a taxi.

The ultimate culinary splash-out is the buffet lunch at the **Dar es Salaam Sheraton**, which costs $32 per person – the food is excellent and you can eat as much as you like.

## Moderate to cheap

The **Chinese Restaurant** in the basement of the NIC Building on Samora Avenue serves a wide range of Chinese, Indian and Western dishes for around $3. The food is tasty and portions are enormous.

The **Motel Agip Snack Bar** is popular with both locals and tourists. Jacket potatoes ($1.50) are a definite attraction and the cappuccino is good, but otherwise it's pretty ordinary. The **Pizza Villa** is the place to go if you want a pizza. Expect to pay up to $5.

For Indian food try **The Shalamar**. The food is tasty but portions are mean (my curry was a lonely chicken wing floating in a pool of sauce). A curry with rice costs $5. The *hoteli*-like **Amgrapoli Restaurant** is much better value. There are two good Indian vegetarian restaurants. The buffet dinner at **The Pandya** is good value at $3.25. The food at **The Supreme** is as good if not better, and a meal shouldn't set you back more than $2.

The **Rendezvous Restaurant** serves a variety of steak and fish dishes for around $4. You can also eat well at several of the moderate hotels. The **Mawenzi Hotel** in particular is very good value, with tasty main courses coming in at

**EAST CENTRAL DAR ES SALAAM**

# KEY TO EAST CENTRAL DAR ES SALAAM

1 ETIENNE'S HOTEL
2 PALM BEACH HOTEL
3 GOLF COURSE
4 NYUMBA YA SANAA GALLERY
5 BUSHTREKKER
6 DAR ES SALAAM SHERATON
7 ETHIOPIAN AIRLINES
8 YMCA
9 SECOND-HAND BOOKSHOP
10 YWCA
11 HOTEL EMBASSY
12 THE CAFETARIA
13 HAPPY SNACKS
14 IPS BUILDING
15 AIR TANZANIA
16 BOTANICAL GARDEN
17 NATIONAL MUSEUM
18 MOTEL AFRIQUE
19 EXTELCOM HOUSE
20 COFFEE SHOP and BURGER BITES
21 PANDYA RESTAURANT
22 COSY CAFE
23 ASKARI MONUMENT
24 TANZANIA TOURIST BOARD
25 SUPERMARKET
26 NEW AFRICA HOTEL
27 AGIP MOTEL
28 BRITISH COUNCIL
29 NIC BUILDING
30 CHINESE RESTAURANT
31 BAKERY
32 SHALAMAR RESTAURANT
33 SNO-CREAM
34 SALAMANDER
35 THE ALCOVE
36 FERRY OFFICES
37 LUTHERAN CHURCH
38 LUTHER HOUSE
39 KILIMANJARO HOTEL
40 MAP OFFICE

under $4. The restaurants at the **Continental**, **Peacock** and **Starlight Hotels** are all worth a try, with the Peacock doing an excellent all-you-can-eat buffet for $10 on Tuesday, Wednesday and Friday nights.

**Cosy Café** has a pleasant atmosphere, and specialises in steaks and other grills. Main courses cost up to $6. **The Salamander** has a deserved reputation for serving the best lunches in town. Meals such as fish and chips and spaghetti bolognese cost $3. Snacks are also served. It is closed in the evenings.

**Happy Snacks** is a fast food joint. The food is erratic but you can fill up for around $1. **The Cafeteria** is similar in price and style, but the food is less greasy.

In the mid-1980s, when the city's other ice-cream parlours served nothing but orange juice spiced with flies, the **Sno-Cream Parlour**'s extravagant interior and marvellous sundaes were decidedly surreal. It looks less out of place these days, but still serves the best sundaes in the country for around $3.

The **TCB Coffee Shop** on the ground floor of Extelcomms House is a good place for a coffee and snack during shopping hours.

# USEFUL INFORMATION

The Tanzania Tourist Corporation (TTC) office opposite the New Africa Hotel is open on weekdays and Saturday mornings. We found the staff helpful, but not that knowledgeable when it came to off-the-beaten-track destinations. The address is PO Box 2485, Dar es Salaam. Tel: (051) 27671/2/3/4/5.

The **telephone area code** for Dar es Salaam is 051.

## Getting around

There are taxis all over the place. A good place to find one is in front of the New Africa Hotel, though you are more likely to be overcharged there than elsewhere. The standard price for a ride within the city centre is about $2. There is a good bus service in Dar es Salaam. Most buses leave from the post office.

## Maps

The Department of Lands and Surveys building is on Kivukoni Front, about 100m past the Kilimanjaro Hotel. Their map office is not in this building but in a small office tucked away behind a building on the block before it. I had been told buying maps could be a drawn-out process, but I found the staff helpful and the office surprisingly well-stocked. If you plan to hike off the beaten track, 1:50,000 maps of areas such as the Pare, Poroto, Usambara and Udzungwa mountains are available.

The kiosk in the foyer of the New Africa Hotel usually stocks maps of Dar es Salaam and Tanzania; if they don't have what you want, try the TTC office or the bookshop in the Kilimanjaro Hotel.

The recently published *Dar es Salaam City Map & Guide* is accurate, and readily available at most tourist class hotels in the city centre.

## Books

Most bookshops in Dar es Salaam (and in Tanzania for that matter) only stock textbooks. For fiction, try the secondhand bookshop on Maktaba Street opposite the post office, or any of several stalls around the Agip and New Africa Hotel. There are shops or kiosks selling books in the foyers of most tourist class hotels. The one in the Sheraton tends to be very overpriced.

The British Council library and reading room has plenty of up-to-date British newspapers and magazines. Membership costs $2.50 per month. You can sometimes buy recent European and American newspapers at the stalls on Samora Avenue near the Salamander Restaurant.

## Hairdressers
There are unisex salons on the ground floor of the Kilimanjaro Hotel and in the YMCA building.

## Shopping
Although it has improved greatly in recent years, Dar es Salaam is some way short of being a shopper's paradise. Locally-produced goods are cheapest at stalls like those lining Maktaba Street. The supermarket on Samora Avenue (see map) is one of many so-called luxury shops, selling a variety of imported foodstuffs and toiletries at inflated prices. I've been told that a supermarket called Supersave, on Kisatu Street, currently offers the best prices on most imported goods. There are several clothes shops and fruit stalls along Zanaki Street. The most colourful place to buy these sort of things is Kariakoo Market (described under *What to Do*). Curio stalls in Dar es Salaam are very expensive when compared to those in Arusha.

## Money
Most people change money at one of the numerous forex bureaux which sprang up after the exchange rate was floated. Forex bureaux give better rates than banks and are open for longer hours. Rates vary considerably, so shop around before you change large sums. I cannot recommend individual bureaux: the one giving the best rate in town when we first visited Dar es Salaam had dropped almost as low as the bank rate three months later. There are plenty of forex bureaux on Samora Avenue and Zanaki Street.

If you need to change money after the bureaux have closed, you can do so at the airport. It's also possible to do this at any hotel which takes payment in dollars, providing you stay at that hotel. Do not change money with street dealers. There is no black market worth talking about in Dar es Salaam, but there are plenty of conmen.

Rickshaw Travel on UWT Street (PO Box 1889, tel: 29125/35079, fax: 46655) is the Tanzanian representative of American Express. It can provide financial services such as emergency cashing of cheques and foreign exchange, and is open from 08.00 to 17.00 Monday to Saturday.

## Embassies and diplomatic missions
Embassies and high commissions in Dar es Salaam are listed below. Most are open mornings only and not at all at weekends. Typical hours are 9.00am to 12.30pm, but this varies considerably.

| Country | Address | Tel |
|---------|---------|-----|
| Algeria | 34 Upanga Road | 46250 |
| Angola | IPS Building, cnr Maktaba & Samora | 46168 |

| Argentina | 953 Msasani Peninsula | 41628 |
| Austria | 20 Samora Avenue | 46251 |
| Belgium | NIC Building, Samora Avenue | 46194 |
| Brazil | IPS Building, cnr Maktaba & Samora | 46191 |
| Britain | Hifadhi House, Samora Avenue | 29601/5 |
| Bulgaria | 232 Malik Road | 23787 |
| Burundi | 1007 Lugalo Road | 46307 |
| Canada | Pan Africa Insurance Building, Samora Avenue | 46000 |
| China | 2 Kajifcheni Close | 67586 |
| CIS (ex USSR) | 73 Kenyatta Drive | 46368 |
| Cuba | 313 Lugalo Road | 46315 |
| Cyprus | City Drive | 23513 |
| Czech Republic | 69 Upanga Road | 46251 |
| Denmark | Bank House, Samora Avenue | 46318 |
| Egypt | 24 Garden Avenue | 32158 |
| Finland | NIC Building, Samora Avenue | 46324 |
| France | cnr Bagamoyo & Kilimani | 46329 |
| Germany | NIC Building, Samora Avenue | 46334 |
| Greece | Parthenon Hall, Upanga Road | 46252 |
| India | NIC Building, Samora Avenue | 46341 |
| Indonesia | 299 Upanga Road | 46347 |
| Iran | Mazengo Road | 32788 |
| Iraq | NIC Building, Samora Avenue | 25728 |
| Ireland | TDFL Building, cnr Upanga & Ohio | 46852 |
| Italy | 316 Lugalo Road | 46352 |
| Japan | 1008 Upanga Road | 46356 |
| Kenya | NIC Building, Samora Avenue | 46362 |
| Korea | 46B United Nations Road | 46831 |
| Libya | 386 Mititu Street | 46254 |
| Madagascar | 143 Malik Road | 46255 |
| Malawi | IPS Building, cnr Maktaba & Samora | 46673 |
| Mexico | 2052 Kimara Street | 23935 |
| Mozambique | 25 Garden Avenue | 46487 |
| Netherlands | ATC Building, Ohio Road | 46391 |
| Nigeria | 3 Bagamoyo Road | 66682 |
| Norway | Extelcomms House, Samora Avenue | 46443 |
| Pakistan | 149 Malik Road | 27971 |
| Poland | 4 Upanga Road | 46294 |
| Rwanda | 32 Upanga Road | 46502 |
| Somalia | 539 Kalenga Road | 50717 |
| Spain | 99B Kinondoni Road | 46506 |
| Sudan | 64 Upanga Road | 46509 |
| Sweden | Extelcomms House, Samora Avenue | 46443 |
| Switzerland | 17 Kenyatta Drive | 66006 |
| Uganda | Extelcomms House, Samora Avenue | 46256 |
| USA | 36 Laibon Road | 66010 |

| Yemen | 353 United Nations Road | 46834 |
| Zaire | 438 Malik Road | 46350 |
| Zambia | Cnr Ohio Road & City Drive | 46383 |
| Zimbabwe | 439 Malik Road | 46259 |

## Tour operators

Most tour operators in Dar es Salaam specialise in visits to the southern reserves described in Chapter Eleven. It is more normal to organise northern safaris in Arusha. It is also cheaper, as most tour operators in Dar es Salaam are in the middle to upper range. Some tour companies can do day trips to Bagamoyo. Safaris can usually be arranged through the owners of various camps in the Selous; see *Chapter Eleven* for details of these.

**Coastal Travels**, PO Box 3052. Tel: 37479; fax: 46045, is a highly regarded company which serves as the main booking agent for many lodges and hotels in southern and central Tanzania. .
**Bushtrekker Safaris**, PO Box 5350. Tel: 31957.
**Holiday Africa**, Africa Street, PO Box 2132. Tel: 30700.
**Kearsley Travel**, Indira Gandhi St, PO Box 801. Tel: 20607/8/9; fax: 35012.
**Savannah Tours**, in the Kilimanjaro Hotel, PO Box 6247. Tel: 25273; fax: 41652.
**State Travel Service**, Samora Avenue, PO Box 5033. Tel: 29291; fax: 29295.
**Takims Safaris**, Jamhuri Street, PO Box 20350. Tel: 25691/2/3; fax: 46130.
**Valji & Alhibai**, Bridge Street, PO Box 786. Tel: 20522; fax: 46401.

# WHAT TO DO

Dar es Salaam is an interesting city, but not one that offers much in the way of conventional sightseeing. It is worth taking a stroll around the harbour area, and through the backstreets between Maktaba Road and the station. There are several old German buildings in the older part of town around the national museum and botanical gardens.

If you have a couple of days to kill in Dar es Salaam, you might want to spend them at Kunduchi Beach (covered later in this chapter) or Bagamoyo (see *Chapter Six*).

## Historical buildings

You can spend a worthwhile couple of hours exploring the several relics of Dar es Salaam's early days which are dotted around the city centre. The oldest surviving building is the **Old Boma** on the corner of Morogoro Road and Sokoine Drive. A plain, rather austere whitewashed monolith, built using coral rubble in the traditional coastal style, the Old Boma is easily recognised by its inscribed Zanzibari door. It was built in 1867 as a hotel to house visitors to the court of

Sultan Majid, whose palace stood alongside it, and has since served as the GEAC's first station and the police charge office.

Several late-19th century German buildings have survived into modern times. The **Ocean Road Hospital,** which lies east of the city centre at the end of Samora Avenue, was built in 1897, and is notable for its twin domed towers. The nearby **State House** also dates to a similar time, though it was heavily damaged in World War I, and the modern building, restored in 1922, bears little resemblance to photographs of the original.

The **Lutheran Church** on the corner of Sokoine Drive and Maktaba Road was built in 1898 in a Bavarian style. Following the recent restoration of its exterior, this is a very striking and attractive church, best viewed from the park on Sokoine Drive. A few blocks down on Sokoine Drive, the Gothically influenced **St Joseph's Cathedral** was built between 1897 and 1902. Other buildings dating from the German Era include the **City Hall** (on Sokoine Road opposite the Old Boma), several ex-civil servants' residences around the botanical garden, and the buildings housing the Department of Lands and Surveys and Magistrate's Court on Kivukoni Front.

## Kariakoo Market

A huge variety of clothes, foodstuffs, spices and traditional medicines can be bought at this lively and colourful covered market which extends on to the surrounding streets in the form of a chaotic miscellany of stalls. The name *Kariakoo* derives from the British Carrier Corps, which was stationed in the area during World War II.

## National Museum

This is one of the better museums I have visited in Africa. The natural history section is a predictable collection of stuffed birds and animals, but the section on early hominid development has some of the world's most important fossils. The history displays upstairs have a good selection of exhibits dating back to the era of European exploration and German occupation. If you plan to visit Kilwa Kisiwani, don't miss the display of coins, pottery and other artefacts found during excavations there. Entrance costs $1.

The area around the museum is notable for its pre-1914 German buildings, recognisable by their red-tiled roofs. The botanical garden, started in 1906, and State House, built by the British in 1922, are both worth a look. From State House, if you walk back to town along Kivukoni Front, you will be rewarded by good views of the city and harbour. You will also pass the 19th century Lutheran Church which is the oldest building in the city.

## Nyumba ya Sanaa
This well-known gallery was founded by a nun, and is now housed in an unusually-designed building, erected in 1983 with the help of Norwegian funding. It exhibits arts and crafts made by handicapped people. A variety of carvings, batiks and pottery items can be bought. The standard of craftsmanship is generally regarded to be high. There is a café in the complex.

## Oyster Bay
This is the closest swimming beach to the city centre. It is a reasonably attractive spot and very popular at weekends. The Oyster Bay Hotel, which overlooks the beach, is a pleasant place to have a drink. Oyster Bay is difficult to get to using public transport. A taxi from the city centre will cost around $2.50.

## Village Museum and Mwenge Market
The Village Museum consists of life-size replicas of huts built in architectural styles from all over Tanzania. It is open daily from 09.30 to 18.00. There is an entrance fee of $0.50 as well as a photographic fee of $1.25 (or $5.00 for video cameras).

The nearby Mwenge market is a traditional Makonde carving community. It is one of the best places to buy these unique sculptures (covered in more detail under *The Makonde Plateau* in Chapter Twelve). Prices are negotiable.

Both are along the Bagamoyo road, about 10km and 13km from the city centre respectively. To get there, you could board a bus heading towards Bagamoyo and ask to be dropped off. City buses and matatus leave from the post office.

## Wildlife Conservation Society
The Wildlife Conservation Society of Tanzania holds monthly talks at their headquarters on Garden Avenue (roughly where the 'a' is on the map.

## Kigamboni
A pleasant escape from the city is to take the ferry from Kivukoni to Kigamboni. This leaves throughout the day and charges less than $1 per person. After disembarking from the ferry, turn left into the road, and after about 2km you will come back to the coast at an attractive beach where there are a couple of bars, and guest houses. Don't walk back to the ferry along the beach, as you will pass through a military area.

## Nightlife
### Bars
The most popular place for an evening drink is the veranda of the New Africa Hotel, scheduled to re-open at the end of 1996. The outdoor bar at the Motel Agip has less character, but it's quieter and the service is better. Further afield, the Oyster Bay and Palm Beach Hotels both get lively at night, but you will need a taxi to get to either of them.

### Discos and live music
The disco in the New Africa Hotel on Wednesday, Friday and Saturday nights is likely to re-open at the end of 1996. The entrance fee is quite steep but there is often a live group. A more earthy place is the disco at the Imperial Hotel on Samora Avenue near the clock tower. There is always the possibility that one of the better-known Zairean groups will be in town for a one-off gig. Ask around. The most popular disco in Dar es Salaam is at the Oyster Bay Hotel; you will need to take a taxi there.

### Cinema and theatre
There are six cinemas in Dar es Salaam. If you are a fan of Indian, kung-fu or gungho American war films you will be in your element. Stallone is a massive figure in Tanzania; his face is printed on shopping bags and painted on shops and restaurants. If enthusiastic kids yell "Rambo" at you don't let it go to your head – they would yell it at Bambi if he happened to be passing.

The only theatre in Dar es Salaam is the *Little Theatre* near Oyster Bay.

The British Council holds weekly film screenings; the programme is posted outside its library.

# KUNDUCHI BEACH

This is Dar es Salaam's major resort. Most people visit it to relax on the sandy beaches, which are marred only by concrete piles at regular intervals, apparently to control erosion. It is possible to hire a boat to one of the many small islands dotted along the coast.

### Getting there
A shuttle bus to the hotels on Kunduchi Beach leaves from in front of the New Africa Hotel at 09.00, 12.00, 14.00 and 17.00 on weekdays, and every other hour between 09.00 and 17.00 at weekends. It stops first at the Kunduchi Beach Hotel, followed by Silversands, Rungwe Oceanic Hotel and the Bahari Beach Hotel. It then returns directly to the city centre.

The trip out takes about an hour. Timings for the return trip are vague. If, for instance, you want to return to Dar es Salaam on the bus which leaves the New Africa at 09.00, it could pass your hotel any time between 09.45 and 10.15.

There are ordinary buses to Kunduchi village, from where you could walk to one of the hotels. This is not recommended; thefts and muggings are a common occurrence on roads between the hotels. Stick to the shuttle service.

## Where to stay
There are four hotels, all on the beachfront.

### *Upper range*
**Bahari Beach Hotel** (PO Box 9312, tel: 47101). This coral and thatch hotel, constructed in traditional Swahili style, is the top of the range. It has attractive grounds. Facilities include a restaurant, swimming pool, and live music on Sundays. Air-conditioned chalets cost $90 s/c double, or $70 for residents. Day visitors are charged a nominal entrance fee.

**Kunduchi Beach Hotel** (PO Box 9313, tel: 47621/23491). This is also a pleasant hotel. All rooms are air-conditioned and sea-facing. There is a restaurant and swimming pool; boat hire can be organised. Rates are cheaper than at the Bahari.

### *Moderate*
**Rungwe Oceanic Hotel** (tel: 47815). Accommodation is in comfortable huts, with a fan, mosquito nets and hot water. Rungwe is a lively place; it has a bar, a restaurant and a disco. $25 s/c double. The campsite is popular with overland trucks.

**Silversands Hotel** This hotel, run by the University of Dar es Salaam, is a bit run-down but nevertheless pleasant. Facilities include a restaurant and bar. Air-conditioned rooms cost $25 s/c double. There is a rather shabby and not very secure looking campsite attached.

## Kunduchi Ruins
These ruins are a short walk from the Kunduchi Beach Hotel. Little is known about their history. One of the ruined buildings is a 16th century mosque. The main point of interest is an 18th century graveyard set amongst a grove of baobab trees. The graves at Kunduchi are notable for being marked by inscribed stone obelisks – a feature not found at any other Swahili graveyard of this period. Pottery collected at the site suggests the town was wealthy and had trade links with China and Britain.

106

Chapter Six

# The North Coast and Usambara

## INTRODUCTION

This chapter covers the coast between Dar es Salaam and the Kenyan border, and the Usambara Mountains between Tanga and Moshi. It is an area with no major tourist attractions, but it offers several minor delights normally bypassed by visitors in their haste to reach Kilimanjaro or the northern safari circuit. Unlike similar destinations in western and southern Tanzania, these are all within easy reach of short-stay visitors.

The largest town on the north coast, Tanga, has been the country's second largest port since German times. The Omani-founded settlements of Bagamoyo and Pangani lie between Tanga and Dar es Salaam, as does the little-visited Sadani Game Reserve.

The Usambara Mountains lie north of Tanga, between the coast and the main Dar es Salaam-Moshi road. The only large town in the mountains is Lushoto, but smaller settlements such as Amani, Soni and Mlalo are all of interest. The most important centres on the Tanga-Moshi road are Muheza, Korogwe, Mombo and Same.

### Climate

The north coast has a typical coastal climate: hot and humid, with short rains in November and December and long rains between March and May. The Usambara is higher and cooler than the coast, but has a similar rainfall pattern.

### Getting around

Regular buses run along the main roads between Dar es Salaam, Tanga and Moshi. Transport off this road is less regular, but there are daily buses to Amani, Lushoto and Pangani, and from Dar es Salaam to Bagamoyo.

The Dar es Salaam-Moshi road was in a sorry state for years, but it has recently been re-surfaced; at the end of 1992, only the 50km stretch north of Mombo still needed work. Buses from Dar es Salaam to Moshi take eight to ten hours. The road between Tanga and Segera is poor, but there are plans to re-surface it. The only other tar road in the region connects Mombo to Lushoto.

Trains between Dar es Salaam and Moshi stop at Korogwe, Mombo and Same, though not at a particularly convenient hour. See *By rail* in *Chapter Three* for details.

In an ideal world you could travel from Dar es Salaam to Tanga along the coast, taking in Bagamoyo, Sadani and Pangani along the way. Unfortunately, transport between Bagamoyo and Pangani verges on the non-existent. Unless you have a 4x4 vehicle, the coastal route is only worth attempting in the dry season, and even then only if you are an optimist with plenty of time on your hands.

# BAGAMOYO

Bagamoyo, 70km north of Dar es Salaam, was the centre of the 19th century slave trade. It was an important base in the first years of German rule, but little development has taken place since then. Bagamoyo is dominated by Arab and German buildings in various states of disintegration. This stagnation has given it a fascinating museum-like quality.

## History

The 12th century town of Kaole, 5km from Bagamoyo, had strong trade links with Kilwa during the Shirazi era, and was evidently wealthy. It must also have enjoyed some prosperity during the Portuguese and Omani periods; most of its decorative graves were erected years after the Portuguese invasion.

Bagamoyo itself was a minor fishing village until the late 18th Century when it became the terminus for the northern slave caravan route. By the mid-19th century approximately 50,000 slaves were shipped from Bagamoyo to Zanzibar annually. Various meanings have been attributed to the name Bagamoyo; *to lose hope* or *where the heart lays down its burden* are two of them. These relate to Bagamoyo being the last place of rest on African soil for captured slaves awaiting shipment.

Many European explorers passed through Bagamoyo, including Burton, Speke, Grant, Stanley and Livingstone. Their publicising of the horrors of the slave trade led to the Holy Ghost Fathers establishing a mission there in 1868. The church they built in 1873 is the oldest in East Africa. It seems fitting that after his death at Lake Benguela in 1873, the preserved body of Livingstone – who called the slave trade the 'open sore of the world' – was carried 1,600km by his porters to the Holy Ghost Mission before being shipped to Zanzibar and England.

The Germans built their headquarters at Bagamoyo in 1888. Stanley arrived there in 1889 after a three year trip to what was then the Equatoria Province of Egypt (the area north of Lake Albert) and was struck by how it had grown since German occupation. He brought with him the Emin Pasha, the German-born British officer who had defended Equatoria since the fall of Khartoum in 1885. Having survived this, the Emin Pasha – drunk at the time, and notoriously short-sighted – celebrated his safe arrival with a near-fatal fall from the balcony of the officers' mess to the street below. He spent the next six weeks in the mission hospital recovering from head injuries.

The Germans deemed Bagamoyo's harbour too shallow for long-term use and moved north to Tanga. The town remained an important regional centre for some years – its most impressive building, the State House, was built in 1897 – but since the turn of the century, its importance has declined steadily.

## Getting there and away
Regular buses to Bagamoyo leave Dar es Salaam from outside Kariakoo Market. The road up is outrageously bad; expect the trip to take four hours. People do visit Bagamoyo as a day trip from Dar es Salaam, but with two long bus trips either side it is not an attractive prospect. In any case, Bagamoyo deserves an overnight stay.

Hitching between Dar es Salaam and Bagamoyo is quite easy over weekends, when a number of expatriates go to Bagamoyo.

## Where to stay
The **Travellers Lodge** is a nicely situated beach hotel with chalets for $14 and $28 self-contained. It has a good restaurant. Another tourist-class hotel is the **Gogo Beach Hotel**, on the beach about 1km out of town. It quite new and rather lacks character, but this should improve with time. It has a restaurant and bar, and the chalets look comfortable.

The moderately-priced **Badeco Beach Hotel** is on the beachfront, a short walk from the town centre. It has a relaxed, friendly atmosphere. Meals are cooked on request and there is a bar. Rooms are basic but clean and have mosquito nets.

The **Alpha Motel** is a basic guesthouse near the bus station, with clean rooms for around $2, and a restaurant. There are other guesthouses, but they are only worth looking at if you are desperate.

## What to see
In the town centre there are a few buildings with carved wooden Zanzibar doors. The most impressive building is the State House, which now serves as a customs office. The unusual two-storey building near the Badeco Hotel, currently being restored, is the one from which the

Emin Pasha fell in 1889. Also near the Badeco is the tree from which the Germans hanged Africans they considered rebellious, and a graveyard for German soldiers. The building which is now the police station used to be where slaves were held prior to being shipped to Zanzibar.

**The Holy Ghost Mission** This 19th century mission should be your first port of call. The church, built in 1873, is still standing and a small museum has fascinating displays on every aspect of Bagamoyo's past. Entrance is free, but a donation is expected. The mission is 3km out of town. The avenue that leads to the mission has a reputation for muggings; leave your valuables behind and go either in a group or with a guide.

**The beach** It is difficult to imagine a beach which conforms more closely to the archetype of a tropical paradise than the one stretching for miles either side of Bagamoyo. We stayed at the Badeco where, unless they have a new cassette by now – or maybe it's deliberate – Bob Marley's *Redemption Song* comes over the speaker perhaps a dozen times a day: a chilling reminder that tens of thousands of slaves were shipped from this beach. If you cannot quite abandon yourself to hedonism in these circumstances, it is still worth wandering along the beach between the Badeco and Gogo Hotels. The old beachfront slave market now sells fish; the white sands in front of it are lined with picturesque fishing dhows. I was enchanted by the legions of ghostly white crabs which scuttle along the beach after dusk.

**Kaole Ruins** In Shirazi times, Kaole was the largest trading centre between Kilwa and Mombasa. The main ruins date mainly from the 13th Century and include what is thought to be the oldest mosque on the East African mainland. There is also an Omani-era graveyard. Kaole is an hour's walk south of Bagamoyo; the most straightforward route is along the beach, but there is a risk of being mugged on the way. Find a guide or leave your valuables behind, preferably both. Kaole can be reached by road. The caretaker is enthusiastic and knowledgeable.

**Bagamoyo Art College** This art college, 100m south of the Badeco Hotel, is housed in a stunning building constructed from traditional materials. Most weekends the students put on a free show of traditional music, dancing and mime. When we visited it, this was attended by what looked like the entire population of Bagamoyo and there was plenty of audience participation.

# SADANI GAME RESERVE

Sadani is the only East African coastal reserve to harbour large mammals and it is said to be the one place where elephant can still be seen bathing in the Indian Ocean. It protects a wide variety of habitats, including mangrove swamps, coastal thickets and acacia woodland. Animal numbers have been depleted by poaching, but this is said to be under control and there is still enough game left in the surrounding area for populations to replenish themselves naturally. Resident mammals include lion, leopard, elephant, zebra, roan antelope, giraffe, oryx and buffalo.

As the nearest game reserve to Dar es Salaam, you might reasonably expect Sadani to be bustling with tourists. In fact, it is one of the least visited and most underpublicised reserves in Tanzania. In 1992, I met only one person who had visited Sadani, a tour operator from Dar es Salaam, and my own attempts to reach the reserve on public transport proved fruitless both from Pangani and from Bagamoyo.

Sadani is considerably more accessible than it was in 1992, provided you have the money to throw at visiting it. An airstrip has been cleared and a tented camp has been erected by Tent With a View Safaris (PO Box 40525 Dar es Salaam; tel: 865934), who do fly-in packages out of Dar es Salaam. But the reserve remains practically inaccessible to independent travellers – a shame, not least because Sadani would otherwise form part of a most alluring coastal route between Dar es Salaam and Tangai.

The small village of Sadani lies within the reserve on the Pangani-Bagamoyo road. In the early 19th Century, Sadani emerged as a major rival to Bagamoyo, but its growth was inhibited by a defensive wall. The wall was built to protect the town's residents from warring Wadoe and Wazigua clans, whose ongoing fighting also dissuaded caravans from passing through the Sadani hinterland. Sadani was briefly considered as a site for the London Missionary Society's first East African mission, but it was passed over in favour of Bagamoyo. If any readers do head out this way, it would be interesting to hear whether there's much to see in the way of old buildings – in addition to the defensive wall and other Omani period relics, one source claims that the original German customs house in Bagamoyo was "transported" to Sadani in 1895.

## Getting there and away

Getting to Sadani on public transport appears to be difficult. If you decide to give it a go, be prepared to get stuck along the way. According to the TTC office in Dar es Salaam, the odd vehicle runs from Bagamoyo to Sadani. This was news to everyone we spoke to in

Bagamoyo; there we were told to catch a bus from Dar es Salaam to Miono (10km east of the Moshi road) where we could catch a pick-up truck to Sadani. The Miono road is favoured by private vehicles so is probably the better one to try. I doubt there is anywhere to stay in Miono and there is a good chance of getting stuck overnight. Take a tent.

Tent with a View Safaris charge between $220 and $300pp for a return flight to Sadani.

## Where to stay

Boldly marked on virtually every map of Tanzania published in the last thirty years, the ex-government resthouse in Sadani village has spent the last two-thirds of this period quietly attempting to biodegrade. It is functional, but camping in the grounds may be preferable to taking a room ($1.50 double). Bring food with you.

The tented camp run by Tent With a View Safaris costs $65pp inclusive of board. Activities run from the camp include driving safaris ($25pp), dhow safaris ($25pp) and foot safaris ($12pp).

## PANGANI

The mouth and lower reaches of the Pangani river have played a major role in coastal trade for several centuries. Pangani itself has been described by one historian as "the Bagamoyo of the first eighteen centuries of the Christian era".

The modern town of Pangani lies on the north bank of the river mouth. It is not particularly ancient, founded by Omani Arabs in around 1820. Throughout the Omani era, Pangani was the main terminus for slave caravans heading to the Lake Victoria region. Although this was a less important caravan route than those to Lakes Nyasa and Tanganyika, Pangani was neverthless one of the most important 19th Century trading centres on the Tanzanian coast, outranked only by Bagamoyo and Kilwa Kivinje.

For several centuries before the arrival of the Omani, Pangani was situated about 4km upstream from its current position on the river mouth. Known as Muhembo, after a nearby hill, this settlement probably dates to the earliest Shirazi times. The oldest coconut plantation in the area is called El Harth, after an Arab family who arrived in the area in around 900AD. Muhembo suffered heavily when it was raided by the Zimba in 1588, and it was practically destroyed by a Portuguese punitive raid in 1635. The probability is that the settlement fell into decline after 1635 and, like many coastal towns, it only recovered under Omani rule.

The most intriguing question about Pangani is whether it was the site of Rhapta, the ancient trading settlement referred to in the *Periplus of the Ancient Sea* and Ptolemy's *Geography*. The case for Pangani as Rhapta is compelling, if largely circumstantial. The *Periplus* places Rhapta four days' sailing south of Lamu and two days south of an island it calls Menuthias. If Menuthias is Pemba, and the landing point used by the ancients was on the north of this island, these directions would fit Pangani. Pointing even more directly to Pangani are the details in Ptolemy's *Geography*, based on the explorations of a Greek merchant called Diogenes, who claimed to have sailed for 25 days up the Rhapta River, where he saw two snow-capped peaks and heard rumours of two large lakes. The Pangani River has its source near Moshi, at the base of snow-capped Kilimanjaro.

No remains of such an ancient settlement have ever been found near Pangani (not entirely surprising if, as Ptolemy implies, the town was at that point some distance upriver from the mouth). Several other possible locations for Rhapta have been suggested, most plausibly the Rufiji mouth, which is so vast that remains of a 2,000 year old settlement would be very difficult to locate, especially if it were now submerged somewhere in the labyrinthine Rufiji Delta. The Rufiji Mouth is about the right distance south of Mafia island but, if the directions in the *Periplus* are to be viewed as implacably accurate (which they might well not be), it's much too far south of Mafia. There are also no snow-capped peaks to be seen upriver.

What does seem certain is that the Pangani River has long formed an important route for exploration of the interior, largely because it provides a reliable source of fresh water as far inland as Moshi. It may well have been the main inland trade route prior to the Portuguese era and quite possibly 2,000 years ago. Ptolemy's information about the African interior, flawed though it may be, is too accurate to be put down to mere coincidence.

Pangani has an attractive situation. The banks of the Pangani River are heavily forested and a gorgeous beach stretches north of the estuary as far as the eye can see. The town itself is Arabic in feel, and several buildings are said to date back to the slave trade. The harbour is quite busy, with the main economic impetus apparently coming from traditional fishing. Otherwise Pangani is relaxed and sleepy, and like so many coastal towns, it does not quite seem to belong in the 20th Century.

## Getting there and away

There are a couple of buses daily each way between Tanga and Pangani. You could also try to hitch; a good place to wait is the turn-off to Baobab Beach (see *Tanga*) as you can stay at the hotel if you have no luck.

The roads heading south from Pangani to Bagamoyo and the Dar es Salaam highway are little-used. There is no public transport along them. If you want to hitch southwards from Pangani, take the ferry across to the south bank of the river and wait there. Don't expect anything to happen in a rush.

## Where to stay/eat
None of the budget lodgings in Pangani has any significant virtue other than cheapness.

The **Pangadeco Beach Hotel** is in a good position and if renovated would be the place to stay, but at present it is dirty, run down, and the rooms don't lock.

The cleaner **Riverside Inn** and **Paradise Guest House** are both on the river front near the bus terminus. A few *hotelis* along the river serve basic meals such as chicken and chips. There is a bar at the Pangadeco.

**Mashado Lodge** (PO Box 8293, Dar es Salaam, tel: 44004/5) is a new upmarket development on the south bank of the Pangani River. The resort is primarily designed to cater for game fishing packages, but other activities which can be arranged include excursions to Amani and Sadani Game Reserve. Accommodation starts at $250pp full board.

**Kingfisher Lodge** (tel: (053) 42491, fax: (053) 46573) lies about halfway between Pangani and Tanga, and is another place specialising in game fishing excursions into the Pemba channel. They also do excursions to several islands and up the Pangani River. Full board accommodation costs $110/195 single/ double or $90/135 for residents.

## Excursions
Most travellers who visit Pangani do so to take a boat up the Pangani River. There is some wildlife in the area, and crocodile are regularly seen. The river is lined with forest so bird watching is good. Pangani District Council charters a boat that carries up to ten people for $4 per hour. Details are pinned up at the Pangadeco's bar. If you want to cut costs by getting a group together, ask around at the Bandorini Hotel in Tanga.

## TANGA

Tanga is Tanzania's third-largest town and second-busiest port. It is one of my favourite East African towns. There is little to do there, but it has a relaxed, friendly atmosphere and is a pleasant place to hang out. If, like many travellers, you never stray beyond the town centre of quiet, potholed streets lined with German and Asian buildings, Tanga is deceptively sleepy. The hub of Tanga's commercial activity lies away from the centre, in the grid of colourful, crowded streets around the bus station. There is also a well-preserved residential area which sprawls attractively along a wooded peninsula east of the town centre.

## History

There is little record of Tanga before Omani times and it was dwarfed by Pangani for most of the 19th Century. Tanga was settled by the Germans when Bagamoyo's harbour proved too shallow. The first school in German East Africa was built at Tanga in 1893, and a railway line to Moshi was started in the same year. When Dar es Salaam replaced Tanga as the capital, the Germans saw no reason to abandon Tanga the way they had Bagamoyo. Its excellent harbour and the coming rail link to the fertile foothills of Kilimanjaro (the Moshi line was only completed in 1911) guaranteed its survival. Tanga remains the second largest port in Tanzania; most of its business comes from sisal exports.

Tanga was the scene of a tragically farcical British raid in the opening stages of World War One. Still seasick after a long voyage from India, 8,000 Asian recruits leapt ashore, got bogged down in the mangroves, stumbled into a swarm of ferocious bees and finally triggered off trip-wires rigged up by the Germans. By the time the raid was aborted 800 British troops were dead and 500 wounded. In the confusion 455 rifles, 16 machine guns and 600,000 rounds of ammunition were left on the shore – a major boon to the Germans. This battle forms a pivotal scene in William Boyd's excellent novel *An Ice-cream War*.

## Getting there and away

Regular buses connect Tanga to Dar es Salaam and Moshi. The bus station is 1km from the town centre. Make enquiries and a booking the day before you want to leave. There are daily buses to Pangani and Lushoto.

There are dhows between Tanga and Pemba every week or so, but they are unreliable and dangerous. There is, however, a motorboat every other day between Tanga, Pemba and Zanzibar, taking around two hours – contact the Bandorini Hotel for details.

## Where to stay

### Upper range

The **Mkonge Hotel** (PO Box 1544, tel: (053) 43440, fax: (053) 45020) is the most upmarket hotel in Tanga. It has recently fallen under the management of the South African Protea Hotel group. The Mkonge is situated about 1km out of town on Hospital Road, in attractive sea-facing grounds. It has a good bar and restaurant and a popular disco at weekends. Air conditioned rooms cost $60/65 single/double.

The **Inn by the Sea** (PO Box 2188, tel: (053) 44613) is next door to the Mkonge, and also has a sea-facing position. Rooms cost $20 double.

The **Marina Hotel** (PO Box 835, tel: (053) 44362) is the most upmarket hotel in the city centre. Self-contained double rooms with hot running water cost $16 (with fan) or $20 (air-conditioned).

## Budget

The **Bandorini Hotel** is well established as the most popular place for travellers, and it's been excellent value for money for over a decade. The owner is a useful source of local travel information, and an excellent cook (for large groups, he does buffets of Indian food which, though not cheap at around $6 per head, put the food at most upmarket hotels in Tanzania to shame). Rooms cost $5/7 single/double with net and fan. The only problem with this place is that it's often fully occupied.

The **Planters Inn** is another well established travellers' haunt. Dating to the pre-First World War German era, the hotel was reportedly the scene of some extravagant gambling on the part of Tanga's predominantly Greek sisal millionaires during the era of British rule. The building retains a strong period charm with its vast balconies and creaky wooden floors. Sadly, though, it has not been maintained with any conviction, and as a result it gets more run-down with each passing year. Nevertheless, it's fair value at $3 for a single or $6 for a self-contained double.

The **Centaur Hotel**, one of the newest in town, is not so strong on character, but it's a clean, well-maintained place, and reasonably priced, with self-contained doubles costing $8 with fan or $16 with air-conditioning.

The **New Era Hotel** lies a short way out of town in a suburban area. Converted from a private house, the rooms look like something out of a how-not-to DIY manual; certainly they are nothing to shout about at $5/10 self-contained single/double. On the plus side, the English man and Asian lady who own and manage the hotel generate a friendly atmosphere. You can camp in the grounds for $3 per person.

For a really cheap room, the **Tanga Central Hotel** is a decent, unpretentious place, geared more to locals than travellers. Ordinary rooms cost $3/5 single/double, and there are also self-contained singles for $5. There are also several cheap guest houses around the bus station and market, though this is not a part of town I'd be particularly keen to wander around after dark.

# Where to eat

Most of the hotels mentioned above have restaurants of a sort. Only those at the **Mkonge** and **Bandorini** stand out in any way, the former serving a variety of western style dishes, and the latter quite wonderful Indian buffets by advance order only.

The **Food Palace** is a new restaurant which serves good Asian and other dishes for around $3-4 per main course. The **Patwas Restaurant** has been around for years, serving great samosas and other snacks, as well as fruit juice and rather ordinary meals. The **Meridian Restaurant**, formerly the Chinese Restaurant, used to be one of the best places to eat in Tanga, but it's now little more than a glorified bar serving a limited selection of local dishes.

## Excursions
### Amboni Caves
These limestone caves 8km north of Tanga are the most extensive in East Africa. Local people knew about the caves years before Europeans discovered them in 1940; they believe the main cave is inhabited by a fertility god and still leave offerings to this deity. The guide has gathered an admirable collection of anecdotes and tall stories. Amboni lies just off the Tanga-Mombasa road; any vehicle heading towards Mombasa can drop you off near the entrance.

### Baobab Beach Hotel
Lying on a baobab-lined beach, 8km from Tanga and 3km from the Pangani Road, this used to be a wonderful coastal retreat with reasonably priced banda and cottage accommodation. In early 1996 it was closed; I understand that the existing management had gone bankrupt. There is some talk of a new purchaser re-opening it in the future. If you're interested, the owner of the Bandorini Hotel should be able to tell you whether or not it's open.

### Tongoni Ruins
These are the ruins of a Shirazi town which peaked in the 14th and 15th centuries. Even in its heyday Tongoni was probably a minor town, but it was certainly prosperous – its graveyard houses the largest concentration of historical tombs on the East African coast, many of which are threatened by the sea. There is also a ruined mosque at the site.

Tongoni is about 20km south of Tanga. To get there catch any bus heading to Pangani and ask to be dropped off at the village of Tongoni. The ruins are 10 minutes walk from the main road. There is a caretaker. Try to get to Tongoni early in the day; there will not be much transport back to Tanga later, and there is nowhere to stay.

## THE USAMBARA MOUNTAINS

This is the most accessible of the Eastern Arc Mountain Ranges, and the best-known scientifically. Research at the botanical garden at Amani started in 1902. Despite severe encroachment in some areas, significant stands of montane forest remain. These forests, like all those in eastern Tanzania, are characterised by a high level of endemism. The general ecology of the eastern Tanzanian mountains is more fully discussed under *Udzungwa National Park* in Chapter Eleven.

The western and eastern Usambara are very different in character. The western Usambara is cultivated and relatively densely populated; the eastern Usambara is forested except where the indigenous vegetation has been replaced by tea plantations. Access to the Lushoto in western Usambara is via a tarred road from Mombo. The most accessible place in the eastern Usambara is Amani, about 30km from Muheza on the Tanga-Moshi road.

## History

The Usambara has been occupied by Bantu-speakers for a few thousand years. The people of the mountains, the Shambaa, have a tradition of welcoming refugees from other areas, and until recent times had a loose political system similar to the *ntemi* of western Tanzania. The probable impetus for forging greater unity was the threat posed by the 18th Century Maasai occupation of the plains west of the range.

The first Shambaa leader was Mbegha, the self-styled *Lion King*, who probably originated from the *ntemi* area of western Tanzania. Mbegha united the area peacefully by taking a wife from each major clan, then placing her son in charge of that clan. His army, formed from refugees, seems likely only to have been used in defence. Under the rule of Mbegha's grandson, Kinyashi, the Shambaa became more militarised. Their greatest leader was Kinyashi's son, Kimweri; under his rule the Shambaa controlled much of the area between the Usambara and the coast.

Kimweri's capital at Vuga, near the modern settlement of Soni, was too deep in the mountains to have had much contact with Kilimanjaro-bound caravans. One of Kimweri's sons, Semboja, the chief of Mazinde, on what is now the main Moshi-Dar es Salaam road, came to exert considerable influence over passing traders. By 1867 he had built up a stockpile of arms large enough to enable him to overthrow Kimweri's successor at Vuga. This event split the Shambaa into several splinter groups, and although the leadership was retained by Semboja, he controlled a far smaller area than did his predecessor. The Shambaa figured heavily in the Abushiri uprising of 1888/9, but after Semboja's son, Mputa, was hanged in 1898, they offered little further resistance to German occupation.

The Usambara was popular with European farmers. Lushoto, originally called Wilhelmstal, was considered a possible capital in the early days of the colony. Evidence of German architectural styles can be seen throughout the region.

# Amani

In 1902 the Germans established an agricultural research station at Amani and set aside the surrounding area as a botanical garden. Amani is now an important medical research centre, housed in buildings dating from the German and British colonial era. The botanical garden, said to be the second largest in the world, still exists. Amani has the genteel appearance of an English country village transplanted to the African jungle: it is surrounded by montane forest and teems with animal life. The area is scheduled to become a nature reserve.

Amani is exceptionally attractive to anyone with an interest in hiking or natural history. Wandering around the forest-fringed village is an ideal way to see species such as black-and-white colobus and blue monkey. The area supports numerous endemic plant species, including nine varieties of African violet, and is renowned for its colourful and abundant butterflies, many of which are also endemic.

The bird life around Amani is fantastic. The conspicuous and beautiful green-headed oriole is restricted to a handful of montane forests between Tanzania and Mozambique. Other Amani specials include the Uluguru violet-backed, banded green and Amani sunbirds, and a variety of robins, bulbuls and starlings. The Nduk eagle owl is only found in the Usambara. Many endemics are forest fringe species, so are likely to be seen in the village. Abercrombie and Kent (see safari company listings in Chapter Eight) do occasional bird watching tours to Amani.

## Getting there and away

Amani is reached from Muheza on the Tanga-Moshi road. There are guest-houses in Muheza should you need to spend a night. The bus to Amani leaves Muheza at 14.00, but it may not run after heavy rains. If you want to try hitching, wait in front of the courthouse 1km from the town centre, opposite a sign that reads *Amani Medical Research Centre 32km*.

The drive to Amani is spectacular. From Kisiwani, 7km before Amani, the dirt road climbs through the forest in a succession of tight hairpin bends. In a bus this is nerve-wracking; I was convinced we were the unwitting victims of a pilot scheme, doomed to failure after a maiden attempt. We got there in the end, however – the bus has been doing this route safely for years.

When we left Amani, we could not find a bus back to Muheza, so walked the 7km to Kisiwani. The road passes through forest all the way; we saw plenty of monkeys, butterflies and birds. It is marginally easier to get a lift at Kisiwani than it is at Amani, as roads to the various tea estates in the area branch off between the two. There is regular transport to Muheza from Bambani, a village about two hours' walk from Kisiwani.

*A balloon safari offers a completely different perspective of the vast plains of the Serengeti (AVZ)*

Above: *Mount Kilimanjaro, the highest free-standing mountain in the world (CH)*

Below: *Rock hyraxes are commonly found on koppies and in mountain areas. Although they may look like rodents, their nearest relative is thought to be the elephant! (NG)*

Left: *The Maasai are nomadic pastoralists who, more than most East Africans, have continued their ancestral traditions (AVZ)*

Above right: *The Gereza Fort at Kilwa. This was built by the Portuguese and renovated in the late 18th Century by Omani Arabs (PB)*

Below right: *The ruins of the Grand Mosque at Kilwa, once the most important gold trading centre in medieval East Africa (PB)*

*Maasai giraffe in Tarangire National Park (CH)*

## Where to stay/eat

The **Amani Club Rest House** is a well-maintained stone building dating to the colonial era. The cosy lounge is heated by a log fire in the evenings, and it houses an improbable collection of yellowing books.

There is also a new **IUCN Rest House** in the village. Both charge between $15 and $20 full board (cheaper for residents) and allow camping for $5 per person.

There is nowhere to eat apart from at the resthouses; the **Welfare Club** is a pleasant place for a drink and conversation, despite its rather Dickensian title.

## Walks and hikes

The East Usambara Catchment Forest Project, established in 1991 and funded by FINNIDA, is charged with implementing a conservation plan to protect the forests of the eastern Usambara catchment area, the source of fresh water to 200,000 people. The development of Amani for ecotourism, with the emphasis on walking and hiking, is a definite priority of this project. The area around Amani is likely to be proclaimed as the Amani Nature Reserve before the end of 1996. Nine trails have been demarcated, ranging in length from 3km to 10km, and leaflets with trail descriptions are in preparation. Other plans include the rehabilitation of the German stationmaster's house as an information centre, and the training of guides to lead visitors on the trails. You can visit the project's office in Tanga for further details of developments, or contact them in advance at PO Box 5869, Tanga; tel & fax: (053) 43820.

A good short walk through the forest – now probably one of the demarcated trails – starts behind the IUCN office. It follows disused and overgrown German roads, then a footpath, to bring you out at a viewpoint over the surrounding hills. We saw some interesting birds, a snake and a giant elephant shrew along this walk. The view when you reach the top gives an idea of the extent of deforestation in the area, and underlines the need to preserve what is left of this vital catchment area.

There is plenty to be seen just wandering around the roads and paths within the research centre and botanical garden. In addition to monkeys, green-headed orioles are common around the gardens, as are several less auspicious birds, including the Amani sunbird.

The following hike is relatively straightforward, covers about 20km, and can be done in two days. From Amani, follow the dirt roads past Derema and Bulwa tea estates. From there you follow disused roads through the villages of Mgambo and Zeria to Kilonga Ngua. From Kilonga Ngua a reasonable dirt road leads to the main Marombo-Korogwe road. You should be able to pick up a lift to Korogwe at the junction. You will need a tent.

A map is recommended for the above hike and essential for any other route. Maps are available from the Department of Lands and Surveys in Dar es Salaam. I'm told a couple of villages are marked inaccurately on the Amani map; someone at the IUCN should be able to point out any errors.

## Korogwe

The largest town on the Moshi-Tanga road is unremarkable except for its Usambara backdrop. It is, however, a useful overnight stop when crossing between the eastern and western Usambara.

The only vaguely upmarket hotel is the **Korogwe Traveller's Inn** on the main Tanga-Moshi road. It is perfectly adequate, and has a well-stocked bar and restaurant. $6 s/c double.

There are several cheaper lodgings to choose from. The **New Savari Guest House**, 100m from the bus station, is very reasonable. Clean double rooms with mosquito nets cost $3. The **Miami Guest House** next door is similar.

You can camp at the Mountain View Resort, which has cold showers, and a bar and restaurant.

## Mombo

This scruffy little town on the Moshi-Dar es Salaam road is the jumping-off point for trips into the western Usambara. Most buses between Dar es Salaam and Moshi stop here for lunch. None of the more basic guesthouses in Mombo give the impression that accommodation is their primary function. Try instead the **Usambara Inn**. Its exterior gives new meaning to the expression run-down (it looks derelict), but the rooms are clean, spacious and have a fan and sink. A restaurant and beer garden are attached.

## Lushoto

The largest town in the Usambara is a strange and slightly anachronistic place. Many buildings on the main street date to the early part of the century, when Lushoto provided weekend relief for settlers farming the dry, dusty Maasai Steppe below. The still-significant settler community adds to the time-warped feel; we drove in on a Sunday and saw a couple of young girls walking to church in clothes that would not have looked out of place in an Edwardian period drama.

If the main street calls to mind an Alpine village, the side roads, lined with mud-and-thatch homesteads, are pure Africa. So, too, is the vibrant market where colourfully-dressed Shambaa women sell their goods. The vegetation around Lushoto reflects these contradictions; papaya trees subvert neat rows of exotic pines and eucalyptus, which in turn are interspersed by patches of lush indigenous forest alive with the raucous squawking of silvery-cheeked hornbill.

You can take in most of what Lushoto has to offer in a couple of hours, but plenty of short walks and day trips can be done using the town as a base.

## Getting there and away
The tar road between Mombo and Lushoto offers splendid views in all directions. Direct buses between Tanga and Lushoto are slow. Instead catch an express bus or train as far as Mombo, from where the odd minibus runs to Lushoto – or you could try to hitch.

## Where to stay/eat
The colonial-style **Lawns Hotel** is the only upmarket hotel in Lushoto. The rooms are comfortable but seem overpriced at $23/double.

**Grant's Lodge** (tel: (053) 42491, fax: (053) 43628) lies 12km from Lushoto near Magambo, the highest peak in the Usambaras. Built in 1934, the lodge is set in an attractive garden, and it contains four bedrooms and a library with a collection of old books and magazines. There are several self-guided trails through the nearby Magambo Forest Reserve, where you can see colobus monkeys and a variety of forest birds. Full board accommodation costs $48 per person.

Back in town, the **Kilimani Guest House** is popular with travellers. Rooms cost $2/3 single/double, and there is a reasonable restaurant and bar. Also recommended in the budget range are the **Lusii Hotel** and **Mkuzi Guest House**. The **Green Valley Hotel** near the market serves good, cheap meals. It also has a few rooms.

Cheap local food and friendly English-speaking staff can be found at the Stop In/Action Safari Café in the corner of the bus station. If you're in town on Saturday, there's a disco at the Hub Club by the football pitch.

## Excursions
The area around Lushoto, riddled with footpaths and winding roads, is open to gentle exploration or – if you have the appropriate maps – longer hikes. The area is scenically varied, with steep-sided valleys covered in euphorbia, pine plantations, small patches of indigenous forest, and cultivated Shambaa homesteads. The Usambara Mountains Tourism Project (UTMP) offers several day and overnight guided walks out of Lushoto, at a cost of $4 per day for a guide plus $4 per person. The guides are knowledgeable, and profits are used for development projects. It is advisable to use their services, due to a number of recent thefts from tourists using private guides to visit places like Irente. The office is next door to the Green Valley Restaurant.

**Irente viewpoint** An attractive short walk from Lushoto takes you to a stunning viewpoint at the edge of the Usambara overlooking the Maasai Steppe. It is possible to organise a guide to take you there, but once you are out of Lushoto it is easy enough to find your own way. Ask people to direct you to Irente farm. From there it is ten minutes' walk through Irente village to the viewpoint. The round trip takes two to three hours. Look out for the Egyptian vultures which apparently nest on the cliffs below the viewpoint. It is also worth scanning patches of indigenous forest en route for forest birds.

## Mtae

This village can be reached from Lushoto by bus, along a road with several terrifying hairpin bends. Perched on a ridged peninsula, with a drop of several hundred metres on either side, the village offers views to Kenya over the Mkomazi Game Reserve, and on a clear day to Kilimanjaro. There are rooms at the Mwivano and Kuna Manena Guest Houses at $1 per person. Buses to Mtae leave Lushoto in the afternoon and take two hours. They return at 05.30 only – if you miss them you'll be stuck for another 24 hours. A café next to the bus stop serves local food and home-made bread – and a few doors down is a bar selling beer.

**Soni Falls** The waterfall at Soni is pretty but nothing special, but the hotel overlooking it is a pleasant base for exploring the Usambara. **Soni Falls Hotel** is clean, friendly, and good value at $5 s/c double. Meals are excellent, but must be ordered in advance. The relaxed bar is lit by a log fire in the evenings.

Of the guesthouses in Soni village, **Msufino Lodgings** looks the best. Rooms are clean, there is a bar and restaurant, and hot water is provided.

Soni village is 30 minutes' drive from Lushoto along the Mombo road. There is a fair amount of traffic; you shouldn't wait long for a lift in either direction. Soni Falls Hotel is signposted from the Lushoto road less than 1km from the village.

## Mlalo

Beyond Lushoto a dirt road skirts the highest peak in the Usambara, Magambo (2,230m), passes through an extensive patch of indigenous forest, then, almost 30km from Lushoto, dramatically descends the side of a valley into a rural sprawl called Mlalo.

Mlalo is bizarre. It has an insular, almost other-worldly feel that made us feel like a pair of Indiana Joneses entering a misplaced Mediterranean mountain kingdom. Initially, I was struck by the unusual style of many of the buildings: two-storey mud houses with intricately-carved wooden balconies which seem to show both German and Arab influences. The town apparently sprawls for miles, yet even in its nominal centre rural homesteads cling precipitously to steep-sided hillocks. There is no electricity; at night the surrounding hills are lit up by lamps bobbing up and down and flickering like fireflies.

The residents of Mlalo seem a bit unsure about tourists; we felt a sense of unease all the time we were there. Wherever we walked people stopped what they were doing to stare at us. In one guesthouse I enjoyed the unique experience of a Tanzanian saying *KiSwahili Kidogo* to me, rather than the other way round. I don't regret visiting Mlalo, but I was profoundly relieved when I left.

### Getting there and away
There are two buses a day between Lushoto and Mlalo, leaving Lushoto in the early afternoon and Mlalo at around 07.00. The bus ride takes two hours or so. This means that you will probably have to overnight in Mlalo if you visit it.

### Where to stay/eat
The guesthouses are near the bus stop. Outside **Lonido Guest House**, a sign proclaims that "Lonido is the only alternative for accommodation in Mlalo. Other alternatives are a mere miscalculation". We gladly risked miscalculation and stayed instead at the **Afilex Hotel**, which was very clean, as friendly as you could hope for in Mlalo, and had the distinct advantage of a manageress who spoke a bit of English.

The restaurant at the Afilex is recommended, despite the fact that the entire staff sat in dead silence and stared at us while we ate. There is a bar and *hoteli* opposite the Afilex.

# MKOMAZI GAME RESERVE

*Many thanks to Nicholas McWilliam for writing to me with current information about this reserve.*

Mkomazi Game Reserve is the southern extension of Kenya's vast Tsavo National Park, covering an area of 3,701km$^2$ east of Kilimanjaro and immediately north of the Pare and Usamtara mountains. The reserve is practically undeveloped for tourism, and it has been subject to considerable pressure over the last 20 years as the human population around its peripheries has grown in number. Together with Tsavaro, Mkomazi forms part of one of East Africa's most important savannah ecosystems, characterised by the semi-arid climatic conditions of the Sahel arc.

In 1992, the Tanzanian government invited the Royal Geographical

Society to undertake a detailed ecological study of Mkomazi. Although mammal populations are low, it has been determined that most of the large mammal species found in Tsavo are either resident in Mkomazi or else regularly migrate there from Kenya, including lion, cheetah, elephant, giraffe, buffalo, zebra, impala and Tanzania's most significant gerenuk population. African hunting dogs were recently re-introduced into Mkomazi, and there are plans to bring in black rhinos from South Africa. Over 400 bird species have been recorded in the reserve, and the recent study has noted at least eight species not previously recorded in Tanzania.

Mkomazi does not at present offer game viewing to compare with other reserves in northern Tanzania, and it is certainly not a conventional safari destination. However, this is compensated for by the wild scenery and the near certainty of not seeing another tourist. Tourist facilities are currently limited to a few 'campsites' (basically just cleared areas) about 2km from Zange Gate and another site about 20km from Zange overlooking Dindera Dam, a good place to see large mammals. The reserve is best avoided in the rainy season, due to the poor roads, and all visitors should be self-sufficient in water, food and fuel.

Because Mkomazi is not a national park, walking is permitted and the fees are relatively affordable ($3 per day for non-residents), making it an interesting and affordable alternative to the Serengeti for adventurous independent travellers. The north-eastern portion of the reserve near Zange Gate is very hilly – tough walking but great scenery – and there is a very real chance of encountering large game animals such as lions and buffaloes on foot. The best way to go about organising a walking trip into Mkomazi would be to walk or hitch the 5km from Same (a moderately sized town on the Moshi-Dar es Salaam road) to Zange Gate, where you can make arrangements with the warden to hire an armed ranger/guide. To stand a chance of seeing a fair range of large mammals, you would need to spend a couple of days walking in the reserve, so you'd need camping gear and adequate provisions.

If you need to spend a night in Same, the **Elephant Motel**, about 1.5km out of town along the road to Dar es Salaam, has moderately priced rooms and an acceptable restaurant. The more central **Amani Lutheran Centre**, situated near the market, has clean, inexpensive rooms, and there are several more basic guest houses around, of which the **Savannah Hotel** is about the best.

Chapter Seven

# Kilimanjaro

## INTRODUCTION

This chapter covers Africa's best-known and highest mountain, Kilimanjaro, and the nearby town of Moshi. Kilimanjaro is the highest mountain in the world which can be climbed by ordinary tourists. Thousands attempt to reach its peak every year. The fertile lower slopes support one of the most densely populated rural areas in Tanzania.

### History

Kilimanjaro's fertile soils have attracted people from all over East Africa for centuries. Ancient stone tools of indeterminate age have been found on the lower slopes, as have the remains of pottery artefacts thought to be at least 2,000 years old. Between 1,000 and 1,500 years ago, Kilimanjaro was the centre of an Iron Age culture spreading out to the coastal belt between Pangani and Mombasa.

Kilimanjaro is now home to the Chagga, a Bantu-speaking group whose ancestors first arrived in the area 500 years ago. The Chagga have no tradition of central leadership. As many as 100 small chiefdoms existed in the mid-19th century. They are efficient agriculturalists, and the lower slopes of Kilimanjaro are covered in their disused dams and irrigation furrows. Because they have always produced a food surplus, the Chagga have a long history of trade with the Maasai and other local groups, and later with Arab caravans.

The first written reference to Kilimanjaro is found in Ptolemy's 4th century *Geography*. It is also alluded to in an account written by a 12th century Chinese trader, and by the 16th century Spanish geographer, Fernandes de Enciso. These allusions fired the curiosity of 19th century geographers, who outdid each other in publishing wild speculations about the African interior.

In 1848, Johan Rebmann, a German missionary working in the Taita Hills, was told about a very large mountain reputed to be covered in silver and to host evil spirits which would freeze anyone who tried to climb it. It was called Kilimanjaro. When Rebmann visited it, he

immediately recognised the silver to be snow. His observations, published in 1849, were derided by European experts who thought it ludicrous to claim there was snow so near the equator. Only in 1861, when an experienced geologist, Von der Decken, saw and surveyed Kilimanjaro, was its existence and that of its snow-capped peaks accepted. Chagga legend suggests that no local person ever successfully climbed Kilimanjaro before Hans Meyer and Ludwig Purstscheller reached its summit in 1889.

## Climate

The higher slopes of Kilimanjaro are cold at all times. Moshi is relatively low-lying (813m) and has a typical equatorial African climate: hot during the day and cool at night. Kilimanjaro can be climbed at any time of year, but the rainier months are best avoided. The heaviest rains fall between March and May.

## MOSHI

Situated at the heart of a major coffee-growing region, Moshi is an attractive if intrinsically unremarkable small town, salvaged from anonymity by one of the most imposing backdrops imaginable. Moshi lies at the base of Kilimanjaro; at dusk or dawn, when the peaks most often emerge from their customary blanket of cloud, they form a sight as stirring and memorable as any in Africa. Despite the teasing proximity of snow-capped Kilimanjaro, Moshi is not the cool highland settlement you might expect. Instead, lying at an altitude of below 1,000m, Moshi has a surprisingly humid, sticky climate, reminiscent of the coast.

Prior to the arrival of the Germans, Moshi was the capital of the area ruled by Rindi, who came into power in about 1860 and, largely through his diplomatic skills, became one of the most important chiefs in the area. By allying with the Maasai, Rindi extracted large taxes from passing caravans. He made a favourable impression on John Kirk, the British Consul in Zanzibar, and signed a treaty with Carl Peters in 1885. When the first German colonial forces arrived at Kilimanjaro in 1891, Rindi assured them he ruled the whole area. At his insistence, they quelled his major rival, Sina of Kibosha.

## Getting there and away

Moshi can be reached by rail, air or road. Air Tanzania flies regularly between Dar es Salaam and Kilimanjaro Airport (off the main Arusha road). A shuttle-bus between Moshi and the airport leaves from the Air Tanzania office next to the Moshi Hotel.

There are two trains every week between Moshi and Dar es Salaam; see *Rail* in Chapter Three for details.

Buses between Dar es Salaam and Moshi take about eight hours. Several buses leave in each direction every morning. There are regular buses between Moshi and Tanga.

There is a steady flow of traffic between Arusha and Moshi. The trip takes under two hours by bus. Buses to Arusha, Marangu and other local destinations leave when they fill up, but buses further afield have fixed departure times and should be booked in advance.

# Where to stay
## Upper range
The government-owned **Moshi Hotel** (PO Box 1819, tel: (055) 3071) is centrally situated. It is, as you might expect, a little run-down, but it's also reasonable value for money at $20/30 for a single/double using communal showers or $50 for a self-contained double.

About 1km from the town centre, the **Keys Hotel** is the only other upmarket option, with self-contained rooms for $40/60 single/double. Both hotels have bars and acceptable restaurants.

The **Lutheran Church Hostel** (tel: 54084) has been recommended by several people as having the best value upper range accommodation in Moshi. There are 60 rooms, ranging in price from $17 to $35 for a single and $20 to $45 for a double (about 30% cheaper for residents). All rooms are self-contained, and have running hot water and private balconies. The food is good. The hostel is about 3km out of town on Kilimanjaro Road; to get there, walk out of town towards the YMCA and continue straight across the roundabout with the main Arusha-Dar es Salaam road. From the roundabout, it's a direct 1.5km walk, but if you get lost, you can ask for directions to the Police School, which is adjacent to the hostel.

## Budget
There is no shortage of inexpensive accommodation in Moshi. A perennial favourite with travellers is the **YMCA** (PO Box 85, tel: (055) 52362). It's a good place to arrange Kilimanjaro climbs, very secure, and has a large swimming pool (which actually had water in last time I was in town – a first!), but it seems a touch overpriced at $10/13 for a small single/double using communal showers.

The **Coffee Tree Hotel** couldn't be more central, and the rooms are very spacious and have mosquito nets. Ordinary rooms cost $5/7 and self-contained doubles (cold water only) cost $11.

Perhaps the best value in town, and a place that's maintained high standards and low prices for several years now, is the **New Kinderoko Hotel** near the market. Ordinary rooms cost $7/8 single/double and self-contained rooms with hot showers cost $9/10. It also has one of the best restaurants in town.

The **Newcastle Hotel** next door is similar in standard but very overpriced at $25/self-contained double.

Another good place near the market is the **Grenada Hotel**, where doubles using communal showers cost $8 and self-contained doubles cost $10. The **Silva Hotel** is similar in standard, a little more expensive, and has cold showers only.

There are plenty of cheaper, more basic guesthouses near the market, of which the **Serengeti Villa** is the stand-out. Doubles cost $4 and self-contained doubles cost $6. The restaurant here is cheap and there's a friendly bar. Even cheaper are the **Safari Guest House** and **New Stand Bar** – both under $4/room – but they're also rather grotty.

The **Kilimanjaro Hotel** is conveniently situated, close to the Railway Station. The rooms get dirtier and shabbier with each passing year, but they are certainly affordable at $3/6 single/double.

There's a cluster of cheap hotels about 1km out of town off the Tanga Road. The **Rombo Cottage Inn** is a friendly, comfortable place, with clean self-contained double rooms and a good restaurant, but its popularity with travellers has caused prices to rocket from around $2 in 1992 to $10 in 1996. The **Suncourt Inn** next door has rooms of a similar quality, and is much better value these days at $6 for a self-contained double with hot water.

Around the corner, the **Jabiru Guest House** is more basic but clean enough and very cheap at $2/single.

The **A&O Royal Crown Hotel** has pleasant rooms, but there's nothing about them to justify the non-residents' rate of $20/double.

### Camping
The Keys Hotel and Golden Shower Restaurant both allow camping, but at $10 per person they seem ridiculously overpriced.

## Where to eat
For a snack, try **Chrisburgers**, which serves eggburgers, samosas and excellent fruit juice. The restaurant on the top floor of the **Coffee Tree Hotel** has a commanding view of Kilimanjaro, and serves solid meals for under $4. **Rombo Cottage Inn** is similar in price and the food is superb.

The best restaurants in Moshi are the **Golden Shower**, 2km out of town on the Marangu road, and **Keys Hotel**. The Golden Shower has a particularly good menu. Main courses cost around $4. Three-course set meals are served at the Moshi Hotel.

The restaurant at the **New Kinderoko Hotel** is currently the best value for money in Moshi, offering large, tasty portions of dishes like chicken and chips or steak and mashed potatoes for around $3.

# Useful information
## Foreign exchange
There was no forex bureau in Moshi in December 1992, but this is likely to change. For now, the best place to change money is the bank opposite the clock tower. You will get a much better rate in Arusha or Dar es Salaam.

## Shopping
There is a good market in Moshi, but shops do not compare to those in Arusha and Dar es Salaam.

# MARANGU

Marangu is 8km south of the main gate to Kilimanjaro National Park. It has an alpine feel, with a babbling mountain stream running alongside the main road. Marangu used to be a popular base for organising Kilimanjaro climbs, but unless you are looking at top-of-the-range prices Moshi is a better bet these days. If you organise a climb in Moshi there is no reason to visit Marangu; most companies will organise transport to the entrance gate. If you are not climbing the mountain, Marangu would be a pleasant place to spend a few days as a base for day walks were it not for the high price of accommodation.

## Getting there
Buses between Moshi and Marangu leave when they are full, which is every hour or so.

## Where to stay/eat
The cheapest rooms in Marangu cost $45. If you have a tent, camping is an option, and cheap rooms are available in Kibo on the Moshi-Dar es Salaam highway.

The **Chinese Restaurant**, on the Dar es Salaam road a few hundred metres from the YMCA, has been recommended as serving decent food at reasonable prices.

**Aleem's Supermarket**, rear of the post office, has a good range of imported goods and foods.

### *Upper range*
**The Kibo Hotel** (PO Box 137 Moshi, tel: (055) 52503 or dial 900 and ask for Marangu 4), is a well-established hotel 1km from the village, with pretty flowering gardens, a relaxed atmosphere, and a good restaurant. Kilimanjaro climbs organised here are not cheap, but have an impeccable reputation. $80/102 HC s/c single/double, or $56/70 for residents.

**The Marangu Hotel** (PO Box 40 Moshi, tel: dial 900 and ask for Marangu 11) is another comfortable old hotel with a solid reputation. It is 5km from Marangu on the Moshi road. $82/110 HC s/c single/double, including dinner and breakfast.

The newer **Capricorn Hotel** is similar in price to these hotels.

### Moderate

**Babylon Bar & Hotel** This is 500m and signposted from Marangu Post Office. In itself, it's a reasonable place, but at $45/75 HC s/c double/triple it must rank as the worst value for money in Tanzania. A similar room in Moshi costs well under $5.

For climbers, there is more reasonably priced accommodation near the Marangu Gate. The **Kilimanjaro Mountain Lodge** lies just inside the gate, and the **Uhuru Peak Lodge** just outside it. Rooms at both are negotiable, but expect to pay between $15 and $20 per person.

### Camping

You can pitch a tent at the Kibo Hotel for $10 HC per person. This entitles you to use the hotel's facilities. You can also camp at the Babylon Bar for $6 HC per person, or at Coffee Tree Campsite for $10.

# MOUNT KILIMANJARO NATIONAL PARK

At 5,895m (19,340ft), Mount Kilimanjaro is the highest mountain in Africa. It is also the highest free-standing mountain in the world, rising 5,000m above the surrounding plains, and the only mountain of its size that can be climbed with comparative ease by non-mountaineers. On the rare occasions when it is not blanketed in clouds, Kilimanjaro's distinctive silhouette and snow-capped peaks are one of the most breathtaking sights in Africa.

Kilimanjaro has three peaks: Kibo (5,895m), Mawenzi (5,149m) and the smaller Shira (3,962m). The area of 756km² lying above the 2,700m contour has been a national park since 1977. Parts of the lower slopes are protected in forest reserves.

No-one knows for sure where the name Kilimanjaro comes from, or even whether it is Swahili, Maasai or Chagga in origin. *Kilima* is Swahili for *little mountain* (a joke?); njaro is similar to the Chagga word for caravan (the mountain was an important landmark on the northern caravan route), the Maasai word for water (it is the source of most of the region's rivers) and the name of a Swahili demon of cold.

In geological terms, Kilimanjaro is a new mountain. The vents which formed its peaks first erupted about one million years ago. Shira collapsed 500,000 years ago, but Kibo and Mawenzi continued to grow until more recently. Shira plateau formed 360,000 years ago, when the caldera was filled by lava from Kibo after a particularly violent eruption. Kibo is now dormant, and no-one knows when it last displayed any serious activity. Chagga myths which suggest there have been eruptions in the last 500 years do not tally with the geological evidence. The myths may have been handed down by previous occupants of the area.

## Vegetation and biology

There are five vegetation zones on Kilimanjaro: the cultivated lower slopes, the forest, heath and moorland, alpine, and the barren summit zone. Vegetation is sparse higher up due to lower temperatures and rainfall.

### Lower slopes

The lower slopes of the mountain were probably once forested, but they are now mainly cultivated. The volcanic soils make them highly fertile and they support a dense human population. The most biologically interesting aspect of the lower slopes is the abundance of wild flowers, seen between Marangu and the park entrance gate.

### Forest

The southern slopes above 1,800m and below 3,000m receive up to 2,000mm of rainfall annually. As a result they are densely forested. This is the most biologically interesting zone. In addition to numerous plant species, the forest supports a fair amount of wildlife. The most commonly seen animals are black-and-white colobus and blue monkey. Antelope species include three types of duiker, and the beautifully marked bushbuck. Leopard, bushpig and porcupine are common but rarely seen. Other large mammals present in small numbers include eland, buffalo and elephant. The forest is home to many varieties of butterfly, and, as with all East African forests, it is rich in bird life. Most forest birds are difficult to spot. An exception is the large, raucous silvery-cheeked hornbill.

### Moorland

This semi-alpine zone lies between 3,000m and 4,000m. It is characterised by heath-like vegetation and abundant wild flowers. As you climb into the moorland, two distinctive plants become common. These are *Lobelia deckenii*, which grows to 3m high, and the groundsel *Senecio kilimanjarin*, which grows up to 5m high and can be distinguished by a spike of yellow flowers. This zone supports low animal densities, but a number of large mammals have been recorded. Klipspringer are quite common on rocky outcrops. Hill chat and scarlet-

tufted malachite sunbird are two birds whose range is restricted to the
moorlands of large East African mountains. Other localised birds are
lammergeyer and Alpine swift. Because it is so open, the views from
the moorland are stunning.

## Alpine
This semi-desert zone lies between 4,000 and 5,000m, and receives an
annual rainfall of under 250mm. The ground often freezes at night,
but ground temperatures may soar to above 30°C by day. Few plants
survive in these conditions; only 55 species are present, many of them
lichens and grasses. Large mammals have been recorded, most
commonly eland, but none are resident.

## Summit
This is the arctic zone above 5,000m. It receives virtually no rainfall,
and there is little permanent life other than the odd lichen. Two
remarkable records concern a frozen leopard discovered here in 1926,
and a family of hunting dogs seen in 1962. The most notable natural
features at the summit are the inner and outer craters of Kibo, a 120m-
deep ash pit, and the Great Northern Glacier, which has retreated
markedly since it was first seen by Hans Meyer in 1889.

# Climbing Kilimanjaro
As Africa's highest peak and most identifiable landmark, Kilimanjaro
offers an irresistible challenge to many tourists. Dozens of visitors to
Tanzania set off for the peak every day, ranging in age from teenagers
to people in their sixties; for those who reach the top, the sense of
achievement is often the highlight of their African trip.

Any reasonably fit person stands a fair chance of ascending
Kilimanjaro. The ascent requires no special climbing skills, consisting
basically of a long uphill slog over four days followed by a more rapid
descent. That said, when people talk about climbing Kilimanjaro as if
it were a prolonged Sunday walk, they seriously underestimate the
mountain. Adequate preparations are a prerequisite for climbing
Kilimanjaro, as is an awareness of the potentially fatal health risks
attached to being at altitudes of over 4,000m.

For many, the single most daunting factor about climbing Kilimanjaro
is the cost – most reliable operators are now charging in excess of $450
per person for a five-day climb. This is a lot of money by any standards,
and especially when you consider that a fairly high proportion of
climbers never get to the top. If you are determined to scale Africa's
highest summit, none of these factors will or should put you off – but
if you're hanging in the balance, my own view is that there are any
number of more enjoyable ways of spending money in Tanzania.

## Routes
The vast majority of people who climb Kilimanjaro use the Marangu Route. There are several other routes, but they are far more expensive to climb, not least because the hut fees along them are almost triple those on the Marangu Route ($40 as opposed to $15). The huts on these routes are in poor condition. Nevertheless, if you have no budget restrictions, it is worth thinking about using another route. Marangu has become busy in recent years and many people complain it is overcrowded.

### Marangu route
**Day one: Marangu to Mandara Hut** On an organised climb you will be dropped at the park entrance gate 8km past Marangu. The path to Mandara passes through forest. There is a high chance of rain in the afternoon, so set off early. Foot traffic is heavy along this stretch, and shy forest animals are rarely seen. If your guide will go that way, use the parallel trail which meets the main trail halfway between the gate and the hut. The walk takes up to four hours. Mandara hut (2,750m) is an attractive collection of buildings with room for 200 people.

**Day two: Mandara Hut to Horombo Hut** You continue through forest for a short time before reaching the heather and moorland zone. There are good views of the peaks and of Moshi from here. The walk takes up to six hours. Horombo Hut (3,720m) sleeps up to 120 people. It is in a valley and surrounded by giant lobelia and groundsel. If you do a six-day hike, you will spend a day at Horombo to acclimatise.

**Day three: Horombo Hut to Kibo Hut** The vegetation thins out as you enter the desert-like alpine zone, and when you cross the saddle Kibo peak comes into view. This six- to seven-hour walk should be done slowly: many people start to feel the effects of altitude. Kibo Hut (4,703m) is a stone construction which sleeps up to 120 people. Water must be carried there from a stream above Horombo. You may find it difficult to sleep at this altitude, and as you will have to rise at around 01.00 the next morning, many people feel it is better not to bother trying.

**Days four and five: Kibo Hut to the summit to Marangu** The penultimate day starts at around 01.00. It is marginally easier to climb the scree slope to Gillman's Point on the crater rim when it is frozen. This is a six-hour walk; an early start improves your chances of reaching the summit early enough to catch the sunrise. From Gillman's Point it is a further two-hour round trip along the crater's edge to Uhuru Peak, the highest point in Africa. From the summit it is downhill all the way to Horombo Hut where you will spend your last night on the mountain, before descending to Marangu the next day. Expect to arrive in Marangu in the mid-afternoon.

### Mweka route

This is the steepest and fastest route to the summit. There are two huts along it: Mweka (3,000m) and Barafu (4,600m). Both are unfurnished uniports which sleep up to 16 people. There is water at Mweka but not at Barafu. This route starts at the Mweka Wildlife College, 12km from Moshi. From there it takes about eight hours to get to Mweka Hut, then a further eight hours to Barafu. You will reach the rim at Stella Point, a six-hour walk from Barafu and one hour from Uhuru Peak.

### Machame route

This is considered to be the most scenic route and is relatively gradual. It starts at the village of Machame, where there is a guesthouse. From Machame it is a two-hour walk to the park gate, a further two hours to the trail head, then four or five hours through the forest to Machame Hut (3,000m). There is water near this hut, which sleeps up to 12 people. It is a five-hour walk to Shira Hut (3,800m) which is near a stream and can sleep up to eight people.

From Shira, a number of options exist: you could spend your third night at Lava Tower Hut (4,600m), four hours from Shira, but the ascent to the summit from there is tricky and only advisable if you are experienced and have good equipment. Another option would be to spend your third night at Barranco Hut (3,900m), then go on to Barafu Hut (4,600m) and ascend to the crater from there (see Mweka route).

### Shira route

This route crosses the Shira Plateau west of Kibo. You need a 4x4 to do it, as it is 19km from the gate to the trail head. You can either camp at the trail head or walk the 4km to Shira Hut. The views from the Shira Plateau are excellent, and there is some game to be seen. If you use this route, spend two nights at Shira in order to acclimatise before you continue. For routes from Shira Hut, see the Machame route.

### Umbwe route

This short, steep route is one of the most scenic. It is often used as a descent route. Umbwe route descends from Barranco Hut, and comes out at the village of Umbwe. It is possible to sleep in two caves on the lower slopes along this route.

### Park fees

The reason why Kilimanjaro is so expensive to climb boils down to park fees. There is an entrance fee of $20 per day ($25 from 1997) and a rescue fee of $20 per person per trip. Huts on the Marangu route currently cost $20 per person per night but are rising to $40 in 1997 – the same as huts on other routes. Each guide and porter costs around $5 per day (this includes their entrance and hut fees). Park fees for one person doing a five-day ascent with two porters and a guide amount to around $210. All these fees are considerably lower for residents.

You are expected to tip the guides and porters. The company you go with can give you an idea of the going rate is, but around $5 per day per guide/porter per climbing party is fair.

## Maps and further reading

A map is not generally considered to be necessary if you use the Marangu Route, but it is for any other. *The Walker's Guide and Map to Kilimanjaro* by Mark Savage (African Mountain Guides, 32 Sea Mill Crescent, Worthing, UK, tel: 01903 37565) is popular and reliable, and has useful information printed on the back. You may be lucky and pick up a second-hand copy in Arusha, but it is better to buy one before you visit Tanzania.

A 60-page national parks handbook, *Kilimanjaro National Park*, has accurate small-scale maps. It is worth buying for its detailed route descriptions and background information, and is available from the National Park office in Arusha for $2.50.

Before you leave home – or as a memento when you get back – try to get hold of *Kilimanjaro* by John Reader (Elm Tree Books, London, 1982). Although it is superficially a coffee-table book, it offers a well-written and absorbing overview of the mountain's history and various ecosystems. The photographs are good too.

## Preparations

Two climatic factors must be considered when preparing to climb Kilimanjaro. The obvious one is the cold. Bring plenty of warm clothes, a windproof jacket, a pair of gloves, a balaclava, a warm sleeping bag and an insulation mat. During the rainy season, a rain jacket and rain trousers will come in useful. A less obvious factor is the sun, which is fierce at high altitudes. Bring sunglasses and sunscreen.

Other essentials are water bottles, a first-aid kit, and solid shoes or preferably boots. Most of these items can be hired in Moshi or at the park gate, or from the company you arrange to climb with. I've heard varying reports about the condition of locally-hired items.

## Health

Do not attempt to climb Kilimanjaro unless you are reasonably fit, nor if you have heart or lung problems. Bear in mind, however, that very fit people are more prone to altitude sickness because they ascend too fast. If you have any cold-like symptoms, wait until you are better before you climb.

Above 4,000m you may not feel hungry, but you should try to eat. Carbohydrates and fruit are recommended, rich or fatty foods are not. You should drink plenty of liquids, and will need enough water bottles to carry several litres of water to Kibo Hut. If you dress in layers, you can take off clothes before you sweat too much, thereby reducing water loss.

Few people climb Kilimanjaro without feeling some of the symptoms of altitude sickness: headaches, nausea, fatigue, sleeplessness and swelling of the hands and feet. You can do a lot to limit these. Give yourself time to acclimatise by taking an extra day over the ascent, eat and drink properly, and try not to push yourself. If symptoms become severe, descend immediately. Even going down 1,000ft is enough to start recovery.

Pulmonary and cerebral oedema are altitude-related problems which can be rapidly fatal if you do not descend. Symptoms of the former include shortness of breath when at rest, coughing up blood, and gurgling sounds in the chest. Symptoms of the latter are headaches, a general lack of co-ordination, disorientation, poor judgement and even hallucinations. The danger is that the sufferer often doesn't realise how sick he/she is and may argue against descending. You are less likely to get these problems if you ascend slowly.

Hypothermia is a lowering of body temperature usually caused by a combination of cold and wet. Mild cases usually manifest themselves as uncontrollable shivering. Put on dry warm clothes and get into a sleeping bag; this will normally raise your body temperature sufficiently. Severe hypothermia is potentially fatal: symptoms include disorientation, lethargy, mental confusion (including an inappropriate feeling of well-being and warmth!) and coma. In severe cases the rescue team should be summoned.

A $20 rescue fee is paid by all climbers upon entering the national park. The rescue team ordinarily covers the Marangu route only; if you use another route their services must be organised in advance.

## Arranging a climb

A number of operators in Moshi and Marangu offer Kilimanjaro climbs. It is also possible to make your own arrangements with a registered guide. Most companies offer a comprehensive package, but I suggest you clarify what you are paying for prior to parting with any money. A package should include a registered guide, two porters per person, park fees, food, and transport to and from the gate. If you are in a group, ensure that one porter is also registered as a guide. Then if someone in your party has to turn back the rest can still continue.

The normal length for a climb is five days. Think about adding a sixth day to acclimatise at Horombo Hut. This will reduce the risk of altitude sickness and increase the likelihood of making the peak. It is daft to team up with strangers just to cut 5% off the price. If you hike on your own or with people you know, you can dictate your own pace and there is less danger of personality clashes developing mid-climb.

You are strongly advised to arrange a climb through an established operator. This will be considerably more expensive than organising a climb with one of the many street touts and fly-by-night operators who will approach you in Moshi, but the extra expense guarantees you a reliable service and experienced guides.

Three companies in Moshi can be recommended without reservation:

**Shah Tours** (PO Box 1821, tel: (055) 52370, fax: (055) 51449)
**Zara International** (PO Box 1990, tel: (055) 54240, fax: (055) 53105)
**Trans-Kibo Travels** (PO Box 558, tel: (055) 52017, fax: (055) 54219)

Reliable climbs can also be arranged through the Keys Hotel in Moshi and the Marangu and Kibo Hotels in Marangu. In all cases, you are looking at around $450-550 for a five-day climb on the Marangu Route, and an extra payment of $80-100 for a sixth day. Climbs along other routes generally cost around $800. With these companies, you can be certain that the price quoted will be inclusive of park and rescue fees, food, guides, porters and transfer from Moshi to the gate – in short, everything but tips.

The alternative to using one of the above companies is to take your chances with a small operator or private individual who approaches you in the street. These guys will offer climbs for around $100 cheaper than the more established operators, but the risks are greater and because they generally have no office, there is little accountability on their side. Many *are* genuine and reliable, but it's difficult to be certain who you're dealing with unless you have a personal recommendation from somebody who has used the same person. A crucial point when comparing this situation to the similar one that surrounds arranging a safari out of Arusha is that you're not merely talking about losing a day through breakdown or something like that. With Kilimanjaro, you could literally die on the mountain – I've heard several stories of climbers being supplied with inadequate equipment and food, or even of people being abandoned by their guides midway through the climb. The very least you can do, if you make arrangements of this sort, is to verify that your guide is registered; he should have a small wallet-like document to prove this.

Chapter Eight

# The Northern Tanzania Safari Circuit

## INTRODUCTION

The reserves between Arusha and Lake Victoria need little introduction. They are the best-known and arguably the finest anywhere in Africa.

The world-famous Serengeti Plain, a vast sea of grass dotted with granite koppies, plays host to Africa's greatest wildlife spectacle: the annual migration of more than a million wildebeest and zebra. Nearby, the Ngorongoro Crater is a spectacular 600m-deep volcanic caldera; its floor supports large herds of virtually every large African mammal.

East of this, Lake Manyara National Park protects a large shallow lake on the Rift Valley floor. The less-celebrated Tarangire National Park preserves an area of acacia woodland notable for its dense elephant population.

The base for exploring this area is the town of Arusha. Northeast of the town, Arusha National Park, though less well-known than the block of reserves described above, protects a wide variety of animals and Africa's fourth-highest peak, Mount Meru.

## Climate

The highlands around Ngorongoro Crater and Mount Meru receive a high rainfall and are cold at night. The rest of the area is warm and relatively dry. Rainy seasons are in November and December, and from March to May. Game viewing in the Ngorongoro Crater and Lake Manyara is good at any time of year. Tarangire is best between July and December, and the Serengeti between November and March.

## Getting around

Access to the Serengeti, Ngorongoro and Manyara is via the B142, a dirt road which leaves the Dodoma-Arusha road at a village called Makuyuni. The B142 bypasses Lake Manyara at the village of Mto wa Mbu, then snakes up the side of the Rift Valley wall, passes through Karatu, and climbs to Ngorongoro Crater rim. From the crater it descends on to the Serengeti plains, passing through the park headquarters in the Seronera valley before reaching Bunda on the main Musoma-Mwanza road.

It is 80km from Arusha to Makuyuni, 37km from Makuyuni to Mto wa Mbu, 25km from Mto wa Mbu to Karatu, and 18km from Karatu to the village on the crater rim. Seronera lies about halfway along the 300km stretch of road between the crater and Bunda.

Tarangire National Park is just off the main Arusha-Dodoma road about 30km south of Makuyuni. Arusha National Park lies off the main Arusha-Moshi road near Usa River.

A couple of buses run every week between Arusha and Mwanza via the B142. These can drop you off along the way, or pick you up if arrangements are made in advance. Buses run daily between Arusha and Karatu, and the Ngorongoro Conservation Authority plans to introduce a service between Arusha and the crater rim, which will run in each direction on alternate days.

## THE MAASAI

The area covered in this chapter is the home of the Maasai, a Nilotic-speaking people who arrived in Tanzania from what is now the Sudan about 300 years ago. The Maasai have aroused western awe and curiosity since the 19th Century, when they acquired a reputation amongst slave traders and explorers as fearsome warriors. Caravan routes studiously avoided them, and areas like the Serengeti were amongst the last parts of East Africa ventured into by Europeans.

Maasai remain the most instantly recognisable East African people, though their modern reputation rests as much on their continued proud adherence to a traditional lifestyle as on any of their past exploits. Maasai men drape themselves in red blankets, carry long wooden poles, and have red-ochred hair. The women's actual dress is not dissimilar to the *Vitenge* favoured by most Tanzanian women, but they cover themselves in all manner of beaded jewellery.

Maasai are traditionally pastoralists. They believe their God, who resides in Lengai Volcano, made them the rightful owners of all the cattle in the world; a view which, in the past, has made life difficult for neighbouring herders. This arrogance does not merely extend to cattle. They scorned agriculturalist and fish-eating peoples, and were equally disrespectful of Europeans, calling them *Iloredaa enjekat* – Those who confine their farts with clothing. The Maasai now co-exist peacefully with their non-Maasai compatriots, but they show little interest in changing their lifestyle.

The Maasai's main diet is a blend of cow's milk and blood, the latter drained – it is said painlessly – from a strategic nick in the animal's jugular vein. They are reluctant to kill their cattle for meat; the animals are more valuable to them alive. Despite the apparent hardship of their chosen lifestyle, many Maasai are wealthy by any standards. Our safari driver pointed out a not unusually large herd of cattle that would fetch the market equivalent of three new Landrovers.

Despite appearances, the Maasai, like us, are living in the 1990s. Large parts of their traditional grazing grounds have been given over to conservation; in the Serengeti and Tarangire they are no longer allowed to graze their cattle.

In some ways, the Maasai are just another cog in the tourist industry, albeit an unwilling one. Herds of snap-happy tourists leap out of minibuses and landrovers to capture their image on film, on the one hand swooning at their noble savagery – *Real Africa!* – on the other shoving a camera at them as though they were just another one of the big five.

There are Maasai who deliberately hang around at places like Ngorongoro waiting for tourists. If you want to photograph a Maasai, you must ask permission and should also be prepared to pay for the privilege. Because of this, many tourists complain that the Maasai are 'overcommercialised'. I don't know whether such people believe the Maasai's first priority should be to pander to the aesthetic requirements of tourists, or whether they are just outraged at not getting something for nothing. Either way, we create the demand and the Maasai satisfy it. If they expect us to pay, that's just good capitalism, something the West has been keen to encourage in Africa. If you don't like it, save your film for another subject.

# ARUSHA

Arusha is the gateway to Ngorongoro and the Serengeti, and like Moshi its skyline is dominated by a mountain: the 4,556m-high Mount Meru. In itself, Arusha is a very ordinary medium-sized African town. It was founded as a German garrison in 1900, and grew rapidly as it became the centre of an important farming area and, more recently, the country's safari industry.

Everything in Arusha seems to revolve around safaris. The competition is fierce; there are touts on every street corner offering the best price in town. This can become wearing, but on the whole business is conducted in a leisurely manner. I found Arusha very relaxed and pleasant once I settled in.

Electricity and water are both problems in Arusha. I have never spent a day in the town when there wasn't an electricity and/or water cut at some point.

## Getting there and away

The most popular way to get between Arusha and Dar es Salaam is via

KEY TO ACCOMMODATION, RESTAURANTS AND BARS

| | | |
|---|---|---|
| 1 MT MERU NOVOTEL | 14 ARUSHA TOURIST | 23 JOHNNY'S RAVIALA |
| 2 PRIMA HOTEL | INN and | 24 PALLSON'S HOTEL |
| 3 KIRIA | URA LODGINGS | 25 McMOODY'S |
| 4 MIAMI BEACH | 15 ROBANNYSON | 26 PIZZERIA |
| 5 MIDWAY | 16 YMCA | 27 BINDAYA |
| 6 AM 88 | 17 NEW SAFARI | 28 AMAR |
| 7 GOLDEN ROSE | 18 EQUATOR | 29 SAFISONS |
| 8 ARUSHA BY NIGHT | 19 KAKA | AND MAYUR |
| - ANNEXE | RESTAURANT | 30 CHINESE |
| 9 SAFARI HOTEL | 20 ARUSHA | RESTAURANT |
| 10 MONJE'S | BY NIGHT | 31 GREENLAND |
| 11 BLUEBIRD HOTEL | 21 CONTINENTAL | 32 NAAZ HOTEL |
| 12 AMAZON | HOTEL | 33 NEW ARUSHA |
| 13 SPLENDID | 22 AXUM | HOTEL |
| | RESTAURANT | |

the railway which terminates at Moshi. You can book for trains to Dar es Salaam at Arusha's otherwise unused station.

Arusha is connected to Dar es Salaam, Moshi and Nairobi by good tar roads. These carry regular transport. Express buses between Arusha and Dar es Salaam are worth the extra expense.

Air Tanzania fly regularly between Dar es Salaam and Kilimanjaro Airport (halfway between Arusha and Moshi).

There are daily buses between Dodoma and Arusha. The road is in a poor state and the ride can take up to 20 hours.

Getting between Arusha and Mwanza is covered in detail under Mwanza in Chapter Nine.

# Where to stay
## *Upper range*
Only one hotel in Arusha meets international standards: the **Mount Meru Novotel** (PO Box 877, tel: (057) 8545/7). This lies within walking distance of the town centre along the Moshi road. Set in landscaped gardens overlooking the golf course, facilities include a large outdoor swimming pool, two restaurants, and a relatively efficient business centre. Rooms are large, with en suite bathrooms, private balconies and satellite television with an in-house movie channel. $110/140 single/double, with a 30% discount for residents.

There are two government-owned tourist class hotels in the city centre, both of which are in need of renovation:

The **New Arusha Hotel** (PO Box 88, tel: (057) 3241) is probably the better of the two, though not particularly great value at $65/70 single/double.

Rooms at the **New Safari Hotel** (PO Box 303, tel: (057) 8545/7), cost $40/60 single/double.

A couple of kilometres along the Moshi Road, the **Hotel Saba-Saba (77)** (PO Box 1184, tel: (057) 3822, fax: (057) 8407) claims to be the largest tourist village in East or Central Africa, a title that is not so much meaningless as downright misleading. The hotel consists of several cheerless concrete quadrangles, reminiscent of a borstal or prison more than any village I've encountered. The rooms are adequate, and sensibly priced at $50/60. All the same, I feel nothing but pity for any tourist who happens to spend their first night in Africa in such an austere environment.

The **Impala Hotel** (PO Box 7302, tel: (057) 8448, fax: (057) 8220) is altogether more appealing, and rated by many tour operators as the best value in its range in the immediate vicinity of Arusha. Situated about 1.5km out of town along Uhuru Road, the rooms here are pleasantly decorated, and have television, hot showers and in some cases fridges. $60/72 single/double.

**Ilboru Safari Lodge** (PO Box 8012, tel: (057) 7834) is another place favoured by tour operators, set about 2km from the town centre in leafy suburban grounds below Mount Meru. It's a pleasant, peaceful retreat, if a little overpriced at $88/127 single/double.

Cheaper tourist class hotels in Arusha include:

**Golden Rose Hotel** (PO Box 361, tel: (057) 8860 – $40/50 single/double)

**Hotel AM88** (PO Box 10045, tel: (057) 7873, fax: (057) 7168 – $40/60 single/double)

**Eland Hotel** (tel: (057) 7868/6892 – $30/40 single/double)

**Hotel Equator** (PO Box 3002, tel: (057) 8410, fax: (057) 8085 – $45/double)

More interesting than any of the hotels immediately around Arusha is the cluster of accommodation in the Usa River area, about 20km out of town on the Moshi Road, near the turn-off to Arusha National Park.

**Mount Meru Game Sanctuary** (PO Box 659, tel: (057) 7179) consists of a main stone building and a few semi-detached wooden cabins surrounded by bougainvillaea-draped gardens. The sanctuary includes a large open enclosure in front of the rooms, stocked with a variety of antelope, and also the site of a large papyrus heronry where hundreds of cattle egrets roost at dusk. Behind the main building, a small zoo is home to a leopard and elephant (taken into captivity because they were ill) and there is potentially good birding in the stretch of forest that fringes the Usa River. Despite the artificiality of the surrounds, the sanctuary sets the tone nicely for a safari, particularly if you stay in rooms one and two, where the animals are practically on your doorstep and the evening air reverberates with the incessant squawking from the heronry. The food's good, too. $96/164 single/double full board.

**Ngere Sero Lodge** (PO Box 425, tel: (057) 3629, fax: (057) 8690) is a small, exclusive retreat set in an old colonial residence on the foot slopes of Mount Meru, with views to Kilimanjaro on a clear day. The grounds are noted for their prolific bird life, and enclose a waterfall and a small lake stocked with trout. Accommodation costs $100 per person full board.

**Mountain Village Lodge** (PO Box 376, tel: (057) 2799, fax: (057) 8907) lies on a coffee farm on the verge of Duluti, a gorgeous forest-fringed crater lake. On a clear day, there are views to Mount Meru and Kilimanjaro. The main building is a converted thatch farmhouse dating to the colonial era, and accommodation is in self-contained chalets. $62/75 B&B, with meals an extra $10 each.

The **Dik Dik Hotel** (PO Box 1499, tel: (057) 8110) is a Swiss-owned hotel set in attractive grounds with a swimming pool and a restaurant rated by some as the best in the Arusha area. $78/116 single/double full board.

The cheapest accommodation in the Usa River area is:

**Tanzanite Hotel** (PO Box 3063 Arusha, tel: (051) 44568, fax: (051) 46762), which has rooms for $40/50/60 single/double/triple B&B, as well as camping for $3pp. Meals cost $7.

## Moderate

One of the best and most conveniently situated hotels in this range is the recently renovated **Pallson's Hotel** (PO Box 773, tel: (057) 2485, fax: (057) 7263), where clean, pleasant self-contained rooms with hot water cost $20/30 single/double.

The **Arusha Resort Centre**, 150m from the Clock Tower, has clean rooms with en-suite kitchens and hot showers for $20 per person ($10 for residents).

A bit tacky by comparison with these two is the **Splendid Hotel**, where cramped rooms cost $30 self-contained double.

The **Naaz Hotel** (PO Box 1060, tel (057) 2087) was once among the most popular hotels in Arusha, but it now seems rather overpriced at $20 for a slightly run-down self-contained double. The **YMCA** has also dropped in popularity. The rooms are not self-contained and seem indifferent value for money at $10/13 single/double – especially as there is no running water in the building. The management of both these places insist on bills being settled in US dollars cash. They're still reliable fallbacks, but they can no longer be recommended with much conviction.

Much better value is the **Arusha By Night Annexe** near the stadium, which has clean self-contained rooms with hot showers for $10/15 single/double.

Also near the stadium, the **Midway Hotel** represents fair value for money at $10/double, though it's looking rather run-down for a hotel that's only four years old.

The nearby **Miami Beach Guest House** has clean, comfortable doubles with nets for $10.

The **Amazon Guest House** is conveniently close to the bus station, and the rooms are large and clean, but it's no better than many other guesthouses with less optimistic pricing policies. Poor value at $10/12 single/double.

## Budget

There are literally dozens of small guesthouses dotted around the bus station and stadium area. Rooms at these places generally cost around $6-7. Standards vary wildly, and new places open all the time, which makes it practically impossible to give firm recommendations in this range. As a rule, the places north of the stadium are generally better than those around the bus station.

If you arrive in Arusha on public transport, the probability is that you'll be met by a few touts offering to find you accommodation. In my experience, there's no reason to avoid these guys; on the contrary, they are generally trustworthy characters who know the best deals in town, and they will save you a lot of footing around. You will not normally be expected to pay for the services of a tout – any question of payment is between them and the hotel to which they take you. But the ultimate reason why you can trust hotel touts in Arusha is that, so far as they are concerned, the real goal is to persuade you to use them as a broker in organising a safari – it's very much in their own interest to ensure they find you a good, reasonably priced room, and it's up to you not to allow this to create an undue sense of obligation when you come to organising a safari.

At the time of writing, **Monje's** and the **Bluebird Guest Houses** are definitely worth heading for, the former in particular, as it has spacious, quiet rooms, hot communal showers and friendly staff.

Also recommended in the $6-7 price range are the **Mashelo** and **Rahaleo Guest Houses**.

The once popular **Safari Guest House** is a little run-down these days, but it's fair value at around $4/double.

Rather different in style, the **Greenland Hotel** is emphatically a tip, and there's rarely any running water in the building, but the rooms are large, idiosyncratically furnished, and quite acceptable value for $3/4 single/double.

**Robbanyson's Guest House** is popular with travellers – goodness knows why as it's no cheaper than most other guesthouses and the combination of dingy rooms, no running water and the stench of open sewers hardly adds up to the bargain of the century. Give it a miss.

**The Outpost** (37A Serengeti Street, tel: (057) 8405) is an Australian-owned backpackers-style hostel in a suburban Arusha garden – it's a nice place to stay though pricier than such establishments tend to be elsewhere in Africa. A bed in a dormitory costs $9 per person and private rooms cost $16/20 single/ double, with all prices being inclusive of a good breakfast. Cheap lunches and dinners are available. To get there from the clock tower, follow Uhuru Avenue east out of town for about 1km, then take the right turn signposted for "The Outpost". The house is about 300m down the road, to your left. It's advisable to ring in advance to check availability of rooms.

## Camping

The **Arusha Vision Campsite** (PO Box 12330, tel: (057) 2894) lies alongside the river next to the Equator Hotel. The management is very friendly and helpful, and the atmosphere is homely and surprisingly rustic for somewhere only 50m from the town centre. Any qualms about the apparently lax security should be put to rest by a flip through the visitors' book, which is full of raves from travellers who ended up staying a week here. Camping costs $2 per person, and you can hire a tent for an extra $1. Food is basic but tasty and there's plenty of it – breakfast costs $1 and dinner less than $2. Black tea is free.

Further out of town, about 3km down the old Moshi Road, **Maasai Camp** is well established and particularly popular with overland trucks. Facilities include an ablution block with hot water, and a good restaurant noted for its pizzas. If you're without transport, you can get a taxi out for around $2. Camping costs $3 per person.

There is a lovely and surprisingly little-used campsite at the **Duluti Club**, on the edge of forest-fringed Lake Duluti, towards Usa River on the Moshi Road. Facilities include an ablution block and a cafeteria serving basic meals and cold drinks. To get there from Arusha, catch any vehicle heading towards Moshi and hop off when you see a large carved wooden giraffe to your left. The turn-off to Duluti Club is signposted to the right opposite this statue; it's about 20 minutes' walk from the main road to the campsite. Camping costs $3 per person.

You can camp in the grounds of the **Tanzanite Hotel** in Usa River for $3 per person. There are good facilities for campers and you can eat in the hotel (meals cost around $6-7).

## Where to eat
There are any number of interesting restaurants in Arusha. The **Mezzaluna Restaurant** does good value Italian and international food. The meals at the **Midway Hotel** have been recommended, and are good value at around $3-4.

The **Safari Grill**, on the ground floor of the New Safari Hotel, has been for several years the most reliable place for filling and relatively inexpensive Western dishes. Most main courses cost around $4-5. The same food can be ordered at the Rainbow Garden at the back of the hotel. Similar in price, standard and antiquity (though not noted for speedy service), the **Chinese Restaurant** does a few indifferent Chinese dishes in addition to a long list of Western standards.

**McMoody's** serves up reasonable hamburgers and cheeseburgers for around $2. Modelled closely on McDonald's, it's a place designed to make fast food junkies feel at home. Rather less successful in its approximation of a Western fast-food icon is **Chickwings**, several branches of which are dotted around town – unfortunately for devotees of Colonel Sanders, the chicken pieces have a rather odd flavour and are very overpriced. There are more tasty snacks available at **Johnny's Raviala Restaurant**. For good, inexpensive ice-cream cones and sundaes, the place to head for is **Safison's Ice-cream Parlour**. **YC Dave** on Swahili Street serves good yoghurt and Indian snacks during the day.

There is no shortage of Indian restaurants in Arusha. The **Shamiara Restaurant**, on the second floor of Pallson's Hotel is one of the best, serving huge, very tasty portions for around $5-7. The service is *terribly* slow – but the food is emphatically worth waiting for.

The **Mayur Restaurant** is an Indian vegetarian restaurant serving cheap snacks as well as main meals for around $7. The **Amul Tandoori Restaurant** is similar in price and standard to the Shamiara.

The **Axum Restaurant** is Arusha's only Ethiopian restaurant. If you're already a fan of sub-Saharan Africa's most distinctive cuisine (a searing, spicy meat or vegetarian stew called *kai wat* served with a flat round sour bread called *injera*) you won't need me to persuade you to give the Axum a try. Vegetarian dishes cost around $4 and meat dishes $6.

# Useful information
The bar next to the Chinese Restaurant used to be a good venue to see live music, but it no longer hosts bands and is instead a darts club with a rather annoying manager. The Barracuda Bar has usurped it as the most lively drinking hole in the town centre – there's a good PA, a fittingly tropical ambience, and a busy, friendly atmosphere. For live music, your best bet is to ask around at the various tourist hotels. The Equator is the most regular venue, but the New Safari and New Arusha Hotels also host bands from time to time. If you prefer to drink in a more sedate environment, try the garden bars at the New Safari Hotel and New Arusha Hotel.

## National parks
(PO Box 3134, tel: (057) 3471 or 3181) The National Park Headquarters is in the Arusha International Conference Centre (AICC). This is the best place to buy booklets on various national parks. They cost $2.50 but are sold for three times the price on the streets and at park entrance gates.

## Ngorongoro Conservation Authority
(PO Box 776, tel: (057) 6091, fax: (057) 3339). The NCA controls the Ngorongoro Conservation Area. Their office is on the corner of Makongoro and Gollondoi roads.

## Books and newspapers
A few vendors usually hang around the clock tower selling secondhand novels, maps and textbooks. The range of novels is poor, but they may sell maps which are unavailable elsewhere.

Kenyan newspapers are available on the day of publication. You won't need to look for them – the people who sell them will find you quickly enough. The news stand in the foyer of the New Arusha has the best range of new novels in the country, as well as a fair selection of postcards, national park pamphlets, foreign newspapers, maps and non-fiction.

## Curio shops

Arusha is one of the best places in East Africa to buy Makonde carvings, batiks, Maasai jewellery and other souvenirs. The curio shops are far cheaper than those in Dar es Salaam, and the quality and variety is excellent. Curio shops are clustered between the clock tower and India Road.

## National Museum

This is the worst museum I've seen in my life. Don't waste your time with it.

# Excursions

There is not a great deal to do in the immediate vicinity of Arusha. If you have a day to kill you could organise a day safari to Arusha National Park.

## Lake Duluti

This attractive forest-fringed crater lake would be a pleasant place to spend a day or two. It is about 2km south of the Arusha-Moshi road. The hotel and campsite by the lake (see *Where to stay* above) are both well signposted and can be reached by foot or vehicle.

## Mount Meru Foothills

The western slopes of Mount Meru are not in a national park, so there is nothing preventing you casually exploring them on foot. The best access point is a dirt road which branches from the main Moshi road opposite the Mount Meru Hotel; a stream next to the junction serves as a carwash. This road continues into the foothills as far as the tree line, passing through bamboo forest on the way. Before you get this far it is possible to divert to a waterfall. About four hours along the road you will reach a plantation of new eucalyptus and pine plantlings. Here you must scramble down to a stream. If you follow the stream for an hour or so, you arrive at the waterfall. There is a short cut back to the main road, but unless you have a map it is probably more sensible to return the way you came. It may occur to you to attempt to climb Meru from the west in order to save on park fees. As Meru Peak is in Arusha National Park this is illegal. If you attempt it and are caught you are liable to be jailed.

A pair of young Tanzanians now offer a guided day walk in the

Mount Meru foothills, stopping at several villages on the way. The walk costs a very reasonable $12 exclusive of meals and water. For further information, contact Japhet or Victor through Sunny Safaris (tel: (057) 7145).

## ORGANISING A SAFARI

There are two basic approaches to organising a safari. The first is to pre-book a package before you leave for Tanzania; the second to make your arrangements after you arrive in Tanzania. The first approach is the one taken by most fly-in tourists, and its advantages are fairly self-evident – it saves you from wasting time once you are in the country, and ensures that you get the itinerary and lodge bookings you want. The second approach is favoured by most budget travellers, the majority of whom cannot predict in advance exactly when they will be in Arusha. It too has several advantages, most significantly that cheaper rates are generally offered to walk-in clients.

Arusha is the most popular and convenient base from which to organise a safari to Tanzania's northern reserves. Although a small proportion of tourists organise safaris from Moshi, Dar es Salaam and even Mwanza, there are few advantages in doing this. The overwhelming majority of safari companies and the most competitive prices are to be found in Arusha.

With literally hundreds of safari companies operating out of Arusha, competition for custom is fierce, particularly at the bottom end of the price scale where there are several unscrupulous and incompetent companies willing to cut any corner and promise anything in order to keep down costs and attract budget travellers. Given that you are likely to face an onslaught of safari touts from the moment that you arrive in Arusha, with the most dubious companies generally being the most pushy, I feel it is important that you give some advance thought to exactly what you want from a safari. The following advice is aimed primarily at people who organise safaris after they arrive in Tanzania, as it is they who are most likely to be taken in by dodgy companies, but the individual company recommendations apply equally to people who organise a safari in advance.

The issue for travellers on a limited budget boils down one simple thing: to what degree should you compromise in order to cut costs? There are several ways you can reduce the cost of a safari – by going as part of a group, by using a cheap but possibly unreliable operator, by camping in private campsites rather than in reserves – but every compromise has the potential to spoil your safari. My own view is that if you've gone to the expense of flying to Africa, and the safari is a once-in-a-lifetime experience, it seems a bit shortsighted to cut corners unless it's absolutely unavoidable. But, as a high number of visitors to Tanzania make economically driven decisions which they later regret, it does seem worth laying out in detail the sort of options that exist.

There are, in essence, two types of safari package on offer: camping and lodge safaris. Camping safaris are cheaper, and sleeping under canvas and eating under the stars will unquestionably make you feel more integrated into the bush environment. Lodge safaris are generally around double the price of camping safaris; for the extra outlay you get a roof over your head, restaurant food, and a far higher degree of luxury and comfort. Whether you elect to go on a lodge or a camping safari is to some extent related to your budgetary restrictions (certainly few people on a tight budget would consider doing a lodge safari), but it's also a question of taste – some people will prefer the extra comfort of staying in lodges, others the more authentic atmosphere of a camping safari.

If you decide to go on a lodge safari, the probability is that the operator will decide which lodges you stay at. If you have the choice, it's worth noting that the TAHI lodges are generally the most atmospheric and have the best natural settings, but the rooms are relatively basic. The Sopa Lodges are far more luxurious and about 30% more expensive, but only the Ngorongoro Sopa Lodge has a setting to compare with its TAHI equivalent. The food at both lodge chains is good, with TAHI serving large buffets and Sopa opting for set menus. The three Serena Lodges should be open by the time you read this: judging by price and by the Kenyan lodges owned by the same group, they should be similar in standard to the Sopa lodges. There are also luxury tented camps in most reserves, which offer a similar standard of accommodation to lodges, but have a far more authentic bush atmosphere. Tented camps are recommended to people who want to avoid the package tour atmosphere which to some extent permeates most of the lodges.

If you decide to go on a camping safari, you can save money by camping in sites outside of the national parks. Tarangire, Manyara and Ngorongoro Crater can all be visited from private campsites, and doing this as opposed to camping within the national parks will cut around $15 per night from the cost of a safari. The disadvantage of doing it this way is that camping outside the parks will inevitably dilute the safari experience – arguably a false economy unless you're on a very tight budget. You can assume that any cheap safari company will use campsites outside of national parks (except for in the Serengeti, where there is no alternative to the national park campsite), so the onus is on you to specify that this isn't what you want – and to be prepared to pay the extra cost to camp in the parks.

A factor that all visitors should consider is the size of the group doing the safari. It is invariably cheaper to go on safari as part of a group, as the operator can divide most transport-related costs between a greater number of people. Typically, a group of four people will pay about 30% less per head than will a group of two people – a considerable saving. The problem with forming an impromptu group is the obvious one of compatibility, something you should be particularly aware of if you have a special interest such as birdwatching or serious photography. My own experience of going on safari as part of a group has generally been good, but I've also had one horrendous experience with a mother and daughter who did nothing but bicker, moan and ask moronic questions (is that an African or Indian elephant? How can you tell...?). Had this been a once-in-a-lifetime experience, they would have ruined it. It's also the case that safari drivers tend to be more responsive to the specific needs and interests of one or two people than they do to those of a larger group, when you often feel they are merely going through the motions.

The majority of safari companies use 4x4 vehicles, such as Landrovers, in which case a group of more than four people will get very cramped. Some companies are willing to take five or even six people in a Landrover, but the slight saving of an extra person really isn't worth the squeeze (and bear in mind that with more than four people, some passengers won't be next to a window). A small proportion of companies – generally the large package tour operators – use minibuses as opposed to conventional 4x4s. In my opinion, minibuses have several disadvantages, notably that the larger group size (typically around eight people) creates more of a package tour atmosphere, and that it is difficult for a large group to take proper advantage of the pop-up roofs which are usually found on safari vehicles. In any event, bouncing around rutted roads in a Landrover is an integral part of the safari experience – it just wouldn't be the same in a minibus.

In all categories, the price you are quoted should include the vehicle and driver/guide, fuel, any camping equipment, food and a cook, and park fees. You are expected to tip the driver and cook. Around $5 per day per party seems to be par, but you should check this with the company. Drivers and cooks are poorly paid; if they have done a good job be generous.

You could put together your own safari by hiring a vehicle and driver, but most budget safari companies operate on a minimal profit margin. You will save little.

## Itinerary
Your itinerary will depend on how much time and money you have, and also the time of year. There are endless options. Most safari companies will put together the package you ask for. They know the

ground well and can advise you on what is possible, but tend to assume you will want to cover as many reserves as possible. This is not always the best approach.

A typical five or six-day trip takes in Ngorongoro, Serengeti, Manyara and Tarangire. A typical three-day trip takes in all these reserves except for the Serengeti. In the dry season (March to October) there is little game in the Serengeti; most safari companies will suggest you spend more time in Tarangire.

The distances between these reserves are considerable and the roads are poor; you will have a more relaxed trip if you visit fewer reserves. On a five day safari, I would drop either the Serengeti or Tarangire. To visit all four reserves, six days is just about adequate, seven or more days would be better.

I didn't find three days long enough to get a good feel for Tarangire, Manyara *and* Ngorongoro; four days would have been better. The combination of Ngorongoro and Tarangire would make an unhurried three-day safari. If you are limited to two days, you could either visit Tarangire on its own or do a combined trip to Manyara and Ngorongoro. If your budget is really limited, Tarangire can be visited as a day trip from Arusha; it is less than two-hours drive each way.

At the other end of the time scale, there is enough to see and do in the area to warrant a safari of two weeks in duration, or even longer. You could easily spend a few days exploring the Serengeti alone. In a two week package, you could also visit Lake Natron, the Kondoa-Irangi rock art and/or the northern part of the Ngorongoro Conservation Area.

## Which company?

I cannot overstate the need for caution in your dealings with safari companies, especially if you are shopping around for a cheap price. There are, of course, any number of reputable companies to choose from, but putting together a reliable safari costs money – at the bottom end of the price scale, reputable companies are overwhelmingly outnumbered by the incompetent and the unethical.

Before you panic, I should stress that in Arusha you generally do get what you pay for. If you organise your safari with an operator asking middle to upper range prices, there is no cause for concern – the problem is pretty much confined to the bottom end of the price scale. It is also the case that the attitude of many budget travellers is largely responsible for allowing this problem to develop. If a significant proportion of travellers will take the cheapest price offered, it is only to be expected that some companies will cut corners in order to undercut their rivals' prices – likewise, if, after having been warned, you still choose to go on a cheap safari with an unknown quantity, you have little legitimate cause for complaint if the vehicle and service aren't up to scratch. You could even argue that such companies offer a legitimate service – high risk, low cost safaris – and that the only question is whether you want to make use of it.

At the time of writing, the lowest price you'll pay for a camping safari is around $70-80 per person per day for four people. Superficially, this price may seem extortionate, but when you consider that it covers park entrance fees, camping fees, petrol and car maintenance (both of which are expensive in Tanzania), food, and the services of a cook and driver, it is difficult to see how a company could charge any less and still make a reasonable profit. At the time of writing, Sunny Safaris and Roy Safaris (see below) serve as a reliable benchmark for the lowest price offered by a reputable company. If you are offered a safari for less than this, you can be certain the company is cutting corners, most commonly by providing a sub-standard vehicle or avoiding paying park fees.

There is little point in naming individual offenders – most companies will change their name if they get any negative press. I've met several people who booked with a "new" company and, after they had paid, found themselves going on safari with a company they knew to be disreputable. Likewise, I've met many people who asked to look at the vehicle before they paid, and were shown a different vehicle to the one that was used. Once you've paid, any thoughts of a refund belong in the realms of fantasy. To give some idea of the extent of deceit to which some companies will go to attract custom, one blacklisted company recently changed its name to that of another company which gets a rave recommendation in another guide book, and thus duped many travellers into thinking they were using a recommended company. The long and short of it is that you should not take anything at face value.

The situation in Arusha creates a slight dilemma for me. I would ideally like to be able to provide a list of every reputable safari company in Arusha, but there is no practical way of checking them all out myself. Nor is it possible to rely on the experiences of other travellers – even the worst company will get it right some of the time. I've met at least four victims of the most high-profile and unscrupulous cheap company that was operating between 1992 and its closure in 1995 – yet I've also met a good number of satisfied customers who used this company. The best source of information is other safari companies. Within the industry, everybody knows who is and isn't reliable. Ask around, and you'll find the same names keep cropping up with surprising regularity whoever you speak to.

The best advice I can give is to allow yourself a full day or longer in order that you can shop around and feel out the situation before you rush into a decision. Despite the fact that so many travellers get caught out by dodgy operators, sorting the wheat from the chaff is primarily a question of common sense.

The companies recommended below provide a fair cross-section of what's on offer. Most of them have maintained high standards over several years, and there is no reason to think this will change. There are, no doubt, many other good operators in Arusha, but with so many fly-by-night companies around, I would prefer to stick to a few select companies with proven track records, and in which I have total confidence. If alert readers notice that this list includes all the Arusha-based companies advertising in this book, there's no sinister explanation – I only offered advertising space to companies that I would personally endorse.

If keeping down costs is your main concern, the first company to head for is **Sunny Safaris** (office opposite the Golden Rose Hotel, PO Box 7267 Arusha, tel: (057) 7145, fax: (057) 8094). In early 1996, they were offering camping safaris for around $70 per person per day for four people and around $100 per person per day for two people. At this sort of price, you won't be camping within the national parks, and you might find your driver to be inflexible about doing any excursion that puts extra kilometres on the clock. In all other respects Sunny provides a reliable service, with good vehicles and drivers. No matter how much you shop around, you'll be pushed to find significantly cheaper safaris than this, and I'm certainly not aware of any other reputable company offering such cheap rates. Sunny can also organise lodge-based safaris at very competitive rates.

**Roy Safaris** (opposite Sokoine/Golondoi Road, PO Box 50 Arusha, tel: (057) 2115, fax: (057) 8892) is another very competitively priced and reliable company. Like Sunny, they tend to use private campsites and to be rigid about mileage, but their vehicles are in excellent condition, and the drivers are competent and knowledgeable. Camping safaris start at around $85 per person per day, and they can also arrange reliable Kilimanjaro climbs and relatively affordable lodge safaris.

**Hoopoe Adventure Tours** (India Street, PO Box 2047 Arusha, tel: (057) 7011, fax: (057) 8226) is one of the most highly regarded companies in Arusha. Their prices for camping safaris are significantly higher than those of the companies listed above (around $110 to $150 per person per day, depending on group size) but the quality of service is much higher, for instance there are no kilometre restrictions, you will camp within national parks, the driver-guides and food meet a higher standard, and portable showers will be provided at national park campsites, which generally have no washing facilities. Their prices for lodge-based safaris are very competitive – around $30 per person per day more than camping safaris – and they can also arrange safaris using special campsites.

**Let's Go Travel** (Goliondoi Road, PO Box 12799, tel: (057) 7111/2814, fax: (057) 8997/4199) is new in Arusha, but as a branch of the well-established company of the same name in Nairobi it can be considered to have a proven track record. Their prices and services are comparable with Hoopoe, and they are especially worth contacting if you're basing your East Africa trip out of Nairobi. Aside from the conventional safari packages, they also offer camel safaris, either a two-day trip into northern Maasai land and Arusha National Park, or a half-day excursion appended to their shuttle service between Nairobi and Arusha. This is the only company that I'm aware of which has established trips to the Kondoa Rock Paintings – a four-day trip, with an optional excursion into Tarangire National Park, costs $520 per person for two people or $380 per person for four people.

**Tropical Tours** (India Street, PO Box 727 Arusha, tel: (057) 8353, fax: (057) 8907) is a German-run company that specialises in walking and mixed walking/driving tours in northern Tanzania. Most of their trips are in off-the-beaten-track areas, and are run in collaboration with local communities. Areas they visit include the Monduli Mountains (35km hike over three days through mountain forest and acacia woodland where there is a good chance of seeing elephants, buffaloes, and various antelope and monkey species); the Longido Mountains (20km hike over three days through pristine montane forest where elephants and buffaloes are still common); northern Maasai land; Mount Meru; and Kilimanjaro (using the less popular routes). They also do a most attractive semi-safari package, which combines walking and motorised transport in and around the Ngorongoro Crater, Lengai Volcano, and the game-rich plains immediately east of the Lobo part of the Serengeti. Prices vary from around $75 per person per day to double that, depending on the level of organisation required, and on whether park fees are involved. If you're looking for something different, this company is highly recommended, and the people who run it are very flexible and knowledgeable, and enthusiastic without being pushy – if the idea of a walking trip appeals, it's well worth popping in for a coffee and a chat.

Several other tour operators, mostly branches of UK or US companies, can put together tailor-made safaris based on staying in lodges. Prices start at around $100 to $150 per person per day (more if you fly in to the reserves). Some names and addresses follow:

**Abercrombie and Kent**, PO Box 427 Arusha, tel: (057) 7803, fax: (057) 7003.
**Kingfisher Safaris**, PO Box 701 Arusha, tel: (057) 3181.
**Ker & Downey**, PO Box 2782 Arusha, tel: (057) 7755.
**State Travel Service**, PO Box 1369 Arusha, tel: (057) 3300, fax: (057) 3113.
**Takims Safaris**, Suite 421, Ngorongoro Wing, AICC; PO Box 6023 Arusha, tel: (057) 3174, fax: (057) 8211.
**United Touring Company**, Subzali Building, cnr Ngoliondoi & Sokoine Rd; PO Box 2211 Arusha, tel (057) 7931, fax: (057) 6475.
**Wildersun Safaris**, Jael Maeda Road; PO Box 930, tel: (057) 3880, fax: (057) 7834.

## Hitching and public transport

Hitching into Arusha National Park is a feasible option, but trying to hitch to the other reserves makes little sense. There are few private vehicles, and most safari companies forbid their drivers to pick up hitchhikers. In any case, people who have paid for a safari or are in a private vehicle loaded with supplies are unlikely to want to carry freeloaders. Even if you do get a lift, you may well get stuck in the Serengeti or Ngorongoro and although you will see little game from a campsite or lodge you will still have to pay park fees.

If you cannot afford an organised safari, your best bet is an Arusha-Mwanza bus through the Serengeti. You will get a good look at the scenery and at the right time of year will see plenty of game, but will have to pay $30 in park fees.

There are buses between Arusha and Karatu, passing through Mto wa Mbu. The Ngorongoro Conservation Authority (NCA) plans to introduce a cheap bus service between Arusha and Ngorongoro Crater rim. This runs twice daily in each direction. It is primarily for staff, but tourists will be allowed to use it.

# ARUSHA NATIONAL PARK

Arusha National Park, which lies between Kilimanjaro and Arusha, only covers an area of 137km², but it protects a remarkable diversity of habitats. The eastern slopes and 4,566m-high peak of Mount Meru, the fifth-highest mountain in Africa, lie within the park and are its main attraction. Arusha is decidedly low-key when compared to Kilimanjaro, and it does not quite match up to the Serengeti or Ngorongoro, but it has plenty to offer those tourists who make the effort to visit it.

Often described as a mini-Ngorongoro, Ngurdoto Crater is in itself worth the entrance fee, a fully intact 3km-wide, 400m-deep volcanic caldera with a forest-fringed rim and lush green floor. Tourists are not permitted to descend into the crater, but points on the rim offer stunning views across it.

Another attraction is the Momella Lakes, a group of shallow alkaline lakes fed by underground streams. They all have different mineral contents and are slightly different in colour. The lakes are some of the best places to see water birds in Tanzania: flamingo, pelican, little grebe and a variety of herons, ducks and waders are common.

Buffalo, elephant, hippo, giraffe, zebra and a variety of antelope are regularly seen. Blue monkey are common in all the forests, and black-and-white colobus can be seen on Mount Meru and on Ngurdoto crater rim. The only large predators are leopard and spotted hyena; we were lucky enough to see both driving between Momella Lodge and the

campsite shortly after nightfall. In addition to water birds, Arusha is rich in forest species.

From a vehicle, most of the park can be seen in a day. You can walk anywhere in the park accompanied by an armed ranger, whose services cost $10 per outing. Mount Meru can be climbed in two or three days.

An excellent 52-page booklet, *Arusha National Park*, is available from the National Parks office in Arusha for $2.50.

A park entrance fee of $15 per 24-hour period is charged.

## Geology
The formation of both Meru and Ngurdoto resulted from the same volcanic activity that formed the Great Rift Valley 15 to 20 million years ago. Ngurdoto is long-extinct, but Meru remains dormant; lava last flowed from it 100 years ago. Until about 250,000 years ago Meru was similar in size to Kilimanjaro, but a massive eruption at that time tore out the entire eastern wall.

## Getting there and away
Momella gate and camp are 20km from the main Arusha-Moshi road. The turn-off at Usa River is clearly signposted. Ngurdoto gate and campsite are 8km from the turn-off. The approach road is in fair condition and can be driven in an ordinary saloon car.

If you do not have a vehicle, the park can be visited as a day tour from Arusha. Any company can organise this. Most companies can also organise a three-day climb up Meru.

If you want to organise your own climb or spend some time exploring the park on foot you will have to find your own way there. You could hire a taxi in Arusha, but if you are patient you should be able to hitch. Any vehicle heading to Momella Lodge or the village of Ngare Nanyuki will go past the main entrance gate. To get an early start, camp or stay at the Tanzanite Hotel the night before you want to hitch in.

Plenty of locals walk along the main road through the park. It is a long walk from Usa River to Momella gate, but there's nothing stopping you from doing it.

## Where to stay
In the upper range, a visit to the park could be based at any of the hotels near Usa River (see *Where to stay* in Arusha). The most convenient place to stay is **Momella Lodge** (PO Box 418 Arusha, tel: (057) 4648), 3km past Momella Gate, a cosy hotel with an alpine feel enhanced by the log fires in the bar and television lounge. Meals cost $12. Accommodation in chalets costs $80/122 HC s/c single/double, or $10.60/15.35 for residents.

The **National Park Rest House** 2km from Momella Gate sleeps up to five people and costs $20 HC per person per night. You can book it in advance through The Warden, Arusha National Park, PO Box 3134, Arusha, or enquire directly about availability at the gate or the National Parks office in Arusha.

There are four **National Park campsites**: three at the foot of Tululusia Hill, 2km from Momella Gate, and one in the forest near Ngurdoto Gate. All are scenic and near streams, have drop toilets and firewood, and cost $20 per person.

You may not walk between the campsites and the entrance gates without an armed ranger, so unless you have a vehicle it may be more practical to pitch a tent at **Momella Lodge**. This costs $8 per person and entitles you to use the lodge's facilities. The lodge will organise somewhere for you to wash, and can provide firewood.

## Climbing Mount Meru

Meru is not the highest mountain in Africa; for the achievement-orientated it is no substitute for Kilimanjaro. On the other hand, those people who climb both invariably enjoy Meru more. It is not as crowded, considerably less expensive, and although it is steeper there are none of the problems associated with Kilimanjaro's altitude.

Meru is just as interesting as Kilimanjaro from a biological point of view and, because comparatively few people climb it, you are more likely to see forest animals. A lot of big game can be seen on the lower slopes. Meru can technically be climbed in two days, but three days is more normal, allowing time to explore Meru Crater and to look at wildlife and plants.

Most people arrange a climb through a safari company in Arusha. The going rate for three days is around $150 per person. You can make direct arrangements with park officials at the gate, but won't save much money by doing this. The compulsory armed ranger and guide costs $20 per day ($10 park fee and $10 salary), hut fees are $10 per night, and there is the usual park entrance fee of $15 per day. A rescue fee of $20 per person covers the entire climb. The minimum cost for a three-day climb is therefore $85 per person plus $65 divided between the party. Food and transport must be added to this, and porters are another $5 per day each.

Meru is very cold at night; you will need adequate clothing. In the rainy season, mountain boots are necessary. The rest of the year, good walking shoes are adequate. The best months to climb are between October and February.

If you arrange your own climb, check hut availability at the National Park Office in Arusha before you head off to the gate. At present the huts are rarely full, but Meru is growing in popularity, and this could change.

**Day one** The trail starts at Momella Gate (1,500m). From there it is a relatively gentle three-hour ascent to Miriakamba Hut (2,600m). On the way you pass through well-developed woodland where there is a good chance of seeing large animals such as giraffe. At an altitude of about 2,000m you enter the forest zone. If you leave Momella early, there will be ample time to explore Meru Crater in the afternoon. The crater is overlooked by the 1,500m cliff rising to Meru Peak. The 3,667m ash cone in the crater is an hour from Miriakamba Hut, and can be climbed.

**Day two** It is three hours to Saddle Hut (3,600m), a bit steeper than the previous day's walk. You initially pass through forest, where there is a good chance of seeing black-and-white colobus, then at about 3,000m you will enter a moorland zone similar to that on Kilimanjaro. It is not unusual to see Kilimanjaro peeking above the clouds from Saddle Hut. If you feel energetic, you can climb Little Meru (3,820m) in the afternoon. It takes about an hour each way from Saddle Hut.

**Day three** You must rise early to ascend the 4,566m peak. This takes four to five hours. It is then an eight to nine hour walk back down the mountain to Momella Gate.

**Note** Some people prefer to climb from Miriakamba Hut to Saddle Hut *and* do the round trip from Saddle Hut to Meru Peak on the second day (eleven hours altogether), leaving only a five hour walk to Momella on the third. Others climb all the way up to Saddle Hut on the first day (six hours), do the round trip to the peak on the second (eight hours), and return to Momella from the Saddle Hut on the third (five hours).

# LAKE MANYARA NATIONAL PARK

Lake Manyara is a shallow, alkaline lake at the base of a cliff-face that is part of the western Rift Valley wall. The northwest of the lake and the land around it are protected in a 330km² national park. In the 1970s, Lake Manyara was famous for its elephants, immortalised by Ian Douglas-Hamilton in his book *Amongst the Elephants*. Poaching has reduced the numbers in recent years; you are unlikely to see a large tusker these days. The park's other claim to fame is its lions, which have a reputation for tree-climbing, behaviour that has also been observed in the Queen Elizabeth National Park (Uganda).

A visit to Lake Manyara National Park kicks off a high proportion of Tanzanian safaris. It is, in truth, a rather low-key introduction to a complex of game reserves that is arguably the best in the world. From the entrance gate, which lies near a village called Mto wa Mbu, a road winds for several kilometres through a cool, lush, mature fig forest. With appropriate jungle noises supplied by silvery cheeked hornbills, this is the one part of the northern safari circuit which might conjure up images of Tarzan swinging into view. But, unless you're hoping for a rare glimpse of a leopard, the forest isn't really big game territory – you can expect to see baboons and with a bit of luck a few samango monkeys, but otherwise the main point of faunal interest is the diversity of birds and butterflies.

Most safari vehicles emerge from the forest at the hippo pools, where several dozens of hippos can be seen soaking and yawning. This is a lovely spot, with the Rift Valley escarpment rising to the west, and the sparsely vegetated flood plain of Lake Manyara stretching to the distant shore. Giraffes are common in this area – many of them so dark in colour that at a distance they appear almost melanistic. The hippo pools also offer excellent birding, with several varieties of heron, waterfowl and waders usually present, as well as more unusual species such as crowned crane, snipes and pratincoles.

The best mammal viewing is along the road towards the hot springs in the south of the park. En route, you pass through tangled acacia woodland with views over the flood plain, where you should see large herds of zebra and wildebeest, the occasional impala and giraffe, and in the marshy area around the springs, plenty of buffaloes. This is also a good road for elephants, the population of which is visibly on the increase since it hit its nadir in the late 1980s.

For all the hype that surrounds the tree-climbing lions, you'll be lucky to see them in arboreal action – the only lion I've ever seen in Manyara was an impressively maned but mundanely terrestrial male plodding across the flood plain. But, whatever you read elsewhere, this unusual behaviour does still occur in the park (Janet Mears of Bradt Publications is a first-hand witness), especially during the dry season when lion concentrations are highest. *Acacia tortilis* trees are particularly favoured.

I've read elsewhere that Lake Manyara is frequently a disappointment to visitors. Certainly, if your expectations are formed by Douglas-Hamilton's book and talk of tree-climbing lions, you're probably in for a slight let down. In my opinion, Manyara is a valuable addition to a safari of several days' duration, but I could understand that somebody with limited time might elect to forsake its biological diversity for an additional day on the predator-rich plains of the Serengeti.

Worth noting is that Manyara is a *great* birding reserve – it's perfectly feasible for a casual birder to see 100 species in a day, ranging from the forest-dwelling crowned eagle to a variety of colourful bee-eaters, barbets, kingfishers and rollers. There are, too, the large flocks of flamingos which collect on the shallow alkaline lake – on my most recent visit, their numbers rivalled those on Kenya's famous Lake Nakuru.

A 44-page booklet, *Lake Manyara National Park*, published by Tanzania National Parks, costs $2.50 and gives detailed coverage of the park's flora and fauna. Like all national parks, an entrance fee of $15 per 24-hour period is charged.

## Mto Wa Mbu

This village near the entrance gate to Lake Manyara sees a lot of tourist traffic and most organised safaris stop at its huge curio market. When you get out of your vehicle expect to be swarmed around by curio dealers. Bear in mind that prices here are double what they would be in Arusha. Mto Wa Mbu means River of Mosquitoes. If you spend a night, you will be in no doubt as to how it got this name.

## Where to stay/eat

There is no accommodation in the park, presumably because it is so small. There is plenty of accommodation outside the park.

### *Upper range*

Tahi's **Lake Manyara Lodge** (PO Box 877 Arusha, tel: (057) 2711/2, fax: (057) 8221) is barely recognisable from its shoddy, run-down state of a few years ago. In most respects it is the equal of any lodge in Kenya, and the buffet dinner is better than any I've eaten at a Kenyan lodge. The rooms are still a bit spartan, and the absence of netting is surprising – the mosquitoes here are terrible – but the en suite bathrooms do at least have running hot water. A definite attraction of the lodge is a large swimming pool, but its single best feature remains its position. Perched right on the edge of the escarpment, the grounds have a panoramic view over the forest and lake, with the Rift Valley hills fading to the horizon. With binoculars, you should be able to pick out elephants, giraffes and buffaloes on the Rift Valley floor; closer to home, there is good birding within the lodge grounds. $137/190 single/double full board.

The other established tourist-class accommodation near Lake Manyara is **Kirurumu Tented Lodge**, owned and managed by Hoopoe Adventure Tours (PO Box 2047 Arusha, tel: (057) 7011, fax: (057) 8226). Perched on the escarpment a short distance north of Lake Manyara, this also offers a grand view across the plains of the Rift Valley, particularly from the bar, though it's a bit too far from the park to pick out much game. The atmosphere is more rustic than at the lodge, and it will be more attractive to people who prefer to feel close to nature. The food is good and the service friendly and efficient. Accommodation is in luxury double tents, each of which has a private verandah, shower and toilet. $146/212 single/double full board.

The **Lake Manyara Serena Lodge** (PO Box 2551, Arusha, tel: (057) 8175/ 6304; fax: (057) 8282), which lies on the escarpment between the older lodge and tented camp, is due to open in mid-1996. $170/260 single/double full board.

### Moderate, budget and camping

There's no shortage of affordable lodgings and campsites in Mto Wa Mbu, the village that lies on the main road outside the park entrance.

The longest serving of these places, **Holiday Fig Camp**, has always been rather cramped and is also rather overpriced these days, with ordinary doubles for $15 and self-contained doubles with fans for $30. Camping costs $5 per person. Facilities include a restaurant and bar, as well as a swimming pool which I've yet to see in a functional state.

**Jambo Campsite** is a pleasant place with camping for $3 per person and adequate double rooms with mosquito netting for $8.

Better value, and very quiet and friendly, is the **Camp Vision Lodge**, which has bright little rooms with nets for $3.

**Twiga Campsite and Lodge** is arguably the most attractive place to stay in the village: the rooms aren't particularly great value at $20 for a self-contained double, but the large, grassy campsite is the best in town and only costs $3 per person. There is a bar and restaurant in the grounds.

There are also a few lodges in the village at the junction to the Lake Manyara Lodge, though these are generally scruffier than the ones in Mto Wa Mbu. Still, malaria and mosquitoes are less of a threat at this altitude, and if you happen to be that most optimistic of souls, somebody trying to get around the parks on public transport or by hitching, you're well positioned to wander up to the lodge for a beer and some long-distance game viewing.

# KARATU

This small, dusty town on the Manyara-Ngorongoro road is often used as a base for visiting the crater. There is a daily bus between it and Arusha.

## Where to stay
### Upper range
**Gibb's Farm** Built on a coffee farm bordering a patch of indigenous forest, many people rate this hotel the best in the Ngorongoro region. Accommodation is in idiosyncratic bungalows. The restaurant is good. Gibb's Farm is 4km from the main road. $139/204 HC s/c single/double, full board.

### Budget and camping
Most people stay at one of the places listed below. There are guesthouses in the town which would no doubt be cheaper.

**Safari Junction Campsite** This is popular with safari companies, but unlike the Holiday Fig Resort it is some way out of town and has spacious grounds. Facilities include showers, a restaurant and a bar, where we were entertained by two men playing a zeze (a one-stringed instrument similar to a violin) and a bongo. It is 1km out of town and signposted. Camping costs $3 per person, hired tents and log cabins cost $8/18/24 single/double/triple.

**Karatu Campsite** This is just off the main road towards Ngorongoro, about 10km from Karatu at Njiapanda. Facilities are good. Camping costs $5 per person.

# LAKE EYASI

This little-visited and scenic lake lies on the remote southern border of Ngorongoro Conservation Area, at the base of the 1,000m-high Eyasi Escarpment on the western Rift Valley wall. There is plenty of wildlife in the area. Eyasi is notable for the hunter-gatherer Hadza people who live near the shore. The road to Eyasi branches from the Kidatu-Ngorongoro road. There are no tourist facilities, so visitors should be entirely self-sufficient.

# NGORONGORO CONSERVATION AREA

The central feature of the 8,300km² Ngorongoro Conservation Area is the crater after which it is named. Ngorongoro Crater is the largest intact caldera in the world and one of the most spectacular sights in Africa. The nearby Olduvai Gorge is the site of some of Africa's most important hominid fossil finds.

Most people are familiar with Ngorongoro's status as a wildlife sanctuary – it has been the subject of countless television documentaries – but the crater is also magnificently scenic. The road from Karatu climbs through densely forested slopes to the rim where, at Heroes Point, there is a spectacular view over the 260km² crater floor 600m below.

With the notable exception of impala and giraffe – the latter being unable to scale the steep walls – just about every species of African plains mammal lives on the crater floor. The crater has the densest predator population in Africa; because of the plentiful game you'll never see a skinny lion or hyena here. It is normal to see elephant, buffalo, lion and black rhino in the course of one game drive, and there is a fair chance of seeing leopard. Ngorongoro is one of the last remaining rhino strongholds in East Africa. Large herds of grazers, mainly zebra and wildebeest, are resident on the crater floor.

The forested crater rim is worth exploring. There are stunning views back across to the Rift Valley along the road between the main village and Sopa Lodge. Bushbuck and leopard are sometimes seen on this road.

Some people complain Ngorongoro Crater is like a zoo. This is

nonsense. The animals are used to vehicles, but they are free to enter and exit as they please. A fairer criticism is that the high tourist traffic robs the crater floor of some of its atmosphere. It is a relatively small area and very open; most animal spotting is done by looking for a group of vehicles clustered together in the distance. Personally I felt the scenery and abundance of animals more than made up for the mild congestion. If crowds put you off there are other places to visit in the Ngorongoro/Serengeti area. Instead of adding to the crowds then moaning about them, give the crater a miss.

An 84-page booklet, *Ngorongoro Conservation Area*, similar in style to the national park booklets, is readily available in Arusha and has good information on the crater and Olduvai Gorge. It is especially worth buying if you plan to visit some of the off-the-beaten-track parts of the conservation area.

The crater rim gets very cold at night. Take a jumper or two, especially if you are camping.

An entrance fee of $20 per 24-hour period is charged. This must be paid even if you just pass through between Arusha and the Serengeti.

## Geology and history

The mountains in the Ngorongoro region date from two periods. The Gol Mountains, to your left as you descend from Ngorongoro to the Serengeti, are exposed granite blocks over 500 million years old. Ngorongoro and other free-standing mountains are volcanic in origin, formed during the fracturing process that created the Rift Valley 15 to 20 million years ago. When Ngorongoro peaked in size two to three million years ago, it was a similar height to Kilimanjaro today. There are two other volcanic craters in the area: Olmoti and Empakaai. A volcano just north of the conservation area, Oldionyo Lengai (Maasai for *mountain of God*), last erupted in 1983.

Evidence found at Olduvai Gorge and Laetoli (discussed more fully later in the chapter) show hominids have occupied the area for at least three million years. It was occupied by hunter-gatherers until a few thousand years ago, when pastoralists moved in. There are, however, still hunter-gatherers living in the Eyasi Basin south of Ngorongoro. These people, called the Hadza, have strong linguistic links with the San of southern Africa.

The fate of the early pastoralists is not known; a succession of immigrants replaced them. The ancestors of the Cushitic-speaking Mbulu arrived 2,000 years ago. The Nilotic-speaking Datoga arrived 300 years ago. A century later the Maasai drove both groups out in a violent conflict; the Datoga to the Eyasi Basin and the Mbulu to the highlands near Manyara. Most place names in the area are Maasai. I have heard several explanations of the name *Ngorongoro*; the most believable, told to me by a Maasai, is that it is named after a type of Maasai bowl that it resembles.

Europeans settled in the area around the turn of the century. The crater floor was farmed by two German brothers until the outbreak of World War I. One of their old farmhouses is still used by researchers working in the crater. Tourism began in the 1930s when the Ngorongoro Crater Lodge was built on the crater rim. Ngorongoro was part of the original Serengeti National Park proclaimed in 1951, but it was made a separate conservation area in 1956 in order that the Maasai could graze their cattle there. Ngorongoro Crater was made a World Heritage Site in 1978.

# Getting there

The Ngorongoro Conservation Authority runs a bus service between Arusha and the park headquarters. The bus goes twice daily in each direction, and stops at Karatu and Mto Wa Mbu. Though primarily intended as a staff vehicle, travellers are welcome to make use of the service, and they pay normal fares. This service will be very useful if you have permission to hike in the area (see *Hiking in Ngorongoro Conservation Area* below), but otherwise the value of arriving at Ngorongoro on a bus is questionable. You could hire a park vehicle to take you into the crater, but unless you are part of a large group this is expensive: $140 for a full day, plus $1 per kilometre, plus a $10 crater fee. Add on park fees and you would be better off organising a safari in Arusha.

# Where to stay/eat

Except for Sopa Lodge, the lodges and campsite on the crater rim are within a couple of kilometres of the park headquarters. The village near the headquarters has bars and basic shops.

## *Upper range*

The **Ngorongoro Sopa Lodge** (PO Box 2551, Arusha. Tel: (057) 8175/6304) is the most upmarket place on the crater rim. It lies some 20km distant from the park headquarters and other lodges, and is reached via a forest-lined road where leopards are frequently observed in the early morning. Accommodation is in large semi-detached rooms resembling stone rondavels from the outside. Each room has two double beds, a heater, a large bathroom with running hot water, a fridge, and a large bay window facing the crater and Ol Mokarot Mountain. There is a swimming pool in front of the bar. The food at the restaurant is excellent. The large, forested grounds are a good place to look for characteristic montane forest birds, with sunbirds (tacazze, golden-winged and eastern double-collared) well represented and a variety of weavers, seedeaters and robins present. $155/240 single/double full board.

The main cluster of lodges is around the park headquarters.

First up, coming from Arusha, is **Rhino Lodge,** run by and bookable through the Ngorongoro Conservation Authority. This isn't the most exciting place to stay, and it has no view worth talking about, but it is certainly the cheapest option in the area at $55/80 single/double.

**Ngorongoro Wildlife Lodge** (PO Box 887, Arusha, tel: (057) 2711/2, fax: (057) 8221) is run by TAHI. Like other hotels in this group, services have greatly improved in the last few years, particularly the catering. The lodge has a beautiful position on the rim of the crater directly above the yellow fever forest. The rooms are comfortable, with piping hot baths (welcome at this chilly altitude) and windows facing the crater. You can pick out animals on the crater floor using a telescope fixed on the patio. The grounds, though smaller than those of Sopa Lodge, support a fair range of forest birds, and they're also one of the few places where I've seen tree hyraxes. $137/180 single/double full board.

**Ngorongoro Crater Lodge** was built in the 1930s and has plenty of period character – a rustic dining room overlooks the crater rim and the verdant lawn apparently doubles as a retirement home for aging buffalo. This lodge was closed for renovation in early 1996, but it should be open by the end of the year, when rooms will cost $106/164 single/double full board.

Also due to open in mid-1996 is the new **Ngorongoro Serena Lodge** (PO Box 2551, Arusha, tel: (057) 8175/6304; fax: (057) 8282), which lies on the crater rim several kilometres past the main cluster of lodges towards the Serengeti. Rooms here will cost $170/260 single/double full board.

On the Serengeti border south of the main road to Seronera, **Ndutu Lodge** is a low-key retreat set amongst the acacia woodland overlooking Lake Ndutu. Accommodation in self-contained bungalows costs $139/204 single/double full board.

### Budget and camping

Simba Campsite on the crater rim costs $20 HC per person. The only cheap rooms are at the driver's lodge in the village, but tourists are not normally allowed to stay there. Your best bet for a cheap room is in Kidatu. It used to be possible to camp on the crater floor, and may become so again, but at the time of writing it is forbidden.

# Hiking in Ngorongoro Conservation Area

You are permitted to walk in the conservation area providing you have an authorised guide. Tropical Tours in Arusha (see *Organising a safari*) specialise in this kind of thing, but it is possible to make your own arrangements. You could, for instance, hike all the way from Lake

Natron to the crater rim, taking in Lengai volcano and other places of interest along the route. This would take at least a week and would probably cost around the same as a Kilimanjaro climb. Another area worth exploring on foot is the Lake Eyasi border.

If you want to do something along these lines, contact the Assistant Conservator of Tourism at the Ngorongoro Conservation Authority in Arusha. At present, few people hike in the area so the chances of getting permission are reasonable, but it is very much at the discretion of the NCA and obviously dependent on what resources are available (guides, porters, transportation within the area etc). If you get permission, you will have to organise food yourself. You should also clarify arrangements for a tent, sleeping bag and other equipment. Remember to take warm clothes; parts of the area become cold at night.

## The crater floor

A sheer dirt road descends from Malanja Depression on the crater rim to the crater floor. At the top of the road, Maasai women and children allow you to photograph them for a small fee. The Malanja depression is grassy and open – a good place to spot typical highland antelope such as mountain reedbuck and Kirk's dik-dik, and birds such as the striking auger buzzard and Schalow's wheatear.

The dominant feature of the crater floor is Lake Magadi, a shallow soda lake which supports large flocks of flamingo. Much of the crater floor is open grassland, making animal spotting relatively easy: black rhino, lion, hyena, gazelle, wildebeest and zebra are all commonly seen. The hippo pool near Mandusi Swamp is a popular picnic spot. Lunch is enlivened by a flock of black kites which have become adept at swooping down on tourists and snatching the food from their hands. Lekai Forest is another attractive spot, made up of yellow fever trees, and the favoured haunt of the crater's elephant.

The ascent back up to the rim passes through patches of forest similar to that on the crater rim.

## Olduvai Gorge

The significance of Olduvai Gorge was first recognised by one Professor Katwinkle, an entomologist who stumbled across it in 1911. In 1913, he led an expedition which unearthed a number of animal fossils. The site was abandoned at the start of World War I.

In 1931, Louis Leakey arrived at Olduvai. He thought it an ideal place to uncover traces of early hominids. The gorge cuts through rock beds layered in time sequence from two million years ago to the present and their volcanic origin makes carbon-dating easy. Leakey found ample evidence of human occupation, but without backing his investigations went slowly. It was only in 1959 that his wife, Mary, uncovered a 1.75 million year old *australopithecus* jawbone. This was the first conclusive evidence that hominids had existed for over a million years and that they had evolved in Africa. After this, the Leakeys received proper funding. They unearthed several more fossils, including *homo habilis*, a direct ancestor of modern man. Leakey died in 1972, but Mary continued working in the area until she retired in 1984. In 1976, at the nearby site of Laetoli, she discovered fossil footprints over three million years old, the most ancient hominid footprints yet discovered.

Birders should definitely divert to the gorge: red-and-yellow barbet, slaty coloured boubou, speckle-fronted weaver and purple grenadier are practically guaranteed to be seen around the museum.

Olduvai Gorge is 3km from the main Ngorongoro-Serengeti road. You may only explore the diggings with a guide, and there is an excellent site museum.

## Lake Ndutu
This alkaline lake lies south of the B142 on the Ngorongoro-Serengeti border. When it is full, Maasai use it to water their cattle. In the rainy season it supports large numbers of animals, so Ndutu Lodge (see *Where to stay* above) is a good base for game drives. The acacia woodland around the lake supports different birds to those in surrounding areas. The campsite on the lake shore costs $40 per person.

## North of Ngorongoro Crater
Few tourists venture into the northern part of the Ngorongoro Conservation Area, as it does not fit comfortably into the standard three- to five-day safari. There are, however, a few places which would be attractive additions to your itinerary if you had time or wanted to head to less touristed spots.

Permission from park headquarters is needed to visit the northern Ngorongoro Conservation Area. The roads in the region are poor and may be impassable after rain. If you plan to explore the area, allocate time generously.

If you visit this area in your own vehicle, treat it as you would any wilderness trip: carry adequate supplies of food, water, and fuel. You should also have essential spares for your vehicle. If you go with a safari company, avoid those on the lower end of the price scale.

### Olmoti Crater
This sunken caldera is near the village of Nainokanoka. A track leads from the village to a ranger's post west of it. The crater can only be reached on foot, so at the ranger's post you will have to organise an armed ranger to guide you. From the ranger's post it is a half-hour walk to the rim. This is a shallow crater, covered in grass, and it offers

good grazing for Maasai cattle and a variety of antelope. From the rim you can walk to a pretty waterfall where the Munge River leaves the crater.

### Empakaai Crater

Almost half the floor of this 6km-wide, 300m-high crater is taken up by a deep soda lake. A road circles the forested rim and another leads to the crater floor. Bushbuck, buffalo and blue monkey are likely to be seen on the rim, which also boasts good views across to Lengai Volcano and, on clear days, Kilimanjaro and Lake Natron. The crater floor is home to a variety of antelope and water birds. With permission from park headquarters, you may camp wild on the crater rim or sleep in a cabin on the southern shore of the lake.

### Engakura Ruins

The ruins of a terraced stone city and complex irrigation system, estimated to be over 500 years old, lie on the eastern side of Empakaai. Nobody knows who built the city – there is no tradition of stone building in this part of Africa – but it was almost certainly occupied by the Mbulu people immediately before the Maasai came into the area. There is a road from Mto Wa Mbu to Engakura.

### Lake Natron

This spectacular soda lake, north of Lengai Volcano, is set in very harsh surroundings, and has a quality that verges on the primeval. The concentration of sodium carbonate dissolved in the lake is so high that it is often viscous to the touch. As well as being highly scenic, the lake is the only known breeding ground for East Africa's flamingoes.

Kamakia Campsite lies about 2km from Lake Natron, near a Maasai village with a bar and shops. There is a toilet and shower at the campsite.

## SERENGETI NATIONAL PARK

There is little I can say about the Serengeti which has not been said already. This is Africa's most famous game reserve, renowned for its dense predator population and annual wildebeest migration. Considering the hype which surrounds it, I half-expected the Serengeti to disappoint, but it didn't. The vastness of the plains and the number of animals which live on them are incredible. I would rate it the best game reserve I have visited anywhere in Africa.

Serengeti National Park covers an area of almost 15,000km², but the Serengeti ecosystem – which includes a number of game reserves bordering the national park as well as Kenya's Maasai Mara Game Reserve – is more than double that size. Most of the national park is open and grassy, broken by isolated granite koppies and patches of acacia woodland. There is little permanent water, so animal migration in the area is strongly linked to rainfall patterns.

The Serengeti was little-known to Europeans until after World War I, when hunters moved in. The national park was created in 1951 and became famous through the work of Professor Bernard Grzimek and his son Michael. At the age of 24, Michael died in an aeroplane crash over the Serengeti. He is buried at Heroes Point on the Ngorongoro Crater rim. Published in the late 1950s, Grzimek's book *Serengeti shall not die* remains worthwhile reading.

Using figures from the 1984/5 census, the Serengeti's most common antelope species are wildebeest (1,300,000), Thomson's gazelle (250,000), impala (70,000) topi (50,000), Grant's gazelle (30,000), kongoni (15,000) and eland (10,000). Other antelope species include Kirk's dik-dik, klipspringer (often seen on koppies) and small numbers of roan, oryx, oribi and waterbuck.

After wildebeest, the most populous large mammal is zebra (200,000), and the two are often seen in mixed herds. There are significant numbers of buffalo, giraffe and warthog. Elephant are relatively scarce, and the few remaining black rhinoceros are restricted to the Moru Koppies area. A few primate species are present, of which baboon are the most common and widespread.

Ultimately, the success of any safari lies in the number and quality of encounters with big cats. There is something infinitely compelling about these animals, a fascination that seems to affect even the most jaded of safari drivers – many of whom are leopard obsessives, content to drive up and down the Seronera Valley all day in the search for a tell-tale tail dangling from a tree.

When it comes to big cats, the Serengeti rarely disappoints. Lions are a practical certainty: some 250 to 300 of these animals stalk the plains around Seronera, with the main concentration around Simba Hills north of the Ngorongoro road. It's normal to see two or three prides in the course of one game drive. Sociable, languid and deceptively pussy-cat-like, lions are most often seen lying low in the grass or basking on rocks. The challenge is to see a lion exert itself beyond a half-interested raising of the head when a vehicle stops nearby.

Cheetahs, too, are regularly sighted in the grasslands around Simba Hills, though in direct contrast to their languid cousins, these streamlined, solitary creatures are most normally seen pacing the plains with the air of an agitated greyhound. The Seronera Valley is also home to a healthy population of leopards, which are most often seen lounging in the canopy of the sausage trees and acacias along the Seronera River. Leopards are more easily seen in this area than practically anywhere I've visited in Africa, largely because there are too few trees for them to hide in as successfully as they would in more lush riverine woodland.

Of the other predators which can be seen in the Serengeti, spotted hyenas are very common, perhaps more numerous than lions. Golden jackals and bat-eared foxes appear to be the most abundant canine species on the plains around Seronera, while black-backed jackals are reasonably common in the thicker vegetation towards Lobo. Driving at dusk or dawn, you stand the best chance of seeing nocturnal predators such as civet, serval, genet and African wild cat. The real rarity among canines is the African hunting dog, which may well be extinct in the Serengeti.

Considering its open nature, I was surprised at how rewarding the Serengeti's bird life is. Ostrich are common, as is the kori bustard, claimed by some to be the heaviest flying bird in the world. A variety of larks, finches and raptors can be seen, but perhaps the most distinctive small bird is the lilac-breasted roller, an exquisitely coloured bird often seen perched on trees alongside the road. In the Seronera area, you can be reasonably certain of seeing three bird species which are thought to be endemic to Tanzania: the beautiful Fischer's lovebird, the grey-rumped spurfowl, and the deceptively babbler-like rufous-tailed weaver.

Maasai, who traditionally occupied the Serengeti plains from the 17th century, are no longer allowed to graze their cattle in the Serengeti. Evidence of their previous occupation of the area can be seen at Moru Koppies, where there are well-preserved Maasai rock paintings.

A 72-page booklet, *Serengeti National Park*, is sold at the National Parks office in Arusha for $2.50. Like all the national park booklets, it contains good maps and is an excellent introduction to the local ecosystems.

An entrance fee of $20 per 24-hour period is charged.

## When to visit

Unlike Ngorongoro, the Serengeti's animal populations are highly seasonal. There is less game in the park during the dry season, although some species (including most predators) are resident and territorial, so do not stray far.

### The wildebeest migration

The wildebeest migration follows a fairly predictable pattern, though there are minor variations from year to year. Wildebeest disperse in the southern part of the Serengeti during the rainy season (December to May), calving near the beginning of this period. On game drives around Seronera at this time of year it is not uncommon to see herds of 10,000 animals.

In April or May the animals congregate in preparation for an 800km migration to the western Serengeti and Maasai Mara, which takes place sometime between April and June. During this time, a herd of over a million migrating animals forms a column up to 40km long, one of the most impressive spectacles in the world.

From July to October, the animals spread out into the northern and western Serengeti. The best base is the Lobo area (not really practical for a camping safari). The animals return to the southern plains in November.

## Balloon safaris

Serengeti Balloon Safaris run balloon safaris from Seronera at 06.00 daily, departing from the lodge at around 05.30. The package includes transfer to the balloon site, a balloon trip of roughly one hour, and a champagne breakfast set out at a table in the bush. This costs $300 per person.

A balloon safari is definitely worth the expense if you can afford it. Gliding serenely above the trees as the sun rises allows you to see the expansive plains from a new and quite thrilling angle. It also offers the chance to see secretive species such as bushbuck and reedbuck, and, because you leave so early in the morning, you are likely to spot a few nocturnal predators (we saw hyenas in abundance, civet twice and had a rare glimpse of an African wild cat). That said, any images you have of sweeping above endless herds of wildebeest and zebra may prove a little removed from reality. You'll only see large herds if you're fortunate enough to be in the area during the exact week or two when animals concentrate close to Seronera; for us, the absence of plains animals was a mild disappointment after having spent the day before we got to Seronera driving through thousands upon thousands of wildebeest in the Olduvai area.

The champagne breakfast is set up in the bush, at a different site every day, depending on which way the balloons are blown. It is presented with some flourish: the immaculately uniformed waiters in particular conjure up images of the safaris of old. Our particular mad-hatters' breakfast party was enlivened by the arrival of three male lions, who strolled less than 100m from the table apparently oblivious to the unusual apparition of twenty four people eating scrambled eggs and sausages at a starched table cloth in the bush. Presumably, this sort of thing doesn't happen every day, whether you're lion or human.

Balloon safaris can be booked at Seronera on the night before departure, but if you want to be certain of a place it's advisable to book in advance, either through your safari company or directly through Serengeti Balloon Safaris at PO Box 12216, Arusha, tel: (057) 8578, fax: (057) 8997. The UK office can be contacted at Unit D9, Harleston Industrial Estate, Harleston, Norfolk, IP20 9EB, tel: (01379) 853129, fax: (01379) 853127.

# Getting there

The only practical way to get to the Serengeti is in your own vehicle or with a safari company.

# Where to stay/eat

The main park headquarters are at Seronera, where there is also a small village, a lodge and camping facilities. On a camping safari you will almost certainly be based at Seronera – all the other campsites in the park are so-called special campsites and cost $40 per person per night. Lodge safaris have a wider choice of bases.

## *Upper range*

**Seronera Wildlife Lodge** (PO Box 877, Arusha, tel: (057) 2711/2, fax: (057) 8221) is the most central and popular lodge in the Serengeti, lying only a couple of kilometres from the park headquarters. Seronera was built between 1970 and 1974, and it is a fine example of a lodge utilising natural features to create an individual and unmistakably African character. The lodge is built around a granite koppie: the bar, frequented by bats and rock hyraxes, is reached through a narrow corridor between two boulders, while the restaurant is sited in a cavernous space, its natural rock walls decorated with traditional paintings. For some years, the service and facilities at Seronera were significantly inferior to the architecture. However, since being taken over by TAHI, there has been a great improvement on these fronts, and the lodge is now among the best I've stayed at in East Africa. Rooms are small but comfortable, with en suite bathrooms and large windows facing the surrounding bush. The food is also very good. $137/190 single/double full board.

In the northeast of the park, **Lobo Wildlife Lodge** is another TAHI possession and bookable through the same address. Older than Seronera, Lobo was built between 1968 and 1970, when the majority of tourism to the Serengeti came directly from Kenya, and it has dropped in popularity now that visitors to the Serengeti come through Arusha. This is a shame – Lobo is, without doubt, the most attractive lodge in Tanzania. Like Seronera, it's built around a koppie, but the design is even more impressive and imaginative than that of the more southerly lodge, spanning four floors and with a fantastic view over the surrounding plains. Incredibly, the building is barely visible until you enter the hotel grounds. Lobo lies in a beautiful part of the park, characterised by rolling hills and large granite outcrops covered in lushly foliated trees. The area is particularly worth visiting in September and October, when the wildebeest migration passes through. At other times of the year, game is generally less prolific here than in the Seronera area, though it supports the park's main concentrations of elephants, and is also noted for large prides of lions. For some, the low volume of game will be compensated for by the scenery, abundant birds, and wilderness feel – you can drive for hours here without seeing another vehicle. $137/190 single/double full board.

Not far from Lobo, **Migration Camp** (PO Box 12095 Arusha, tel: (057) 2814, fax: (057) 8997) is a luxury tented camp which opened in June 1995. Built around a koppie overlooking the Grumeti River, where perennial water supports resident populations of lions, leopards, elephants and buffaloes, this is a secluded, exclusive retreat with a swimming pool, Jacuzzi, cocktail bar, library and lounge. $295/460 single/double full board.

The ostentatious **Serengeti Sopa Lodge** (PO Box 1823, Arusha, tel: (057) 6896/6886; fax: (057) 8245), lies in the southern part of the park on the side of a hill near the Moru Koppies. The rooms here are practically suites: each has two double beds, a small sitting room, a large bathroom complete with bidet, a private balcony and a large window giving a grandstand view over the plains below, perfectly appointed to catch the sunset. The building itself is an idiosyncratic, faintly preposterous construction, with the appearance of an unfinished Greek villa, presumably meant to blend into the rocks. The food is good and facilities include a swimming pool.

The new **Serengeti Serena Lodge** (PO Box 2551, Arusha, tel: (057) 8175/ 6304; fax: (057) 8282) should be open by the time you read this. Similar in standard to the Sopa Lodge, rooms will cost $170/260 single/double full board.

### Moderate and camping

**Kijireshi Tented Camp** Near Bunda, on the western border of the Serengeti, this is a good base if you are exploring the area from Mwanza. Furnished tents cost $75 s/c double. It has a bar and restaurant.

There are seven campsites about 5km from Seronera Lodge. The only facilities are long-drop toilets, but you may be able to organise a shower and fill up water containers for a small fee at the lodge. There is a good chance of seeing nocturnal scavengers such as hyena and genet after dark. $20 HC per person. There are special campsites at Lobo, Kiwara, Moru Koppies, Lake Ndutu and Naabi Hill. They are little-used, so offer relative solitude, but have no facilities. The most special thing about them is the price. $40 per person.

# TARANGIRE NATIONAL PARK

Tarangire is less famous than the other northern reserves, but it is no less rewarding. Like the Serengeti it is part of a wider ecosystem within which there is a great deal of migratory movement. During the wet season, most of its animals disperse to the Maasai Steppe, while wildebeest and zebra move northwest to the Rift Valley floor between Lakes Natron and Manyara.

In direct contrast to the Serengeti, Tarangire comes into its own during the dry season. Between June and November, Tarangire abounds in game attracted to the permanent water of the Tarangire River. During these months it is likely to prove more rewarding than the Serengeti. Vegetation is denser than in the Serengeti, comprising acacia and mixed woodland and, near the Tarangire river, dense elephant grass and the occasional palm tree. Baobab trees are abundant. Tarangire has a wild character, reminiscent of reserves in southern Tanzania.

Tarangire supports similar large mammals to the Serengeti, but the denser vegetation makes predators such as lion and leopard more difficult to see. It is famous for its elephant, with herds of 20-odd animals relatively common. Two localised antelope found in Tarangire are the fringe-eared oryx and gerenuk. According to the 1980 census the greater Tarangire ecosystem supports 25,000 wildebeest, 30,000 zebra, 6,000 buffalo, 3,000 elephant, 2,700 giraffe, 5,500 eland, 30,000 impala and 2,000 warthog. Tarangire's reputation as the best of the northern reserves for birds is, in my experience, a little overstated. Lake Manyara has a far greater habitat diversity, and there is a considerably greater variety of birds to be seen, at least when compared to the parts of Tarangire which are normally visited by tour vehicles. That said, you should see a good variety of raptors and acacia-associated birds, as well as three bird species which are endemic to Tanzania, the ashy starling, rufous-tailed weaver and black-collared lovebird.

Most people spend a day in Tarangire and concentrate on the northern circuit. If you have longer, Lake Burungi circuit offers your best chance of seeing black rhinoceros, bushbuck and lesser kudu, the Kitibong Hill area is home to large herds of buffalo, Lamarkau Swamp supports hippo and numerous water birds during the wet season, the southern plains are favoured by cheetah, and Mkungero Pools is the place to look for waterbuck and gerenuk.

A 56-page booklet, *Tarangire National Park*, is available from the National Parks Headquarters in Arusha. A park entrance fee of $20 per 24-hour period is charged.

## Getting there and away
Tarangire lies about 7km off the main Arusha-Dodoma road. Coming from Arusha, this road is tarred as far as the Tarangire turn-off. Most people tag a visit on to the end of a longer safari, but if your time or money is limited, a one- or two-day safari to Tarangire is a viable option.

## Where to stay
**Tarangire Safari Lodge** is the oldest lodge in the park. Situated on a bluff overlooking the Tarangire River, it's a pleasant and pretty place, with accommodation in standing tents ($90/136 single/double full board) and bungalows ($96/146 single/double full board).

The new **Tarangire Sopa Lodge** (PO Box 1823, Arusha, tel: (057) 6896/

to the customary high standards of this chain of lodges. The rooms are luxurious and the food is excellent. My one reservation is the rather indifferent location, alongside a small and normally dry watercourse below a baobab-studded slope – surely a more scenic site could have been chosen?

**Oliver's Camp** (PO Box 425 Arusha, tel/fax: (057) 8548) is another new place, comprising six furnished tents set amongst the Kikoti koppies. The emphasis here is not so much on overnight stays incorporated into a more wide-ranging safari, but on packages of five to seven nights' duration, which allow you to explore the area fully on foot and by vehicle, including a few nights at a mobile wilderness camp and a night drive to seek out nocturnal predators. $220/320 single/double full board.

There are couple of campsites within Tarangire – strong on bush atmosphere but also rather costly at the customary $20 HC per person. The alternative is to pitch a tent outside the park, at **Kigongoni Campsite**, where you can camp for $3 per person or rent a room for $10 per person. To get to Kigongoni, turn off from the Arusha-Dodoma road as if heading towards Tarangire's entrance gate. After about 2km, you'll see the campsite immediately to your left. There is also a small local guesthouse in the village on the junction of the Arusha-Dodoma road and the turn-off to Tarangire.

# KONDOA IRANGI ROCK PAINTINGS

Lying off the main Arusha-Dodoma road, the rock paintings found in the Kondoa region of Tanzania are the most numerous in East Africa. There are over 100 known sites, the most accessible and interesting of which are reached from the small centre of Kolo. African rock art is overlooked by many tourists, despite the aesthetic value of many paintings, and the numerous questions the art raises about the artists, their beliefs and their lifestyle.

The paintings of the Kondoa region are between 200 and 4,000 years old. Rock art weathers quickly in African conditions. Many older paintings are badly faded, and the tradition may be more ancient than these dates suggest. Most rock paintings are found in caves or rock overhangs. In the Kondoa region east and west-facing sites were favoured.

Paintings are in a variety of styles and cover a range of subjects. Giraffe and various antelope were favoured subjects and eland seem to have held a special significance. Other paintings depict religious ceremonies. There are also abstract paintings of geometric figures whose significance can only be guessed at. Style changes have been recorded at many sites, with newer paintings superimposed over older ones.

The identity of Kondoa's artists is a mystery. Most southern African rock art is accredited to San hunter-gatherers. San-like people occupied all of East and southern Africa prior to the arrival of Bantu-speakers 2,000 to 3,000 years ago. The Hadza of the Lake Eyasi region and the local Sandawe are thought to be remnant populations of these early hunter-gatherers. Some Sandawe clans claim their forefathers were responsible for the paintings, but there is no tradition relating to them amongst the Hadza. The Wa-Gogo of Dodoma make the improbable claim the paintings were done by the Portuguese!

Whoever the artists were, their decimation was relatively recent. It could be linked to the Maasai invasion north of Kondoa 300 years ago. This caused displacement of the local Bantu-speaking people, and may have had a knock-on effect in Kondoa.

Before you visit the paintings, try to get hold of the National Museums of Tanzania Occasional Paper No. 5, a booklet by Fidelis Masao called *The Rock Art of Kondoa and Singada*. I picked up a copy for $1 at the National Museum in Dar es Salaam.

## Getting there and away

Several accessible and highly-rated sites are near the village of Kolo on the Arusha-Dodoma road. The Antiquities Department in Kolo can organise a guide. The paintings are about 10km from the main road. There is no accommodation in Kolo, so a tent would be useful. There are guesthouses in Kondoa and Babati, 25km south and 80km north of Kolo respectively. Some Arusha-based companies will include Kondoa in a safari itinerary and Let's Go Travel can organise tours specifically to see the rock paintings. The paintings could then be visited as a full day trip from Tarangire.

WESTERN TANZANIA

Chapter Nine

# Western Tanzania

## INTRODUCTION

This chapter covers the vast western part of Tanzania. It is divided into four sections: the Central Railway, Lake Victoria, Lake Tanganyika, and southwest Tanzania.

With international ferry services to Uganda, Burundi and Zambia on its lakes, both of which are also linked to the coast by the central railway line, it is not surprising that large numbers of overland travellers pass through western Tanzania. What is surprising is how few bother to explore it. The region is also rarely visited by short-stay visitors, largely because of the distances involved, and so it is a great destination for travellers with a sense of adventure and few time restrictions.

Africa's largest lakes, Victoria and Tanganyika, dominate western Tanzania. They are totally dissimilar in character. Victoria is vast and amorphous, shallow, muddy and, for the most part, scenically indifferent. The 675km-long Tanganyika is deep and narrow, with a green mountainous shore and crystal clear water. There is good transport on both lakes and plenty of opportunity for imaginative travellers to get well away from the usual tourist beat.

There are four national parks in western Tanzania: Katavi, Gombe Stream, Mahale Mountains, and Rubondo Island. Gombe Stream is well-known for its chimpanzees and for the work done there by Jane Goodall, but the other three are remote and little-visited. All are reasonably accessible, however, provided you are not in a rush and are prepared to rough it a bit.

### Climate

Western Tanzania is relatively flat and low-lying. Rain falls between November and May. The vast central plateau between Dodoma and Tabora is hot and dry, while the Lake Tanganyika area is hot and humid and supports extensive areas of lowland forest. The Lake Victoria region is more temperate, but can be humid.

## Getting around

Main access to the area is via the central railway. This runs from Dar
es Salaam to Tabora before branching to Mwanza, Kigoma or Mpanda;
see *Rail* in Chapter Three for schedules.

A second important link is the Lake Tanganyika steamer, which does
a weekly run between Mpulungu (Zambia), Kigoma and Bujumbura
(Burundi). Boats on Lake Victoria link Mwanza to Port Bell (Uganda)
and various Tanzanian ports. Details of lake ferries are given under
the relevant lake later in the chapter.

Roads are generally in poor condition, and best avoided. I met
someone who took 48 hours to travel between Mwanza and Tabora by
bus. (Geert Clauwert, who drove from Arusha to Mwanza via Singida
and Tabora in July 1996, confirms that this road is still in appalling
condition, though a new asphalt highway between Mwanza and Tabora
is under construction – due for completion in the year 2002.) There
are exceptions: the Mwanza-Musoma road is tarred and for the most
part in good condition, and the road connecting Mpanda to Mbeya via
Sumbawanga, though not surfaced, is in reasonable condition – and
the only direct way of getting between these towns.

# THE CENTRAL RAILWAY

The 1,238km railway line between Dar es Salaam and Kigoma was
constructed by the Germans between 1905 and 1914. It follows the
old slave caravan route through Dodoma and Tabora, the same route
used by Burton and Speke in their search for the source of the Nile.
The British-built Tabora-Mwanza line was completed in 1928.

The central line is the only sane alternative to flying between the
coast and western Tanzania, and it gives travellers a rare opportunity
to see central Tanzania in something approaching comfort. Between
Dodoma and Tabora, the line passes through the most barren scenery in
the country, a seemingly endless drought-prone plain of baked red sand
and sparse woodland. It stops at several small villages, the livelihood
of which evidently revolves around selling food to train passengers.

The scenery becomes more lush as you approach Kigoma. It is worth
waking early to see the patches of indigenous forest, swamp and dense
miombo woodland along the line. Between Tabora and Mwanza the
scenery remains arid until the approach to Lake Victoria, where strange
granite formations break the monotony.

The most important towns along the line, Tabora and Dodoma, are
covered below. See *Rail* in Chapter Three for schedules.

## Dodoma

Dodoma is now the official capital of Tanzania, displacing Dar es
Salaam. it was an important village on the 19th century caravan route.

When the railway reached it, the Germans built a station and administration centre, and planned to make it the capital of German East Africa. During the war the area suffered two famines, killing over 30,000 people, and these plans were shelved.

Dodoma grew steadily between the wars. It was a staging post on the Cape to Cairo flights of the 1930s. Its position on the railway and Trans-Tanzania road before the Iringa-Morogoro stretch was built in the 1950s made it a major internal crossroad.

Whatever its past and future claims to importance, Dodoma in its present incarnation is unremittingly smalltown in atmosphere, and one of the few places in Tanzania where I sensed a slight undercurrent of hostility to *wazungu*. You'd be unlikely to come here from choice, and if for some reason you do wash adrift in Dodoma, it won't be long before you think about moving on.

## Getting there and away

Dodoma is strategically positioned in the centre of Tanzania, a consequence of which is that many travellers are tempted to cut between other parts of the country through Dodoma, based solely on the information contained on a map. It is emphatically worth stressing that almost any plan which involves bussing through Dodoma should be nipped in the bud – the main roads south to Iringa and north to Arusha are in appalling condition and the latter in particular is among the most gruelling bus trips in Tanzania, taking up to 18 hours. If you insist on trying these routes, buses between Dodoma and Iringa and Dodoma and Arusha leave in either direction in the early morning – you're advised to book a seat an afternoon in advance and to check the exact time of departure bearing in mind you'll almost certainly be quoted Swahili time.

The 350km road between Dar es Salaam and Dodoma is surfaced in its entirety. A fairly steady stream of buses runs between the current and future capitals, generally leaving before midday and taking around seven to eight hours. You can also pick up buses between Dar es Salaam and Dodoma at Morogoro.

Most travellers who pass through Dodoma are on one of the trains crossing between Dar es Salaam and Kigoma or Mwanza. If you feel an overwhelming need to take a more lingering look at Dodoma, or you simply want to cut the two-night train trip by one night, then (coming from the west) there's nothing stopping you from buying a ticket as far as Dodoma, spending the night there and bussing on to Dar es Salaam the next day. Coming in the opposite direction, it's possible to buy a ticket out of Dodoma from the railway station in Dar es Salaam. Westbound trains pass through Dodoma between 08.00 and 10.00 the morning after they leave Dar es Salaam.

## Where to stay/eat

The **Dodoma Hotel** (tel: (061) 20451), formerly run by TRC but now in private hands, is an attractively designed building directly opposite the railway station. Rooms have dropped considerably in price since 1992, and they are now excellent value at $13/17 s/c single/double. This is also the best place to eat in Dodoma, at least if your culinary demands stretch much beyond *ugali* or rice and slop. The restaurant serves good, sensibly-priced meals, for instance steak and chips for $4, as well as a three-course set menu for $7. There is live music in the bar on some nights.

The **Kilimanjaro Villa** is probably the most attractive of the cheaper options, in a leafy suburban property about 500m from the railway station. Large self-contained rooms cost $5/7 and rooms using communal facilities cost $4/5.

The **CCT Hostel** is a church-run place about 300m from the railway station next to a large domed church. A variety of rooms are available, for between $5 and $7. It's a very clean and reasonably pleasant place to stay, and food is available, though alcoholic drinks are banned from the premises.

Otherwise, there are at least ten basic resthouses clustered around the market and bus station. It's difficult to make any specific recommendations – for starters, half of them are likely to be full on any given day – but you should have no problem finding a room for around $2. Most places have nets and communal showers – I'd tend to pass over a room that doesn't.

# Tabora

This hot, dusty town is where the railway lines to Kigoma, Mwanza and Mpanda meet. If you travel around western Tanzania, you are likely to spend a day in Tabora at some point, and may even have to spend a night. Tabora is a friendly place, and quite attractive with its shady roads lined with mango and flame trees.

## History

Tabora is the home of the Nyamwezi, Tanzania's second-largest tribe. In the mid-19th century, under the leadership of Mirambo, they controlled the area between Tabora and Lakes Tanganyika, Rukwa and Victoria. They were actively involved in the slave trade and provided many porters for the central caravan route.

Mirambo, a natural diplomat, kept good relations with Arab traders and European visitors. After his death in 1884, his successor clashed with the Germans, who captured Tabora in 1893. The large fort overlooking the town dates from this period.

The 19th century Arab slave-trading post, Kazeh, was a few kilometres from Tabora. Burton and Speke stopped there on their way to becoming the first Europeans to see Lake Tanganyika. In 1872, between his famous meeting with Stanley at Ujiji and his final, fatal expedition to Lake Benguela, Livingstone stayed in Kazeh for five months waiting for supplies from the coast. His restored house is now a museum.

## Getting there and away

Tabora is an important railway junction; most people who spend time there do so to make a train connection. Buses run between Tabora and most parts of western Tanzania, but they are not a pleasant option. The twice-weekly bus service between Tabora and Mbeya could be useful to travellers. It takes at least 20 hours.

## Where to stay/eat

The best option for an upmarket hotel is probably the **Wilca Hotel** on Boma Road. I don't have current prices but you shouldn't be looking at more than $10 for a self-contained double. The more central **Golden Eagle Hotel** is similar in price and standard. Both hotels serve reasonable meals.

TABORA  (sketch map)

(Hн = cheap Guest Houses)

The **Furaha School for the Blind** (Shule ya Furaha) has acceptable doubles for $4. Also recommended is the **Pentecostal Church Hostel** on Lumumba Road.

The main cluster of guesthouses is along School Road, and there are also a few, generally more scruffy, rest houses near the bus station and near the Wilca Hotel, with rooms for around $2-3. Most of these places are full most of the time, so at the bottom end of the price range it's not so much a case of which place is the best but of taking a room wherever you find one. The **Vatican** and **Morovian Guest Houses** have been recommended.

### Excursions
**Livingstone's House** This museum 6km out of town holds various exhibits relating to Livingstone's stay in Tabora and is worth a look if you have a day to kill. There are no buses, so you will have to negotiate a price for a round trip by taxi.

**Rungwa Game Reserve** Rungwa is an extension of the Ruaha ecosystem and protects similar animals to Ruaha National Park. It is ten hours from Tabora by bus, and there is no guarantee you will be allowed in. To get there, ask a bus to Mbeya to drop you at Rungwa village on the park boundary. At the village, speak to the head ranger for permission to walk in the park and to organise a guide. Bring a tent and food with you.

## LAKE VICTORIA

Lake Victoria, the largest lake in Africa and the second-largest freshwater lake in the world, is split between Uganda, Kenya and Tanzania, with the lion's share in Tanzania. The lake lies in an elevated basin between the major forks of the Great Rift Valley, and, unlike Lake Tanganyika, it is shallow – only 70m deep on average – and its muddy water is plagued with bilharzia. The most important Tanzanian ports are Mwanza, Musoma and Bukoba.

Most of the people who live around Lake Victoria are fishermen by tradition. The lake's future as a fishery is far from assured. In 1956, Nile perch were introduced to it in order to increase its food yield. These voracious fish have preyed on the cichlid species which naturally occur in the lake. Most Lake Victoria endemics are now extinct or heading that way.

Perch are fished through necessity, but as they are too large to roast on a fire and too fatty to sun-dry, they do not meet local needs. As the number of algae-eating endemics has dropped, the lake's algae level has risen. This is a type of environmental change that perch are known to be sensitive to. Worse still, perch cannibalise their own young when

other prey runs out. There is concern that Lake Victoria will become a vast expanse of dead water, leaving a huge gap in the subsistence of lake shore villages and the economy of towns such as Mwanza.

## Lake Victoria Ferries

The Tanzania Railway Corporation (TRC) runs an excellent network of ferry services out of Mwanza, with international routings to Port Bell in Uganda and Kisumu in Kenya, as well as internal services to Bukoba, Nyamirembe, Nkome and Ukerewe Island. Most of the ferries are in unexpectedly good condition, with first and second class cabins offering a level of comfort matched in East Africa only by the train between Nairobi and Mombasa in Kenya. The restaurants serve good, inexpensive meals and chilled beers and sodas. Though first or second class are definitely preferable if you can afford it, there is no reason why you cannot travel third class – the ferries are not particularly crowded and, unlike on the trains, theft is reportedly not a major cause for concern.

Fares and timetables for individual routings follow below. In addition to these fares, a port tax of US$5 must be paid in hard currency upon leaving any Tanzanian port. On international services, you may be required to show a vaccination certificate and, if required, a visa for the country you intend to enter.

Timetables shown below were accurate for February 1996, and in general differ little from the timetables as of 1992, but nevertheless you should be prepared for the occasional timetable change, especially if further ferries are diverted from internal routings to cover international ones.

**Mwanza – Port Bell (Uganda)** This direct overnight service runs twice a week in each direction and it takes 15 hours. The *MV Bukoba* leaves Mwanza on Sunday and Tuesday at 16.00, and it leaves Port Bell on Monday and Wednesday at 18.00. Leaving from Mwanza, there are officially two fare scales: residents pay the Tanzanian shilling equivalent of $20/16/12 for first/second/third class, and non-residents pay $35/25/20 in hard currency. In practice, however, it seems that travellers can pay the lower rate in local currency. Leaving from Port Bell, where the residents' fare would work out at the equivalent of $22/18/14 in Ugandan shillings, foreigners are invariably required to pay the higher non-residents' rate.

**Mwanza – Kisumu (Kenya)** The *MV Bukoba* started doing this run once a week as of January 1996, and the frequency may well increase if the service proves to be popular. At present, the ferry leaves Mwanza at 15.00 on Thursday and it leaves Kisumu at 18.00 on Friday, taking

20 hours in either direction. As with the ferry to Uganda, there are two rates: residents pay the equivalent of $24/19/12 in local currency and non-residents pay $45/30/25 in hard currency. As this is a new service, I've not met anybody who has used it, but again it seems likely you'd be able to pay local rates leaving from Mwanza but have to pay the higher rate leaving from Kisumu.

**Mwanza – Bukoba** There is one overnight ferry in each direction five days a week, with duties split between *MV Serengeti* and the larger *MV Victoria*. Ferries leave Mwanza at 21.00 or 22.00 every day except Wednesday and Friday, and they leave Bukoba at a similar time every day except Thursday and Saturday. The trip takes around 12 hours. Fares are $11/7/5 first/second(sitting)/third on *MV Serengeti* and $14/10/8/5 first/second/second(sitting)/third on *MV Victoria*.

**Mwanza – Nyamirembe** *MV Clarius* leaves Mwanza at 08.00 on Monday and arrives in Nyamirembe at 18.00 the same day. The return

---

## STOP PRESS

In May 1996, the *MV Bukoba*, the boat which normally covers international routes on Lake Victoria, capsized outside Mwanza after sailing overnight from Bukoba while the *MV Victoria was* in dry dock. Fewer than 120 survivors were found by rescue teams, and it has been estimated that as many as 1,000 passengers drowned, most of them trapped in the boat.

So soon after a tragedy on this scale, it is difficult to find the will to discuss its practical implications for travellers. But nor can I responsibly ignore the questions raised by the disaster. Regarding international ferry services, I think it's safe to assume that another boat will take these over from the *Bukoba*, but the bigger question in many travellers' heads will be whether the disaster was a one-off freak or an inevitable result of shoddy safety practices – in other words, is it likely to happen again?

This is a question that's difficult to answer until such time as official investigations are complete. Initial reports suggest that the *Bukoba* was carrying twice its legal capacity of 450 passengers when it sank, and they have thus cited overloading as the most probably cause of the accident. If this is the case, then a repeat incident is a real possibility unless more rigid ticketing practices are enforced. However, overloading alone doesn't explain why the boat capsized without warning, in calm weather, and after it had already been on the water for ten hours.

The sinking of the *Bukoba* was the first major disaster in almost 100 years of steam and motor navigation on Lake Victoria, a statistic which offers little reassurance if its cause lay in a recent decline in maintenance, training or ticketing practices. On the other hand, it makes it difficult to quantify whether using a ferry on Lake Victoria is any more or less dangerous than road travel, which claims thousands of lives in East Africa every year.

trip leaves Nyamirembe at 08.00 Tuesday and arrives in Mwanza at 18.00 the same day. The fare is $6 second class sitting or $4 third class.

**Mwanza – Nkome** *MV Clarius* leaves Mwanza at 08.00 on Wednesday and Saturday and arrives at Nkome Island at 18.00. In the opposite direction, the boat leaves Nkome at 08.00 Thursday and Sunday and arrives at Mwanza at 18.00. The fare is $4 second class sitting and $3 third class. Ferries stop at Mchangani and Lugata on Kome Island, and at Lushamba and Itabagumba.

**Mwanza – Nansio (Ukerewe Island)** There is at least one ferry in each direction daily, taking three hours and costing $3 second class sitting or $2 third class. They usually leave Mwanza at 08.00 and Nansio at 13.30, but the schedule varies slightly from day to day so check it an afternoon in advance.

## Mwanza
According to the 1988 census Mwanza is the second largest town in Tanzania. It is a relaxed place, which, after years of stagnation, seems to have picked up in ecomonic terms far more quickly than most Tanzanian towns. Mwanza has a reasonably cosmopolitan flavour; it has a large Indian population, good links with Kenya and Uganda, and is a focus for overland travellers and expats. Scenically, Mwanza is notable for the bizarre granite outcrops which surround it, the best known of which is the precariously perched Bismarck Rock at the harbour entrance.

### Getting there and away
Relatively few fly-in tourists to Tanzania visit Mwanza, as it is rather removed from the main tourist centres of the northern and coastal districts. The town is, however, a major transport hub for people travelling more widely in East Africa, boasting rail connections to the coast and to Lake Tanganyika, and direct ferry services across Lake Victoria to Kenya and Uganda.

Trains between Mwanza and Dar es Salaam on the coast run four days a week in each direction, stopping at Tabora where you can disembark to connect with rail services to Kigoma on Lake Tanganyika. See *Rail* in Chapter Three for timetables and fares. Details of ferry services to Kenya, Uganda and elsewhere on Lake Victoria are under *Lake Victoria Ferries* earlier in this chapter.

Buses connect Mwanza to several other parts of the country, but the only routes where these services are quick and reliable are along the eastern shore of the lake, to Musoma and Kisumu in Kenya. Roads

which follow the lake shore west of Mwanza are in poor condition as far as Bukoba, so if you're heading this way catch the ferry to Bukoba and use road transport from there. I would advise strongly against catching buses headed towards Kigoma, Tabora, Dodoma or Dar es Salaam, as the roads are in terrible condition – wait for a train.

A fair number of travellers arrive in Mwanza wanting to cross directly to Arusha. This is a problematic route, and there is no quick and cheap way of doing it. If time is a greater factor than money, the best thing to do is to go directly across the Serengeti. At least three buses do this trip every week, as do a number of private Landrovers which carry passengers – ask about a seat in advance at the bus station in Mwanza or Arusha. The problem with this route is that you cross two conservation areas and so must pay $40 in park entrance fees overland above the bus fare. This is a waste of money if you already plan to go on safari. On the other hand, for those who can't afford to do a safari proper, it actually makes for a cheap way of seeing the Serengeti – the road passes right through the heart of the reserve and game viewing will be excellent for the six months of the year when animals are concentrated in the southern part of the Serengeti ecosystem. Landrover drivers (but not bus drivers) are reportedly happy to stop for the occasional photograph!

The cheap and nasty way of getting between Mwanza and Arusha is to use a bus which crosses south of the Serengeti through Singida and Shinyanga. This is a hellish ride, taking at least 36 hours and sometimes as long as three days, through dry, unattractive country where stops are dictated by breakdowns and flat tyres as much as any other factor. Looking on the bright side, there is nothing much along the way to spend your money on – just take plenty of food and water with you.

Otherwise, you're pretty much restricted to heading towards Dar es Salaam by train and bussing to Arusha from there (you could, of course, catch a train as far as Dodoma and then bus through to Arusha, but this involves another unappetising bus trip). This could be a sensible option under some circumstances (basically if you want to visit Dar es Salaam or Zanzibar en route to Arusha), but otherwise it seems rather pointless as it probably means four days travelling and you'll end up spending as much money as you would have crossing the Serengeti in a day.

A final, arguably rather convoluted option would be to cross via Kenya: buses to Kisumu take ten hours, then you could bus or take the overnight train to Nairobi, and finally a minibus through to Namanga border post. This route is only worth considering if it doesn't require additional visa expenses (which will depend on your nationality), but by using the train to Nairobi you could conceivably get through in less then 36 hours, and it should work out to be a lot cheaper than crossing the Serengeti.

MWANZA

KEY TO ACCOMMODATION

1 TUMAINI
2 BARIADI
3 KISHAMAPANDA
4 GEITA
5 DELUX
6 NEW MWANZA
7 PAMBA HOSTEL
8 SENGERENA
9 MLANGOWA MUTINDI
10 MAJAKUNA
11 IKO
12 LAKE
13 SHINYANGA
14 MASWA
15 NEW GARDENIA
16 IMPALA
17 NYANGUGE
18 BUNGASOLWE
19 ZIMBABWE
20 VICTORIA ANNEXE
21 VICTORIA
22 NSIMO
23 TILAPIA

# Where to stay
## Upper range
The **Hotel Tilapia** (PO Box 82 or 190, Mwanza, tel: (068) 42109/50517, fax: 50141) is Mwanza's one truly upmarket hotel: a relatively new private development on the Lake Victoria shore near the jetty for Saa Nane Island. Large, comfortable, air-conditioned rooms are very reasonably priced at $60/double or $90/suite ($42 and $60 respectively for residents), and facilities include a swimming pool, a well-regarded restaurant, and an attractive wooden bar and patio overlooking the lake and Saa Nane.

In the town centre, the government-owned **New Mwanza Hotel** (PO Box 25, tel: (068) 3202) cannot compete with the Tilapia in terms of facilities or setting, and it could certainly do with a facelift, but it's convenient enough and not bad value at $40 for an air-conditioned double.

## Moderate
The **Lake Hotel** (PO Box 910, tel: (068) 3263), conveniently situated between the railway station and town centre, is an excellent hotel in this range. The large, nicely furnished and well maintained rooms wouldn't look out of place in a government hotel, and they are all self-contained with hot water and mosquito nets. Rooms cost $12/14/16 single/twin/double, including a poor breakfast. The hotel's restaurant has apparently closed for good, but the outdoor bar remains one of the better drinking holes in Mwanza.

The **Delux Hotel** is another sensibly priced place, a little run down when compared to the Lake Hotel, but correspondingly cheaper at $8/10 self-contained single/double. At one time it used to be difficult to find a vacant room after midday, but there were rooms available whenever I asked on my most recent visit to Mwanza. There is a good restaurant, two bars, and a disco attached, the latter generating a level of noise that may become annoying if you've no intention of joining in.

The **Iko Hotel** (PO Box 2469, tel: (068) 40900) is a pleasant little place, on a rocky hill overlooking the lake near the golf course and Hotel Tilapia. Open less than a year when I visited in February 1996, the rooms already showed some signs of wear, but for the time being they are pretty good value at US$20 for a comfortable double. There is a restaurant and bar attached, and the surrounding suburban lanes make for attractive rambling and birding.

The **Tema Hotel**, 5km out of town on the Shinyanga Road, has acceptable self-contained doubles for $14.

## Budget
There is no shortage of affordable accommodation in Mwanza, with perhaps 20 guesthouses dotted around the city centre.

A place which currently stands out is the **Panda Hostel** – once rather scruffy, it has recently been bought by the Tema Hotels Group (who do all the catering on trains and ferries in Tanzania). The rooms have received a much needed coat of paint, and they seem very good value at $4/6 self-contained single/double with mosquito net, while the communal showers no longer leave anything to be desired. There's a restaurant on the ground floor (if you've already eaten on a train or ferry, you know what to expect) and a rooftop bar where you can get cold beers and sodas.

Another reliable place is the **Kishamapanda Guest House**, opposite the Delux, which has bright rooms for $4/5 single/double and self-contained doubles for $6. As with the Delux, it used to be practically impossible to find a vacant room here, but this seems no longer to be a problem.

Near the bus station, the **Victoria Hotel** is looking ever more run down, but the rooms are adequately clean, have mosquito nets and fans (the latter not working when I last checked) and seem fair value at $4/5 single/double. Altogether better are the large self-contained rooms for $6/8 in the adjoining **Victoria Hotel Annexe**.

In 1992, the then newly built **Nsembo Hotel** had some superficial pretensions to superiority, though it was already showing signs of rapid wear and tear, and the toilets were overrun with cockroaches. Come 1996, the hotel is looking very tired, the staff remain as unfriendly as ever, but the rooms seem worth a try at $6 for a self-contained double.

Most of the other places marked on the map are standard guesthouses with rooms in the $3-5 range. The best of a fairly ordinary bunch are probably the **Zimbabwe**, **Tumaini**, **Nyanguge** and **Shinyanga Guesthouses**. The first in particular is popular with travellers and conveniently close to the bus station, though a little difficult to find – just keep asking directions.

## Camping

The **New Blue Sky Campsite**, formerly a discotheque (the owner says he's too old for loud music), had only just opened up when I was in town. At the time of writing, facilities are limited to bucket showers, but the owner hopes to install proper ablution facilities and a restaurant by the end of 1996. The property is in a lovely spot on the shore of Lake Victoria, about halfway between the town centre and Hotel Tilapia, and if properly developed it could be a real gem (though at this stage it could as easily be that the whole enterprise has fallen apart by the time this book goes to print). Camping costs $3pp.

## Where to eat

The **Sizzler Restaurant**, opposite the New Mwanza Hotel, is the newest restaurant in the town centre. In my estimation, it is also the best. It serves a variety of Indian dishes for around $5, supplemented by a few western and

Chinese items. In the evenings, an outdoor barbecue does mishkaki, chicken tikka and fresh chapatis and roti bread. The restaurant is open for lunch and dinner every day except Thursday.

The food at the **New Mwanza Hotel** is similarly priced, and there's nothing wrong with it, but it's rather ordinary by comparison.

The **Sitar Restaurant** has been around a while now, and it remains fairly popular with travellers, though last time I ate there I thought the food looked and tasted as if it had been cooked in Brylcream. What feedback I've heard since tends to confirm this is still the case.

For sheer value for money, you won't beat the restaurant on the ground floor of the **Delux Hotel**, where massive portions of a variety of Asian and African dishes cost between $2 and $3.

Similar in price, but not nearly as good, the **Tivoli Restaurant, Fourways Restaurant**, and the restaurant on the ground floor of the **Panda Hostel** are all worth a try if you're in town long enough to want a change of scene.

**Salma Cone** serves great ice-cream sundaes and fresh popcorn at reasonable prices.

Fresh brown bread can be bought at Pizzeria Mgahawa near the New Mwanza Hotel.

## Excursions
### Saa Nane Island
This small, rocky island in Lake Victoria has been set aside as a game reserve and zoo. On both accounts it is a bit of a washout; re-introduced buck wander around aimlessly and several listless predators are confined in small cages, as is a decidedly pissed-off looking chimpanzee.

All this detracts from the island's real attraction, the small animals which inhabit it naturally. It is crawling with lizards such as the gaudily coloured rock agama. We also saw a few water monitors, the largest African lizard, crash gracelessly through the undergrowth. Bird life is profuse. Fish eagle, pied kingfisher and white-bellied cormorant are common near the lake shore. Twitchers will have little difficulty spotting such localised species as swamp flycatcher, yellow-throated leaflove, grey kestrel and slender-billed weaver. Rock hyrax are the most visible mammal.

The motorboat to Saa Nane leaves from a jetty 15 minutes' walk from Mwanza town centre. It departs at 11.00, 13.00 and 15.00 and 1700, and returns an hour later. You can spend as long as you like on the island for an admission fee of $1. At present, you may not stay overnight.

## Sukoma Museum

Tanzania's largest tribe, the Sukoma, live in and around Mwanza. The Sukoma Museum, 20km out of town, displays exhibits relating to their lifestyle. Try to visit it on a Saturday, when the Sukoma Snake Dance is performed in tandem with a live python. If you visit the museum on weekdays it may well be deserted. You can camp for $2 per person, but facilities are limited to running water and one toilet.

The Sukoma Museum is a short walk from Kissesa on the Mwanza-Musoma road. Any bus to Musoma can drop you off there.

## Ukerewe Island

Ukerewe Island is two to three hours from Mwanza by ferry; see *Lake Victoria Ferries* for details. The island's largest town, Nansio, is also the ferry terminal. The round trip to Nansio is a good way to see some of Africa's largest lake.

Nansio is a scruffy little town. You will have an hour to wander around while you wait to re-embark the ferry, which is more than adequate. The island itself is very pretty, however, and the sandy beaches west of Nansio are said to be bilharzia-free. If you have a couple of days spare in the Mwanza area, you could do worse than spend them exploring Ukerewe using Nansio as a base.

The **Gullu Beach Hotel** (PO Box 308 Nansio, tel: (068) 50764, fax: (068) 41726) lies on the lake shore about 500m from Nansio Port. A variety of rooms are available: singles, doubles and triples using communal showers cost $5/7/10 for residents and $8/13/17 for non-residents, while self-contained doubles cost $10 for residents and $16 for non-residents. All rooms have mosquito nets and rates include breakfast. Camping costs $3pp resident or $6pp non-resident. There is a restaurant and bar. Fishing boat hire costs $150 per day.

If this is too expensive, there are several local guesthouses in Nansio, of which the **Panda Hostel** and **Island Inn** are about the best. The Island Inn has a restaurant.

There are occasional vehicles between Nansio and Bunda on the main Mwanza-Musoma road.

## Kome and Maisome Islands

Adventurous travellers may be intrigued by these two large islands on Lake Victoria, both of which can be reached by ferry from Mwanza. According to maps, both islands have substantial areas of forest; it seems likely they will harbour similar animal species to those which occur naturally on Rubondo Island National Park. It's less likely there will be any formal accommodation; assume you'll need a tent. A survey map might also be handy. Depending on who you speak to, the staff at the ferry office in Mwanza can be very helpful with information about places where ferries stop.

Ferries from Mwanza to Nyamirembe/Nkome stop at both islands on Monday, Wednesday and Thursday; ferries returning to Mwanza stop at both islands on Tuesday, Thursday and Friday (see *Lake Victoria Ferries* for details).

## Bunda

Bunda, the largest town on the Mwanza-Musoma road, is a route focus of sorts. It is where Arusha-based safari companies drop off passengers heading to Mwanza, and the best place to catch a pick-up to Ukerewe Island.

The scenic road between Mwanza and Bunda is in good condition. It passes first through dry, flat country dotted with small koppies and Sukoma homesteads and offers regular glimpses of Lake Victoria. Before reaching Bunda it skirts the Serengeti; at the right time of year there is some wildlife to be seen.

Bunda is no more than moderately intriguing. More substantial than maps suggest, it has a scenic position at the foot of a range of steep granite hills. If you have the inclination to climb one of these, you would have a superb vantage point over Lake Victoria and the Serengeti plains.

There are several guesthouses and *hotelis* in Bunda. Rooms cost less than $2.

## Musoma

Musoma lies on a pretty part of the Lake Victoria shore, but apart from strolling around town or lazing at the Silver Sands Inn, there is little to do there. Travellers coming from Kisumu (Kenya) used to stop in Musoma to pick up a ferry to Mwanza, but since the Musoma-Mwanza road was re-surfaced the ferry service has been discontinued. Musoma now sees few tourists.

### Where to stay/eat

The colonial-style **Railway Hotel** lies on the lake shore about 3km from the town centre. In the town centre, the **Orange Tree Hotel** is clean, has a bar and restaurant, and is a bit cheaper.

The best budget hotel is **Silver Sands Inn**, overlooking the lake 1km from the town centre. Meals are served on request and soft drinks are available. The **Mennonite Centre** is clean, friendly and popular with travellers, and it has a canteen, but it is often full.

There are several guesthouses. **Butata Lodge** is basic, but it is clean and friendly, and rooms have mosquito nets. The livelier **Banana Bar Lodge** has a bar, a restaurant, and video shows in the evening; not the place to stay if you want an early night, but fun if you don't.

The restaurant at the **Orange Tree Hotel** is fair. **SK Restaurant** serves Western and Indian meals. Several bars and *hotelis* line Mukendo Road; the **Banana Bar** and **Embassy Lodge** look reasonable.

## Rubondo Island National Park

This national park protects the 240km² Rubondo Island. The predominant vegetation type is rainforest, but there are also patches of grassland and papyrus swamp. Several large mammal species are present: sitatunga, bushbuck, vervet monkey and hippopotamus are indigenous, elephant, chimpanzee, roan antelope and black rhino have been introduced. Rubondo is rich in forest- and water-associated birds.

Game viewing is done either on foot or from a boat, which makes the island attractive to budget travellers. A round trip from Mwanza takes the best part of a week, so few people visit it. If you do, you could well have it to yourself.

An entrance fee of $15 per 24-hour period must be paid in hard currency.

### Getting there

If you can afford it, the simplest way to get to Rubondo is to charter a flight from Dar es Salaam or Arusha.

Coming by boat or by road, the normal base for reaching Rubondo is Nyamirembe Port. Ferries from Mwanza to Nyamirembe run twice a week; see *Lake Victoria Ferries* for details. Getting to Nyamirembe by road is only feasible with your own 4x4. There is no public transport beyond Geita. Some Arusha-based safari companies will include Rubondo in a safari itinerary.

At Nyamirembe, you will have to organise a boat across to the island. The best place to do this is at the Fishery Department. The ride across takes about two hours.

If you are using the ferries, you will spend four nights in the area. There are guesthouses in Nyamirembe, so you could spend a couple of nights there to save on park fees. Exploring the roads around Nyamirembe could well pay dividends. The port borders Biharamulo Game Reserve, which provides sanctuary for 30 large mammal species including elephant, zebra, buffalo and hippopotamus. Biharamulo is the northern extreme of the miombo woodland belt. Two antelope species – roan and common reedbuck – also reach the northernmost extent of their range there.

## Where to stay
The basic camp on the island has bandas and a campsite. Both cost $10 per person. All food should be brought from Mwanza.

# Bukoba
This quiet, attractive port is situated on green hills which roll down to the Lake Victoria shore. It is the centre of a thriving coffee industry, but otherwise has a distinct air of decline. There are a number of impressive Indian-style buildings in the town centre, but most are in poor condition. Bukoba is said to have been founded by the Emin Pasha in 1890.

There is no sightseeing in Bukoba, but it is an agreeable place. We arrived after two months in Uganda, and enjoyed the town simply for the relaxed air that is so typical of Tanzania. To wander around a town and not have *Mzungu!* yelled at us from every direction was indescribably pleasant.

If you have time to kill, take a walk along the marshy area between the town and the lake. A surprisingly large variety of water birds can be seen.

## Getting there and away
Travellers who visit Bukoba generally do so on their way to or from Uganda. Details of this route are in Chapter Three. Details of ferries between Bukoba and Mwanza are given under *Lake Victoria Ferries* in this chapter. Occasional buses connect Bukoba to Mwanza and Kigoma. Personally, I think you would be crazy to contemplate using them.

Lake Victoria

Lake [H]

Ferry (2 km) ⟶

Coffee Tree [H]

Kahawa Guest House

[H]

Cathedral ◆

SOKOINE

JAMHURI

MKT

[H] Mayday

MOSQUE

◆ Mosque
BOOK SHOP ■

[✉]

[H]

Lutheran Youth Hostel

New Banana [H]

[H] Arusha

Rwazibi [H]

KASHOZI

[£$]

[Ⓥ]TWR

[H]

Guest House

[H] Victoria

KENYA

◆ Lutheran Church

Urafiki Bar

Ⓑ

[H] New Rombo

(Uganda) ⟶

**BUKOBA**

## Where to stay

In the town centre, the most upmarket accommodation – or so they say – is to be found at the **New Banana Hotel**, which has dingy self-contained doubles without running water for $10. Altogether more alluring are the meals, notably the excellent whole tilapia and chips for $2.

On the lake shore, out towards the ferry jetty, the **Lake Hotel** has a faded colonial charm and a scenic position, though the rooms are nothing special and a bit overpriced at $12/16 self-contained single/double. You can camp in the grounds for $3pp.

The nearby **Coffee Tree Hotel** is similar in price, but lacks character.

Much better value than any of the above is the **Rwabizi Hotel**, with oddly-shaped but comfortable and for once brightly painted self-contained doubles for $8 and suites for $12.

The indisputable pick of the cheaper accommodation is the **Lutheran Youth Hostel**, where clean, secure four-bed dormitories and double rooms cost under $2 per person. Excellent value for money. The nearby **Catholic Youth Centre** has self-contained rooms for $7/8 single/double, and good business facilities including a fax machine, computer and secretarial services.

If you prefer not to stay in an institution, the **Kahawa Guest House** is the best of the more basic places, followed by the **Mayday Hotel** and then a string of rather dismal also-rans.

# LAKE TANGANYIKA

Africa's deepest and second-largest lake is 675km long, an average of 50km wide, over 1,400m deep, and holds a volume of water seven times greater than that of Lake Victoria. It follows the western arm of the rift valley and is very attractive, with green, hilly shores and crystal clear water.

Due to its age and isolation, Lake Tanganyika is one of the richest aqueous habitats in the world. It supports at least 250 fish species, of which 200 are cichlids, most of them endemic. The most important fish economically is the *dagaa*, a plankton-eater which lives in large shoals. It is sun-dried on the lake shore for sale throughout western Tanzania.

## Lake Tanganyika Ferries

The legendary *MV Liemba*, originally called the *Graf Van Goetzen*, was transported to Kigoma by rail and assembled during World War I. Before its maiden voyage, the Germans sank it to prevent it from falling into British hands. The boat was salvaged and re-named in 1924 and has steamed up and down the lake almost continually since then. The oft-repeated story that *Liemba* was used in the filming of *The African Queen* is to the best of my knowledge a myth.

*Liemba* does a round trip every week between Kigoma, Bujumbura (Burundi) and Mpulungu (Zambia). It departs from Kigoma at 16.00 Wednesday and arrives in Mpulungu at 10.00 Friday. It then turns back at 16.00 Friday and arrives in Kigoma at 10.00 Sunday. It leaves Kigoma at 16.00 Sunday and arrives in Bujumbura at 10.00 Monday. The return trip from Bujumbura departs at 16.00 Monday and arrives back in Kigoma at 10.00 Tuesday.

A second boat, *MV Umoja*, operates on the lake within Tanzania. When only one boat is running, as is often the case, it does the Bujumbura-Mpulungu run and the other service is suspended.

Tickets bought in Tanzania can be paid for in local currency. Kigoma to Mpulungu costs $22.50 first class and $18.25 second class. Both classes consist of four-bunk cabins. Tickets bought in Zambia or Burundi must be paid for in US dollars and cost double what they would in Tanzania. Both boats have a restaurant. Meals cost $1.25. A bar serves beer and sodas.

The ferry stops at lake-shore villages such as Mugambo, Ikola, Kalema and Kasanga. If you don't want to go into Zambia, Kasanga is the place to get off. There is a basic guest house and road transport from Kasanga to Sumbawanga and on to Mbeya. The ferry arrives at Kasanga in the early morning, so there is plenty of time to find a lift.

There is nowhere for ships to dock at these villages. When the ferry arrives it is greeted by a floating market selling dried fish and other foodstuffs, while passengers are ferried to and from the shore on rickety fishing boats. Viewed from the upper decks this is richly comic; if you are embarking or disembarking it is a nightmare. The hold seethes with passengers climbing over each other to get in and out; the ticket officer frantically tries to identify and extract a fare from the newcomers; at the exit, the smaller boats ram each other trying to get the best position.

If you have the inclination to explore Lake Tanganyika slowly, small boats do run between minor ports. I cannot vouch for their regularity or reliability.

Most settlements along the lake shore have no formal accommodation, so you are advised to carry a tent.

Lake Tanganyika

Ferry Booking Office

Railway H

Kigoma H  Mapindezi  Lake View  B  MCT.

Ally's Restaurant

to UJIJI

Aqua H.
&
Sunset Tours

KIGOMA          (sketch map)

# Kigoma

Kigoma, the largest town on Lake Tanganyika, was founded in 1915 when the railway line reached the lake. Kigoma is an easy-going and cosmopolitan town, built around a mango-tree-lined avenue that climbs uphill from the lake. When I last visited Kigoma it was crawling with overland trucks, travellers and African businessmen, all waiting for transport connections.

## Getting there and away

The only realistic ways to get to Kigoma are by air, rail or water. You could come by road from Mwanza, but you would measure the journey in days. For details of rail services, see *Rail* in Chapter Three. Details of the lake ferry are given above. Air Tanzania flies from Dar es Salaam to Kigoma once a week.

## Where to stay

There are two tourist hotels in Kigoma, both on the lake shore ten minutes' walk from the town centre. The newer **Aqua Hotel** has comfortable rooms and good facilities. I prefer the older, cheaper and cosier **Railway Hotel**. Two hotels in the town centre are geared to travellers. The friendly **Lake View Hotel** has clean, comfortable rooms with mosquito nets for $2/3 single/double. The similarly-priced **Kigoma Hotel** is scruffier, but just as friendly. There are several guesthouses on the main road towards Ujiji.

## Where to eat

**Ally's** serves a remarkable variety of meals for less than $1 – it also has a good snack menu and fresh bread and pastries. The **Lakeview and Kigoma Hotels** have fair restaurants. The **Railway Hotel** is more expensive, but the food is good.

# Ujuji

Most people who pass through Kigoma make a trip to Ujiji, 10km away. Said to be one of Africa's oldest market villages – whatever that means – Ujiji was a 19th century Arab trading post, and still shows Swahili influences you would not expect in this part of the country. Stanley and Livingstone met in Ujiji in 1872; it is where the famous phrase "Doctor Livingstone, I presume?" was first uttered. A plaque marks where the meeting took place; the adjoining museum displays some inept and absurdly-captioned paintings of Livingstone.

The monument to Livingstone and Stanley stands under a mango tree, and it bears a plaque which was originally set in a large obelisk; the present stone setting was built shortly after World War II. In fact, there was an earlier monument to Livingstone and Stanley, erected by

Belgium after the end of World War I, which consisted of a bland, whitewashed concrete slab covering the base of the original mango tree under which the meeting is said to have taken place. Unfortunately, this concrete eyesore caused the roots of the original tree to decay: photographs taken in 1921 and 1930 show that over the course of a decade a flourishing and thickly foliated tree had been reduced to a bare stump with only a few scraggly branches remaining. In August of 1930, the tree was finally felled, but not before the District Officer of Kigoma, Captain Grant, had the foresight to graft a new tree from the original. It is this grafted tree which now hangs over the monument, where a brass plaque donated by the Royal Geographical Society reads "Under the mango tree which then stood here Stanley met Livingstone 10th November 1871". All of which is rather poignant until you discover that Stanley's journal suggests the meeting took place near the old market, several hundred metres from the monument, and that the tree shown in the 1921 photograph was almost certainly too young to have offered any significant cover 50 years earlier. The probability is that when locals were quizzed by their German colonisers about where the famous meeting took place, they simply invented a plausible site – a scenario that will be familiar to anybody who has regularly asked for directions in Africa.

People who visit Ujiji expecting it to be a thriving, vibrant market town are invariably disappointed. These days it is no more than a large fishing village. It is quite interesting to watch the fishermen and boat builders practise their trades.

There is regular transport between Ujiji and Kigoma. Should you want to overnight in Ujiji, there is a basic guesthouse.

## Gombe Stream National Park

Gombe Stream is renowned for its chimpanzees and the research done into their behaviour by Jane Goodall. It was gazetted as a game reserve in 1943 and made a national park in 1968. Goodall arrived there in 1960 sponsored by Louis Leakey, who felt her lack of scientific training would allow her to observe chimpanzee behaviour without preconceptions. After initial difficulties trying to locate them, Goodall overcame the chimps' shyness through the combination of a banana-feeding machine and sheer persistence.

Since the late 1960s Goodall's work has achieved both popular and scientific recognition. Her painstaking studies of individual chimps and the day-to-day social behaviour of troops have been supplemented by a series of observations confronting conventional scientific wisdom. Observations which initially caused controversy – tool-making, inter-troop warfare and even cannibalism – have since been confirmed and accepted. Much of Goodall's work is described in her books *In the*

*Shadow of Man* and *Through a Window*. The study of Gombe's chimpanzees is now the longest-running study of an individual wild animal population in the world.

Gombe Stream supports a significant baboon population, the subject of research since 1967. Other common primates are vervet, blue, redtail and red colobus monkeys. Most other mammals found there are secretive or nocturnal, so are rarely seen by visitors. Over 200 bird species have been recorded.

To see the chimpanzees you will need to go on a guided walk. They are most frequently observed at a feeding station near the main camp. If they are not there, you will have to go deeper into the forest. The only part of the park where you may walk unguided is along the lake shore. The forest reaches down to the beach, so you should see plenty of birds, butterflies and primates in this area, especially towards dusk when many nocturnal animals come to drink at the lake.

Because they are genetically similar to humans, chimpanzees are susceptible to the same diseases. If you are unwell, do not visit the park. Even a cold has the potential to kill chimpanzees who may not have your immunity.

Gombe is popular and its capacity is limited. Park fees are regularly increased, presumably whenever numbers threaten to become unmanageable. At present the entrance fee is $100 per 24-hour period, and a further $30 to stay overnight. Fees must be paid in hard currency, and are likely to have increased by the time you read this. Before you head off to the park, check up-to-date fees at the Railway Hotel.

A 72-page booklet, *Gombe Stream National Park*, is the most comprehensive in the series published by Tanzania National Parks. It's an essential purchase if you plan you visit the park, and includes checklists and detailed coverage of chimpanzee behaviour. It may be difficult to buy a copy outside of Arusha.

## Getting there and away

Gombe Stream is 16km from Kigoma and can be reached by lake-taxi. These are uncovered and can become uncomfortably hot in the sun. If you have an umbrella, take it along. Lake-taxis leave from a village 3km from Kigoma at roughly 11.00. They take four hours to get to Gombe, and cost $2. From Kigoma, you can hire a taxi to take you to the village from which the lake-taxis leave. Lake-taxis returning to Kigoma pass Gombe Stream at around 05.45.

Sunset Tours (next to the Aqua Hotel) can organise day trips to Gombe on a private boat. The use of a boat for a day costs $120. For a group of three or more, this is worth thinking about, bearing in mind it will save you paying the overnight fee charged at Gombe.

## Where to stay

The camp is not far from the lake shore. Accommodation is in bandas, and there is a communal kitchen. The camp is plagued by baboons, which are likely to attack you if you carry food openly between your banda and the kitchen. You can pitch a tent on the lake shore. Again, baboons are a problem. They may knock down your tent if there is fruit in it. All food must be brought from Kigoma. Avoid bringing fruit.

# Mahale Mountains National Park

Mahale Mountains was gazetted in 1985 to protect a 1,613km² knuckle of land jutting into Lake Tanganyika. The Mahale range, the highest peak of which, Nkungwe, rises to 2,462m, is the park's dominant physical feature. The lake shore west of the mountains is very scenic. The western foothills receive an annual rainfall of 2,000mm, and are covered in lush lowland forest. The drier eastern slopes are covered in miombo woodland. At altitudes above 2,000m there is both bamboo and montane forest.

Over 700 chimpanzees live in Mahale's lowland forest. A group of 100 has been habituated and studied by Japanese researchers since 1961.

Other lowland forest species found at Mahale are similar to those found at Gombe, with the addition of typical west African species such as brush-tailed porcupine and giant forest squirrel. An endemic black-and-white colobus subspecies is found in the park's montane forests. The eastern slopes of Mahale support woodland species: elephant, lion, roan antelope, buffalo and giraffe. These often stray into the forest; lions have killed several chimps, and African hunting dogs have been seen on the beach.

Chimps are less readily seen than at Gombe Stream, but most people feel that Mahale's scenery and wilderness atmosphere make up for this. It is also a lot cheaper to visit than Gombe. All game viewing is on foot, but you may not walk without a guide. Guides can be organised when you arrive at Kasiha. If you want to hike into the mountains or to climb Nkungwe peak, arrangements should be made in advance.

An entrance fee of $20 per 24-hour period must be paid in hard currency. It is not recommended that you visit the park during the rainy season (November to April). Much of the information in the National Parks booklet *Gombe Stream National Park* will be useful to visitors to Mahale.

## Getting there and away

One of the attractions of Mahale is its remoteness. It can only be reached by plane or boat. Any tour operator in Arusha or Dar es Salaam will be able to organise a chartered plane. It is possible to charter a boat from

Above: *The buffalo is considered by many to be East Africa's most dangerous animal (NG)*

Below: *The colourful rock agama is often seen basking in the sun near tourist lodges (AVZ)*

Above left: *Lions are prolific on the plains of Serengeti. The male may spend as much as 23 hours per day sleeping (AVZ)*
Above right: *A cub awaits the reappearance of its mother with part of a kill (AVZ)*
Below: *Lioness with zebra kill. The females of the pride do most of the hunting (AVZ)*

Above: *A leopard in its favourite resting place up a tree. Though less often seen than the other big cats, they are the most widespread (AVZ)*

Below: *A cheetah and her cub. This is the fastest land animal in the world: in a short sprint it can reach 70kph (NG)*

Left: *The maribou stork is the only one of its family that is a carrion-eater, hence its unattractively bare head and neck (NG)*

Right: *The lilac-breasted roller is one of the most eye-catching birds of the Serengeti and other lightly wooded habitats (NG)*

Kigoma to Mahale. Contact Sunset Tours in Kigoma. A three-day trip will cost around $800.

The only way for budget travellers to get to and from Mahale is on the Lake Tanganyika ferry. This stops at Mugambo, the village 15km north of the park boundary, seven hours after it leaves Kigoma. On the return trip, the ferry stops at Mugambo at 04.00 and arrives at Kigoma seven hours later.

From Mugambo, most people hire a private boat to the headquarters at Kasiha. We did, however, receive a letter from someone who walked the 15km to the boundary. He says you are unlikely to get lost as the mountains are in front of you the whole way and the path is flat. You will pass through several villages, where you must exchange greetings with the village chairman, who can usually be found at the school. Unfortunately, he did not say what he did once he got to the boundary. It is another 15km from there to Kasiha.

### Where to stay
There is a guesthouse and campsite at Kasiha. Both cost $10 per person. Bring all the food you need from Kigoma. There is also a privately-run luxury tented camp in the park, which can be booked through Ngare Sero (PO Box 425 Arusha tel: (057) 3629, fax: (057) 2123). It is open between May and October.

# SOUTHWEST TANZANIA

This section follows the little-used B8 from northwestern Tanzania to the southern town of Mbeya. The B8 passes through Katavi National Park and the towns of Mpanda and Sumbawanga.

## Mpanda
This small town is the terminus of the southern branch of the central railway line. It is unremarkable but, presumably because so few tourists pass through, people are helpful and friendly.

### Getting there and away
The obvious way to get to Mpanda is by rail. Three trains run weekly between Mpanda and Tabora; see *Rail* in Chapter Three. The odd truck uses the road connecting Kigoma and Mpanda.

A more interesting but less reliable way to reach Mpanda is via Ikola or Kalema. The Lake Tanganyika ferry passes both villages in the mid-morning. There is no regular transport on to Mpanda and nowhere to stay in either village. Carry a tent. Except after rain when the road becomes impassable, a truck runs between Ikola and Mpanda most days. The trip takes five hours.

Kalema is an interesting little place: not somewhere that would merit a special visit, but certainly worth exploring if you do pass through. Kalema was an important staging post between Mpala (in Zaire) and Tabora during the slaving era. In 1879, it was occupied by Belgians with slaving interests, and then in 1885 it was settled by the White Fathers, who built a church and mission. When I visited Kalema in 1992, I was struck by the incongruity of the mission building, which I remember as having a whitewashed, rather Mediterranean appearance. What I didn't realise was that I was looking at one of the oldest buildings in the Tanzanian interior, dating to 1893, and fortified with ramparts and gun slits, which helped to ward off frequent attacks by the Wabende in the early years of the mission. The White Fathers' church, built in 1890, was certainly still standing at the end of World War II. I imagine that it's still there today.

Surpisingly, the Kalema Mission is the best part of 1km inland from the jetty. The story is that when the White Fathers landed in Kalema, the level of Lake Tanganyika was marginally higher than it is today and so the hill under which the mission was built would then have been right on the shore. This drop in water level is most probably explained by the temporary blockage of rocks and silt in the lake's main outlet, the Lukoga River in Zaire, something that was noted by Stanley when he passed through the area.

### Where to stay/eat
City Guest House, on the Sumbawanga road, is convenient, clean and friendly. It has a restaurant and bar. Rooms cost $1.25. Most truckies use this guesthouse, so it's a good place to ask around for lifts to Katavi.

We stayed at the Stima Guest House in the town centre, which is also basic but fine. Rooms cost $1.00/1.30 single/double. There are other guesthouses around the market.

## Katavi National Park
In *Ivory Knights*, Nicholas Gordon describes Katavi as "isolated and unloved, and in need of support". He does not exaggerate – when we arrived in November 1992 we were only the 18th party of tourists to visit it in over two years, and the first to arrive without a vehicle. Katavi may be Tanzania's most obscure national park, but it offers excellent game viewing and has a real wilderness atmosphere. It is also surprisingly easy to visit independently.

The dominant vegetation type is miombo woodland, broken by the grassy Katavi flood plain and palm-fringed Lake Chala in the south. Most large African mammals are present, including significant populations of elephant (over 4,000), hippopotamus and buffalo, predators such as lion, leopard and spotted hyena, and herbivores such as sable and roan antelope, zebra, giraffe, eland and waterbuck. Over 400 bird species have been recorded.

If you arrive without your own vehicle, a park vehicle can run you from the entrance gate to a cement hut overlooking Katavi flood plain. Game viewing from the hut is fantastic: we saw more than 100 hippo grazing one evening, and herds of 200 buffalo and 50 elephant. There is a good chance of spotting predators as they cross the plain. If you take an armed ranger to stay with you, you can walk on to the plain – an invigorating experience.

There is a fair road network in Katavi. If you have a vehicle, the Lake Chala region is rewarding. A detailed map is pinned up in the ranger's office. Plenty of game can be seen from the Mpanda-Sumbawanga road which bisects the park. No fee is charged for just passing through.

An entrance fee of $20 per 24 hours must be paid in hard currency, as must a camping/hut fee of $30 per person. A park vehicle costs $0.50/km (about $20 to the flood plain and back). An armed ranger costs $10/day. A two-night stay cost us $70 each, all-inclusive.

## Getting there and away

There is said to be the odd bus between Mpanda and Sumbawanga, but you will probably have to rely on lifts with trucks, for which you should expect to pay. Ask at the City Guest House or Agip Garage in Mpanda. The entrance gate is just off the main road, 1km south of Sitalike village. Sitalike is 35km from Mpanda and 200km from Sumbawanga.

Heading south from Katavi may involve a long wait at Sitalike. By the time you get there from the hut at Katavi, most traffic to Sumbawanga will have already come past. There is nowhere to stay at Sitalike, so if nothing comes towards mid-afternoon try to get back to Mpanda. If you got stuck, you could probably camp at the entrance gate and try again the next morning.

If you are heading to Katavi in your own vehicle, make sure you have enough petrol. There is nowhere to fill up between Mpanda and Sumbawanga.

No tour operators yet run regular trips to Katavi, but a recent (July 1993) letter from a friend in Kigoma suggests this is likely to change in the near future. I don't have details, but it's reasonable to assume these will be fly-in packages tied in with visits to Mahale. Ngare Sero in Arusha do bookings for the private camp in Mahale and should be familiar with the latest developments (PO Box 425 Arusha tel: (057) 3629, fax: (057) 2123).

## Where to stay

The only accommodation is in an unfurnished two-room concrete hut overlooking Katavi flood plain 15km from the entrance gate. Bring your own sleeping bag. Firewood is available, but drinking water must be brought from a spring near the entrance gate. The rangers will fill up a jerry-can on request. Bring all provisions from Mpanda or Sumbawanga.

You may camp at a number of places in the park. The best site is at Lake Chala. Campsites are basic, with firewood but no drinking water.

# Uwanda Game Reserve/Lake Rukwa

Uwanda lies 20km southeast of Katavi. Together, they make for one of the most alluring wilderness destinations in East Africa. Uwanda's dominant feature is Lake Rukwa, a shallow alkaline lake with an extensive floodplain which attracts large ungulate herds after the November rains.

Rukwa is subject to seasonal fluctuations. Often it is split into two expanses of open water separated by a marsh. Mammals found are similar to those in Katavi, but one antelope species, the localised puku, is rarely seen anywhere but Uwanda. Rukwa is notable for albino giraffes, unusually-striped zebra, and a high crocodile density. Over 400 bird species have been recorded.

It is only feasible to visit Uwanda in your own vehicle. You must carry adequate spares, fuel, food, water, and camping equipment. Roads are rough and may become impassable after rain. The safest time to visit is between March and October, but there is more game in the wet months. Rukwa can be approached from either Mbeya, Sumbawanga or Katavi.

# Sumbawanga

Due to its name, which sounds like the chorus for a Hollywood musical about Africa, I approached Sumbawanga with some curiosity. Sadly, it turned out to be a dusty, unloveable place. You will probably only want to spend a night before you move on.

## Getting there and away

There is a fair amount of traffic from Mpanda, but what you get is pot luck. Fate dealt us a truck filled a metre deep with timber, which exaggerated the roughness of the road – as did the absence of suspension. Be very, very kind to fate the day before you head out this way.

There are several buses every morning between Sumbawanga and Mbeya. In both directions they leave at 07.00. Book a seat in advance. It is an eight-hour trip on a fair road which passes through Tundumu.

If you are heading to Kasanga on Lake Tanganyika, there are a couple of buses a week. If you ask at the market before midday, you should find a pick-up truck heading that way.

## Where to stay/eat

The only proper hotel is the **Upenda View Inn**, a pleasant place with newly-furnished rooms, a good restaurant and a bar and garden. When we visited, the staff were irritatingly dopey, but this could easily change.

There is no shortage of guesthouses, and most look perfectly adequate. The **Zanzibar Guest House** behind the bus station has acceptable rooms for $2/2.50 single/double.

The food at the Upenda View is good and not prohibitively expensive, but there are plenty of cheaper *hotelis* around if you prefer.

## Excursions

Between Sumbawanga and Lake Rukwa lie the Mbizi Mountains. The little I know about this range whets my appetite, but we didn't have time to explore. According to a ranger at Katavi, you can get from Sumbawanga to the village of Kijiji on the back of a pick-up truck and from there walk to another village called Mpondo, where there are spectacular views over Lake Rukwa. The implication was that this could be done as a day trip, but I wouldn't bank on it. Take a tent.

Maps of the area suggest a road continues on to Rukwa, passing through patches of forest on the way. My feeling is that if you have the appropriate maps and equipment the area could be well worth exploring on foot, but I would suggest you get permission from the district headquarters in Sumbawanga before you attempt it.

Chapter Ten

# The Southern Highlands and Lake Nyasa

## INTRODUCTION

This chapter covers an area bounded by the Tanzam Highway to the west, Songea to the east, Makambako to the north, and Zambia and Malawi to the south. Southern Tanzania is easy to get around and exceptionally pretty, a combination which should make it particularly attractive to budget travellers. Despite this, the only tourists it sees are overlanders dashing between Dar es Salaam and Malawi. At the turn-off to the Malawi border near Kyela, we were virtually forced off the bus: no-one could believe tourists wanted to continue to the Tanzanian part of Lake Nyasa!

The principal town is Mbeya. Other major towns include Tukuyu, Songea, Njombe and Kyela. The most significant physical features are Lake Nyasa and the mountains either side of the lake. The Poroto and Kipengere ranges lie north and east of Nyasa; the Livingstone Mountains rise dramatically to its immediate west.

## Climate

With altitudes ranging from under 500m to over 2,500m this region has a varied climate. Lake Nyasa (478m) is hot and humid, but the rest of the region is temperate. A sweater will come in useful at night. Tukuyu has the highest rainfall in Tanzania, and is best visited during the dry season between May and October.

## Getting around

Mbeya, the main gateway to the region, can be approached by rail or road from Dar es Salaam or by road from western Tanzania. See *Mbeya* for details. Songea can be approached from Mtwara on the south coast, on a road passing through some very wild and spectacular scenery.

Within the region there is plenty of transport along the Mbeya-Kyela road, the Songea-Makumbako road and the Tanzam Highway. Two ferries a week run between Itungi and Mbamba Bay on Lake Nyasa. Transport on side roads is less erratic than in most parts of the country.

## MBEYA

Mbeya was established in 1927 to service the Lupa goldfields near Chunya, which closed in the 1950s. Surrounded by rich agricultural lands and in a strategic position along the Tanzam Highway and Tazara Railway, Mbeya has continued to prosper.

Mbeya is an appealing town. Its skyline is dominated by the impressive – and climbable – Mbeya range. It has an unusually westernised, bustling feel and shows few of the signs of neglect that characterise most Tanzanian towns. Mbeya is mainly used by travellers

KAUNDA

POST

New · NORTH

SISIMBA

Coffee Shop · WEST

Supermarket
Mt. Rungwe
Mbeya Peak
ACACIA
Ice Cream Parlour
P.M. Rest.
EAST
Cathy's Cafe

MKT.

LUMUMBA

Mt. Livingstone

SOUTH · LUPA WAY

Mbeya Inn Annex

Myamba

Mkwanzulu

B

Stand Inn

Central Visitors Lodge

Moravian Y.H.

Holiday Lodge
Rift Valley H.

to CHUNYA

Mbeya

MBEYA

(sketch map)

MBALIZI

Forex Bureau

TANZAM· HIGHWAY

to
TAZARA Rlwy. Sta.

to
IRINGA &
DAR ES SALAAM

as a stop-off point on the way to Zambia or Malawi, but it is a good base for exploring the southern highlands.

## Getting there and away

Most people travel between Mbeya and Dar es Salaam by rail. There are five trains a week on the Tazara line; see *Rail* in Chapter Three for details. There are regular buses between Dar es Salaam and Mbeya. This 893km trip takes around 20 hours. Overnight buses on this route have a bad reputation for theft; it is advisable to split the trip at, for instance, Iringa.

From Arusha or Moshi, you can go either via Chalinze/Dar es Salaam or Dodoma. For reasons discussed elsewhere, the Dodoma route is not recommended.

From western Tanzania, the most comfortable option is to get to Dar es Salaam by train and proceed to Mbeya from there. A more adventurous route goes via Mpanda and Sumbawanga; see Chapter Nine. There are two buses a week along the little-used Tabora-Mbeya road, passing through one of the most remote parts of Tanzania. They take at least 20 hours.

Buses to local destinations such as Kyela, Tukuyu, Njombe and Tundumu leave regularly on a fill-up-and-go basis. Buses to more distant destinations should be booked in advance.

## Where to stay

There is plenty of accommodation in Mbeya, but places tend to fill up early. Almost everywhere we looked at was clean and good value.

### *Upper range*

There are three tourist-class hotels in Mbeya.

The **Mount Livingstone Hotel** ( PO Box 1401, tel: (065) 3331) is generally rated the best, with rooms for $50/80 single/double, and a 50% residents' discount.

The **Rift Valley Hotel** (tel: (065) 3756) is similar in price.

The **Mbeya Peak Hotel** is a little cheaper.

### *Moderate*

The **Holiday Lodge** (Tel: (065) 2821/3375) is the best value in its range, but it fills up early. Rooms are clean and large, but spartanly furnished. The restaurant is good value.

The **Central Visitors Lodge** (Tel: (065) 2507) is the conspicuous brown-and-blue double-storey building behind the bus station, and it also seems good value.

## *Budget*
Two places stand out in this range:

The **Moravian Youth Centre Hostel**, a couple of minutes walk out of town, is clean, secure and popular with travellers ($5 double).

Even better is the cosy and friendly **Mount Rungwe Guest House**, next to the Mbeya Peak Hotel. There are wash basins in the rooms and the communal showers have hot water.

There are also several clean, cheap guesthouses behind the bus station. Try the **Mbeya Inn Annexe Guest House** or the similar **Myambo** and **Stand Guest Houses**.

# Where to eat
The restaurant at the **Holiday Lodge** is the outstanding place to eat in the budget range, serving good, cheap stews with chips or rice. For a proper restaurant meal, the **Mount Livingstone Hotel** is highly recommended, both for the quality of the food and for its varied menu. The restaurant in the **Rift Valley Hotel** was also very good when I last visited Mbeya. **Eddy's** on Sisimba Road has also been recommended. For ice-creams and packaged food items, try **Ramji's Supermarket** in the THB Building near the post office – it's also a good place to pick up recent international newspapers and magazines.

The restaurant at the **Utegele Country Resort** (see *Mbeya Range*), open daily except Monday, is highly regarded. Meals cost around $5.

# Useful information
## Foreign exchange
When we were there, the only forex bureau was Ndigo's, 2km out of town on the Dar es Salaam road. It is likely there will be a forex bureau in the town centre by the time you read this.

## Tazara Railway Station
This is a few kilometres from Mbeya on the Tanzam highway towards Zambia. The booking office is at the station. Your best bet is to either get a taxi or take a bus towards the Zambian border and ask to be dropped off.

## Shopping
Mbeya is the place in which to stock up if you are planning a few days' hiking or camping in the surrounding area. The supermarkets on Market Square sell a fair variety of imported goods. Fruit and vegetables are best bought at the market. Plenty of small *dukas* surround the market.

# Excursions
## Chunya
This intriguing small town, 70km north of Mbeya, was the centre of the 1920s/1930s gold rush. Mining stopped in the 1950s when it ceased to be profitable. Chunya then enjoyed a short-lived tobacco boom before degenerating into something approaching a ghost town. Many of the grander buildings are now boarded up and there is a general air of faded prosperity. You can still see local prospectors panning the river which runs through the town. There is talk of working the gold again using modern methods.

A few pick-up trucks, leaving from near the Mbeya Peak Hotel, ply the scenic road from Mbeya to Chunya every day. You can normally get to Chunya and back in a day, but there are two guesthouses there: the Moonlight and Night Queen.

World's End Viewpoint, just off the Chunya road 21km from Mbeya, offers excellent views across the Rift Valley escarpment to the Usunga Flats.

If you have your own vehicle, it is possible to continue past Chunya to Lake Rukwa (see *Chapter Nine*).

## Mbeya Range
The mountains which tower over Mbeya are of less biological interest than the more extensive ranges covered later in the chapter, but there are good views over the Rukwa region from the peaks and wild flowers are abundant in the wet season. The most accessible peak, Kaluwe (2,656m), can be climbed in a few hours from Mbeya by following a path which starts behind the hospital.

The highest point in the range is Mbeya peak (2,834m). This is most easily climbed from Luiji, a village about 20km from Mbeya town. The climb takes six hours and is steep in parts, so it should only be attempted if you are reasonably fit. To get to Luiji, ask any bus heading south from Mbeya to drop you at the turn-off near Mbalizi. It is 9km from Mbalizi to Luiji. I am not aware of any public transport, so expect to walk.

The only accommodation in Luiji is at Utengule Country Resort, built on a coffee farm ($20 s/c double). A cheaper campsite should be operating at the resort by the time you read this.

If you want to do a longer hike in the area, you can cross from Mbeya Peak to Pungulume (2,230m) at the western extreme of the range. Utengule Country Resort can give you details.

## Mbozi meteorite
This 15-ton meteorite, discovered in 1942, is believed to be the third-largest in the world. It lies 10km off the Tanzam Highway southwest of Mbeya. The turn-off is signposted. It is difficult to get to without transport.

## TUKUYU

Tukuyu is a shapeless small town salvaged from anonymity by having one of the most appealing settings in Tanzania. It is ringed by the Poroto Mountains and lies at the base of Mount Rungwe, a dormant volcano which at 2,957m is the second-highest point in the southern highlands. Tukuyu is the obvious base for exploring the Poroto, a range dotted with waterfalls, crater lakes, and patches of forest – all capped by stirring views to Lake Nyasa more than 1,000m below.

The area between Tukuyu and Nyasa is home to the Nyakyusa people, whose neatly painted homes were described by the explorer Joseph Thomson as "perfect arcadia". It is a fertile region, with rich volcanic soils and an annual rainfall of over 1,500mm. The dirt roads that criss-cross the area are lined with small subsistence farms growing bananas, mangos, tea and coffee.

Tukuyu was founded as a German administration centre in the late 19th century, and originally called Nieu Langenberg. The old Langenberg, on Lake Nyasa near Ikombe, was abandoned due to the high incidence of malaria and is now a mission.

If you plan on hiking, the area is best between May and October. At other times there is rain most afternoons. Tukuyu is cold at night.

## Getting there and away

Tukuyu is on the tarred Mbeya-Kyela road. Regular buses run in both directions on a fill-up-and-go basis.

## Where to stay/eat

The **Langiboss Hotel** is all a traveller could wish for. Rooms are clean and comfortable, the manager speaks English and is well-informed about hikes in the area, and there are even hot showers. It is 1km out of town and has a marvellous view of Mount Rungwe. There is a bar and restaurant (meals must be ordered in advance). If you are hiking, you can leave excess gear at the hotel. $1.50/2.00 single/double. If it is full there are plenty of scruffy guesthouses dotted around the town.

There is a campsite on the grounds of the **Pentecostal Holiness Association Mission**, the turn-off to which is signposted 10km from Tukuyu on the Mbeya road. The priest in charge is helpful and knows the surrounding area well. It is a half-hour walk from the turn-off to the mission.

## Excursions

This area is ideal for casual rambling. Wander along any of its winding dirt roads and you will be rewarded with lovely views and scenery, varied bird life and vegetation, and regular glimpses into rural African life. Even on by-roads there is a fair amount of traffic (expect to pay for lifts, though), so exploring the area over a few days from one base is possible.

The following are some of the more accessible spots, most of which are easily visited as a day trip from Tukuyu. With time, initiative and some 1:50,000 maps from the Department of Lands and Surveys in Dar es Salaam, you can explore further.

### Ngozi Crater Lake

The most spectacular crater lake in the Poroto mountains is over 2km long and circled by 200m-high cliffs. To get to the rim you walk up the forested southeastern slopes, rich in plant and bird life. Ngozi is attributed with magical powers locally. A faded signpost marks the turn-off to Ngozi a few kilometres from Isongole village. From there a driveable dirt track continues for 5km before it reaches the footpath to the rim. From Isongole, the trip takes two to three hours each way by foot. It is advisable to organise a guide; the path is not always clear, particularly during the rainy season.

## Kiwira Natural Bridge

A natural rock bridge, formed 400 years ago by water-cooled lava from Mount Rungwe, spans the Kiwira River further along the same road as the Pentecostal Holiness Association Mission (see *Where to stay*). To walk there from the mission takes a couple of hours. Trucks run most days from the main road to an army base near the bridge, and may give tourists a lift. Ask for details at the mission.

## Mount Rungwe

If you are reasonably fit, Rungwe can be climbed and descended in about ten hours. Alternatively, if you have a tent and are adequately prepared, you could spend a couple of days exploring the slopes. The most popular route starts at Isongole, bypasses Shiwaga Crater, then takes you through extensive patches of forest. A 1:50,000 map of Rungwe is available from the Department of Lands and Surveys in Dar es Salaam.

## Masoko Crater Lake

This attractive crater lake is one of the easiest beauty spots to visit in the Tukuyu area. It also has some interesting historical asssociations: the solid stone building on the rim of the crater was constructed in around 1912 to house the German Fifth Field Garrison, and it was the base from which Germany fought British troops in the neighbouring Nyasaland Protectorate. The stone building housed British troops between the wars, and it now serves as a courthouse.

Masoko, like most crater lakes, has attracted several legends. It is rumoured that towards the end of World War I, the Germans dumped a fortune in gold bars, money and military vehicles into the lake to avoid their falling into British hands – believable enough when you consider the same thing happened to the *Liemba* on Lake Tanganyika, but almost impossible to verify if there is any truth in the story that the lake is over 3km deep. Difficult to say whether there's anything to be read into the fact that the occasional German coin is washed up on the shore of the lake. Locals claim that swimming in the lake is tantamount to suicide, and there are also stories that the courthouse is haunted.

Masoko lies roughly 15km from Tukuyu along the Ipinda/Matema road. A fair amount of traffic heads this way – predominantly overcrowded pick-up trucks. You may prefer to walk out: it's gently downhill most of the way, and very pretty with intimate, cultivated slopes occasionally giving way to magnificent vistas to Lake Nyasa. With an early start, you'll have no problem getting a lift back.

## Kapalogwe Falls

The main attraction of this waterfall is that you can wade through the river to a large cave behind it. Without a vehicle, it's a bit far from the main road to make for a viable day trip (12-15km each way). The turn-off is 10km from Tukuyu on the Kyela road.

## Hiking in the Tukuyu area

The Poroto Mountains extend westwards into the Kipengere Range almost as far as Njombe, creating an extensive highland area with a number of possible access points. I have not heard of anyone who has attempted to hike in this area, but there are some interesting possibilities.

The foremost of these is the Kitulo Plateau connecting the two ranges, on which lie the highest peak in the southern highlands, Mtorwi (2,961m), and the 2,929m Chaluhangi Dome. The plateau is noted for the wild flowers which blanket it after the November rains, and the pastoral Nji people who inhabit it. If you have a vehicle, the approach from Chimala on the Tanzam Highway climbs a succession of dizzying hairpin bends and is said to be very dramatic. There is little in the way of public transport in the region, so access could be a problem for backpackers.

I know of people who have hiked in the Livingstone Mountains near Matema. The manager of the Langiboss Hotel in Tukuyu may be able to advise you on this.

The Department of Lands and Surveys in Dar es Salaam stocks 1:50,000 maps of the region. You would be foolish to think of hiking without them. You should carry proper equipment and be self-sufficient in terms of food. It might be an idea to speak to the police or some other authority in Tukuyu about your plans and try to get some form of written permission, just in case.

If any readers do hike in this area, I would be interested to hear about it so information can be included in the next edition.

# LAKE NYASA

Broadly speaking, Lake Nyasa is the Tanzanian part of Lake Malawi (as explained on page xii, calling it Lake Malawi will not get you very far in Tanzania). Whatever you call it, it is without a doubt the most scenic of Africa's three great lakes, and although most travellers visit the Malawian part, the Tanzanian portion is equally attractive. Lake Nyasa contains 30% of the world's cichlid species. These colourful fish can easily be observed in the lake's clear water.

Lake Nyasa has a bad reputation for cerebral malaria. Take your pills and continue to take them for four weeks after you leave the area. If you show any signs of malaria, get to a doctor quickly.

## Getting there and away
The gateway to Nyasa is Kyela, 10km from Itungi Port on the lake shore. Regular buses between Mbeya and Kyela take about four hours and stop at Tukuyu. The 1,000m descent from Tukuyu to Kyela is breathtaking; make sure you get a window seat. The contrast between the pleasantly cool highlands around Tukuyu and the cloying heat of the lake shore may come as something of a shock.

## Lake Nyasa Ferry
Few travellers are aware of the ferry service between Itungi Port and Mbamba Bay, the best way to see the northern part of Nyasa. The scenery is dominated by the Livingstone Mountains rising sharply on the east shore. The ferry stops at several fishing villages where the locals approach in dugouts, selling fish, fruit and other goods to passengers.

The ferry to Mbamba Bay runs twice a week. It leaves Itungi at 07.00 on Monday and Friday and arrives at Mbamba Bay at around midnight the same day. It turns around more-or-less immediately and arrives back at Itungi at 17.00 the next day. These times are *very* approximate. The ferry stops at Lupingu, Manda, Lundu, Nindai and Liuli.

A third ferry leaves Itungi at 07.00 on Wednesday and arrives back on Thursday afternoon. This stops at most lakeside villages, including Matema, but doesn't go as far as Mbamba Bay. It is about an hour from Itungi to Matema, so you could use the ferry to get there and back if the timing was suitable.

In theory *MV Songea* does the Monday and Friday run and the smaller *MV Iringa* does the Wednesday run. We went on a Friday and *MV Iringa* was used, so this may not always be the case. Lake Malawi can get very choppy, and the smaller boat is not much fun in rough weather. *MV Songea* is said to be much smoother.

There is no accommodation in Itungi. You will have to spend the night in Kyela and get a vehicle to Itungi at around 05.30 on the morning of departure. Vehicles leave from in front of the TRC office, 1km out of town. There is a booking office at the TRC building, but as the ticket officer travels with the ferry it serves no practical function. You can buy a ticket at Itungi while you wait for the ferry to be loaded up.

There is one class, and it is not overcrowded. Tickets cost $4. Meals are available on board, as are sodas and beers.

## Kyela

Kyela is not my favourite town. It is sweaty and scruffy, and has more than its fair share of people who feel an uncontrollable need to yell *Mzungu!* at any passing European. The town centre is a small grid of roads around a central market. The TRC office is 1km from the market in the same direction as Itungi.

### Where to stay/eat

There are loads of indifferent guesthouses in Kyela. Rooms cost under $2. If you are catching the ferry, try either the **nameless lodge opposite the TRC office** or the **New Vatican City Lodge** 300m towards town.

In the centre, the **nameless guesthouse opposite the Ram Hotel** is acceptable. So is **Kyombo Guest House** on the main road 200m towards Tukuyu. **Mkoko's Restaurant**, behind the market, has a shady verandah and a fridge stocked with beer and sodas.

## Matema Beach

This beach on the northern tip of Lake Nyasa is rated the best anywhere on the lake. With the Livingstone Mountains rising sharply to the east and the Poroto Range on the western horizon, it is difficult to imagine a more visually attractive setting. Matema is the kind of place you could settle into for a while: swimming in the warm bilharzia-free water, taking short walks, chatting to the locals – or just waiting for the sun to set behind the Poroto.

### Getting there and away

The daily bus between Mbeya and Matema passes Tukuyu, Kyela and Ipinda on the way. It arrives at Matema after dark, and leaves at 05.00, so is not that convenient.

It is easier to get to Matema in hops. There is regular transport from Kyela to Ipinda, a large village 27km from Matema, and even the odd pick-up truck from Tukuyu (via Masoko Crater Lake). The daily bus aside, you can find private transport between Ipinda and Matema, especially on Saturdays. There is a basic but adequate guesthouse in Ipinda, behind the bank ($1/2 single/double). I have heard you can walk between Ipinda and Matema along a river which comes out at Lake Nyasa 3km west of the mission. I have no idea how long this would take.

The day before you plan to leave Matema, ask the mission if any of their vehicles are heading to Ipinda the next morning.

The ferry which leaves Itungi at 07.00 Wednesday arrives at Matema an hour later. It also stops at Matema on Thursday afternoon on its way back to Itungi. Ferries to Mbamba Bay *do not* stop at Matema.

## Where to stay

The **Lutheran Mission Resort** on the shore has spotless *bandas* with comfortable beds and mosquito nets. A kiosk sells cold sodas and coffee/tea, and a canteen serves enormous buffet-style meals. These must be ordered in advance and cost $2.50 per head. The home-made bread served at breakfast is wonderful. Double *bandas* cost $10, *bandas* sleeping four cost $20. You can camp for around $5 per tent.

## Excursions

In the stifling heat of the lake shore even the shortest stroll feels like a major excursion. The time to explore is the early morning. One warning: if you head further afield, ask before you swim. There are no crocodiles at Matema, but they are common on nearby parts of the shore, where they kill villagers with a frequency that suggests caution is advisable.

There are a few local spots worth looking at. The best-known is Matema Pottery Market, held every Saturday at the village 1km east of the resort. The pots are crafted by the Kisi who live on the northwestern lake shore and are sold as far afield as Dar es Salaam. On weekdays, you could try to arrange for a fisherman to row you to the peninsula where the pottery is made.

About 500m past the village, the shore becomes rockier. This is a good place to see colourful cichlids. Crocodile are common at the river mouth 3km west of Matema and hippo have been seen a short way upriver.

## Liuli

This is the last but one stop on the southbound ferry trip, an attractive natural harbour protected by a rocky peninsula, topped by the sphinx-like formation from which derived the village's German name, Sphinxhafen. Liuli is the site of the largest mission in this part of Tanzania, and the burial place of William Johnson, the Anglican missionary who co-founded the Likoma mission on an island in the Malawian part of the lake. Johnson is one of the most fondly remembered of all the missionaries who worked in the Lake Nyasa area; for 46 years he preached from a boat all around the lake shore, despite being practically blind and well into his seventies when he died in 1928. Johnson's grave was for several decades a pilgrimage site for Malawian Christians.

Liuli's greatest claim to posterity is as the site of the first naval encounter of World War I, an incident which was described by *The Times* in London as "Naval Victory on Lake Nyasa" and by a participant, Mr G M Sanderson, as "pure comedy".

Shortly after war was declared, the British Commissioner of Nyasaland dispatched the protectorate's only ship, the *Gwendolyn,* to destroy its German counterpart, the *Hermann Von Wessman.* The *Gwendolyn's* captain, Commander Rhoades, was informed at Nkhata Bay that the *Wessman* was docked for repairs at Liuli. He arrived at Liuli in the cover of dawn with a somewhat nervous crew: their only gunner was a Scots storeman who had trained several years previously as a seaman-gunner and who freely admitted that he remembered little of his training. After several misfires, caused by a combination of dud ammunition and rusty aiming, a shell finally connected with the German boat.

"Immediately afterwards," wrote Sanderson several years later, "a small white dinghy put off from shore, in which was a European clad in a singlet and a pair of shorts pulling furiously for the *Gwen.* Rhoades ordered "Cease fire" and blessed silence fell. It was his drinking pal [Captain Berndt], the skipper of the *Wessman,* with whom every meeting was a drinking party. The dinghy came alongside and its furious occupant leaped to his feet and, shaking both fists above his head, exclaimed "Gott for dam, Rrroades, vos you drunk?". The news that the war had arrived had not yet reached him. When Rhoades informed him that he was a prisoner, one could see his anger turn to horror as he realised his fatal mistake."

Good enough reason to pause when the boat stops at Liuli, though it's an open question whether you'd think about disembarking. Liuli lies on a lovely stretch of shore; the German mission and Johnson's grave are still there; and, who knows, with a bit of imagination you might even be able to conjure up the image of a semi-naked and infuriated Captain Berndt gesticulating from his dinghy.

More pragmatically, there's nowhere to stay, and when you want to move on you'll be reliant on the occasional mission vehicle heading to Mbamba Bay, or more likely the next ferry. Of course, if you have a tent and you don't mind a couple of days' wait for transport out, this might just add up to a most attractive off-the-beaten-track option – food, at least, shouldn't be a problem on the shore of this most fish-rich of lakes.

## Mbamba Bay

The southernmost town on the Tanzanian part of Lake Nyasa lies on a pretty coconut-lined beach. The only accommodation is the basic but friendly **New Mbamba Guest House**, where single rooms cost $1. If you are waiting for the ferry to Itungi (which can arrive at any time of night) there are palm-leaf shelters on the beach. It is said to be safe to sleep under these if you arrive late with the ferry, but we didn't try it.

## Mbinga

From Mbamba Bay, a 60km dirt road winds its way up the valley wall through well-developed miombo woodland to a grassy plateau and Mbinga. This is a thrilling route, the road clinging to the mountainside and offering dramatic views back to the lake.

There is an erratic bus service along this road. If the bus doesn't show up, you will have to take what you get (a crowded pick-up in all probability). It normally takes three hours, but we did it in light rain and it took closer to seven. Most of this time we spent trudging through mud while the driver tried to free his vehicle; the rest of it we clung terrified and dripping to the sides of the overloaded vehicle while it skidded uncertainly around the precipitous road. I imagine this road is impassable after heavy rain.

Mbinga is an oasis. You can get hot tea there. Had I arrived in a more rational state, I would probably call it a typically dull small African town, but... Whatever else, once you hit Mbinga there is plenty of transport along a well-maintained dirt road to Songea. There is even a "Special Video Bus" to Dar es Salaam three days a week. There are a few guesthouses and *hotelis* around Mbinga's bus station.

# SONGEA

Songea is a large, lively town at the junction of the road to Mbamba Bay and the road connecting the Tanzam Highway to the south coast. If you arrive in Songea from the south coast or Lake Nyasa, its busy market, well-stocked supermarkets and general state of good repair are a welcome re-connection with the modern world. Until the ivory moratorium in 1989, Songea was a major centre for poachers smuggling ivory out of the Selous. This may well account for the town's comparative prosperity.

## Getting there and away

A recently built tar road connects Songea to Njombe and the Tanzam Highway. Regular buses run along it. Buses to Njombe and Mbeya go when they are full; buses to Dar es Salaam should be booked in advance.

A few trucks and 4x4 vehicles run daily along the wild, scenic road connecting Songea to the south coast. If you are heading this way, you may well end up spending a night in Tunduru, a thriving mining town about halfway between Songea and Masasi.

Between 1985 and 1988, according to Nicholas Gordon's *Ivory Knights*, the streets of Tunduru were plagued by man-eating lions. Almost 50 people were killed, including the game warden sent to sort the problem out, and a further 28 wounded. The offending cats have since been shot. There are a few guesthouses and *hotelis* in Tunduru. Rooms start at around $6.

## Where to stay

In the moderate range, **Hotel Angoni Arms** on the Tunduru road is idiosyncratic and likeable, but a bit run-down. The rooms are spacious, there is an attractive view from the balcony, and it has a restaurant and bar.

In the town centre, try the **OK Hotel**, which has a lively bar and the best restaurant in town, or the quieter but similarly priced **Yulander Holiday Lodge**.

As usual there are plenty of guesthouses at the bus station and in the town centre. Two deserve a special mention:

Rooms at the **Deluxe Guest House**, a two-storey hotel in the town centre, are clean and have mosquito nets.

Around the corner, the **New Star Guest House** is clean and friendly, and its rooms have mosquito nets.

A new recommendation is the **Mkomi Guest House**, on the main road near the bus station.

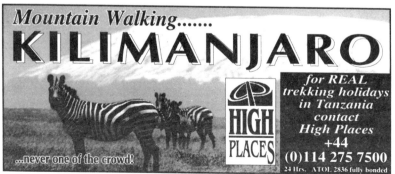

# NJOMBE

There is not much of interest in this quiet, pleasantly situated small town. If you have a spare afternoon it could be a pretty area in which to do some walking. There is an attractive waterfall on the Ruhidji River, next to the main road 2km north of the town centre. Njombe is cold at night.

## Getting there

Njombe is 237km from Songea (the distance is marked incorrectly on some maps). They are connected by a good tar road, so the bus ride between them takes less than five hours. There are regular buses in all directions from Njombe. In fact, for such a sleepy-looking town, it has one of the most chaotic bus stations I have seen. Watch your belongings.

## Where to stay

The two-storey **Milimani Hotel**, 250m from the bus station towards Songea, has a good bar and restaurant. Rooms are inexpensive, clean, comfortable and spacious, and the showers are hot.

The **Lutheran Centre Hostel** offers beds in clean, recently furnished dormitories for less than $1 per person and it has a canteen. It is 50m and signposted from the main road, just before the Milimani

Of the several guesthouses around the bus station, the best is the **Shamba Guest House**.

# MAKAMBAKO

This important junction town is a good place to hitch a lift from in any direction. If you get stuck there is a Lutheran Hostel, and also a couple of private lodges.

## Chapter Eleven

# The Tanzam Highway and the Southern Reserves

## INTRODUCTION

The Tanzam Highway, so-named because it links Tanzania to Zambia, is the main road through southern Tanzania. It starts at Tunduma on the Zambian border, passes through Mbeya, Iringa, Mikumi and Morogoro, then connects with the Dar es Salaam-Arusha road at Chalinze. This chapter picks the road up at Iringa and follows it northwards to Chalinze.

The region's most significant physical features are the Uluguru Mountains near Morogoro and the Udzungwa Mountains near Mikumi. It is passed through by Tanzania's largest river, the Rufiji, and its main tributary, the Great Ruaha. The stretch of road from Iringa to Morogoro is very scenic, first following the Ruaha River through the baobab-clad foothills of the Udzungwa Mountains, then passing through Mikumi National Park.

Some of Tanzania's most alluring conservation areas flank the highway. The Selous, the largest game reserve in Africa, covers a vast area of miombo woodland lying between the Tanzam Highway and the south coast. Ruaha National Park lies west of the highway near Iringa. Mikumi National Park is bisected by the highway between Iringa and Morogoro. The newly-proclaimed Udzungwa Mountains National Park lies south of Mikumi towards Ifakara.

### Climate

Much of the area covered in this chapter is low-lying and hot. The Udzungwa and Uluguru Mountains and, to a lesser extent, Iringa are cooler. The rainfall pattern is typical of Tanzania, with the bulk of the rain falling between November and March.

### Getting around

There is plenty of transport along the Tanzam Highway. The road is tarred and, even though it is potholed in parts, buses are relatively quick. Expect to cover around 50km per hour allowing for stops.

Hitching is a possibility; the only time we tried, however, near Iringa, we waited two hours without any luck.

The Tazara Railway runs roughly parallel to the highway for most of its length. They split at Makumbako and re-connect at Dar es Salaam, so the line is of little use to travellers wanting to explore the area. The Tazara Railway does stop at Ifakara, and is a good way of getting to Udzungwa National Park.

# IRINGA

It would be misleading to describe Iringa as exciting, but the town is both interesting and agreeable. There are several period buildings in the old German quarter near the market, while Majumba Street, the main trading road, is very colourful and lively. Iringa is situated on a hill from which there are good views over the Ruaha valley.

The area around Iringa is not without interest. Day trips can be made to the nearby Isimila Stone-Age Site and to Mkwawa's capital at Kalenga (see *History*). Iringa is the jumping-off point for visits to Ruaha National Park.

## History

Iringa is the home of the Hehe, a relatively modern grouping forged in the 1850s under the leadership of Munyigumba. His son and successor, Mkwawa, achieved a legendary status amongst both his own people and his enemies. Mkwawa was a cunning warrior who expanded his territory to include large parts of the caravan route between Tabora and the coast. The name *Hehe* is believed to derive from the battle-cry he initiated, a loud *hee-hee*.

Mkwawa refused to acknowledge the German administration. When they attempted to treatise with him, he responded by blocking caravans from passing through his territory. In 1891 Emil Zelewski and 1,000 German troops were dispatched to quell the Hehe. After a few skirmishes, Mkwawa ambushed Zelewsky, killing half his men and making off with over 300 rifles and all their ammunition. Over the next three years Mkwawa set about fortifying his capital at Kalenga. Iringa, incidentally, is a European corruption of the Hehe word *lilinga*, which means fort.

In October 1894, Kalenga was attacked and demolished by the Germans, who stood a battery of cannons along the ridge of a hill which overlooks it. Amongst other blows, a direct hit was scored on the arsenal holding the gunpowder Mkwawa had borrowed in 1891. Mkwawa went on the run; for the next four years he fought the Germans using guerrilla tactics. When faced with capture in 1898, he shot himself through the skull rather than be taken alive. His skull, originally taken to Germany, was returned to Tanzania in 1954. It now rests in the Mkwawa Museum in Kalenga.

## Getting there and away

You can get to Iringa easily from anywhere on the Tanzam Highway. Getting away from Iringa is less simple. The apparent busyness of Iringa bus station is deceptive; few buses actually start their journey there and although plenty will be going in your direction it may be difficult to find a seat. It is advisable to book a seat in advance. Iringa is about nine hours from Dar es Salaam by bus.

Seats for Dodoma-bound buses should also be booked in advance. The road is terrible; the trip takes up to 12 hours.

## Where to stay

### Moderate

There is no shortage of accommodation in Iringa, though as you might expect, much of it consists of indifferent to scruffy guesthouses.

A good moderate hotel is the **Isimilia Hotel** (PO Box 216, tel: (064) 2605), which has small but clean double rooms with hot running water for around $8.

The nearby **Iringa Hotel** (PO Box 48, tel: (064) 2039), formerly run by the TRC, is now very run-down and overpriced by comparison.

Another popular place with expats is the **Baptist Mission Guest House**, 4km out of town on Togwa Road, which has clean self-contained doubles for $14. The **Raj Hotel** has also been recommended.

### Budget

The **Lutheran Centre Guest House** remains a reliable bet, with basic but clean rooms for $4.

At the more basic guesthouses rooms generally cost around $3; among the better places are the **Hoteli Ya Kati** and **Lupombwe**, **Tembo**, **Iringa Venus** and **New Akbar Guest Houses**.

## Where to eat

There is a good choice of restaurants in Iringa. For lunch, **Hasty Tasty** and **Hasty Tasty Too** serve a variety of tasty and inexpensive stews, juices, and Indian snacks. The **Raj Hotel**, Iringa's top restaurant, has a varied menu and is open long hours. Main courses cost about $3. The **Iringa Hotel** serves three-course set menus for $2.50. Its bar is well-stocked and cheap; a sociable place to linger for the evening. **Hoteli Ya Kati** is also good. Main courses cost around $1.50.

The **Lantern Restaurant** has great views over Majumba Street and across to the hills surrounding Iringa. The menu lacks surprises but the food is good. After you eat, you can relax and enjoy the view at the attached bar. Main courses cost $2.

# Excursions
## Kalenga
This small village on the banks of the Ruaha was the site of Mkwawa's fortified capital (see *History* above). A small museum houses Mkwawa's bullet-shattered skull and several of his artefacts. The well-informed and enthusiastic caretaker speaks good English and will happily take you around the village.

To the untrained eye Kalenga is an unremarkable African village, but the caretaker can point out several remnants of Mkwawa's capital: the remains of fortified walls, the mound used by the chief to address his people, and the foundations of his home. He will also point out the ridge from where the Germans unleashed the barrage of cannon fire which destroyed the capital. This hill has since become known as Tosamaganga (throwing stones), and is now the site of a quaint 1930s Italian mission.

Pick-up trucks to Tosamaganga and Kalenga leave Iringa every hour or so. They wait for passengers at the end of the surfaced road 200m past Samora Stadium. At Kalenga you will be dropped off next to the market; it is a five-minute meander through the village from there to the museum. Keep asking for directions. If your Swahili is limited, asking for Mkwawa will get you further than asking for a museum.

## Isimila Stone Age Site
In a dry river bed 22km south of Iringa lies one of East Africa's richest stone age sites. Its significance was recognised in 1951 by a schoolboy who collected two rucksacks full of stone implements, amongst them a 40cm-long, 4kg hand axe. Isimila was first excavated by Professor Howell of Chicago University in 1957.

Isimila was inhabited by stone age people of the Late Acheulean culture about 60,000 years ago, at which time it was a shallow lake. A small museum houses a number of their tools, including cleavers and hand axes. You can also see fossilised bones and teeth of the extinct *hippopotamus gorgops*. In another gulley, ten minutes' walk away, a group of striking 10m-high sandstone pillars, carved by a river which dried up years ago, look like the set for a Lilliputian western.

The turn-off to Isimila is signposted on the Tanzam Highway south of Iringa, a few metres past the 20km marker – any bus heading that way can drop you there. It is a 20-minute walk from the road to the site. On the way you pass through a small group of huts where the caretaker lives. Ask for him on your way past.

You can negotiate with a taxi driver to do a round trip to Isimila.

This cost us about $15. The caretaker at the site speaks little-to-no English – if your Swahili is limited an English-speaking taxi driver will be a definite asset.

# RUAHA NATIONAL PARK

Ruaha is Tanzania's second-largest national park, and one of its wildest. Only the area around the Great Ruaha River has been developed for tourism, and even this sees relatively few visitors. There are plans to extend the internal road system from the present 400km to 1,500km.

Ruaha protects a wide variety of habitats, including evergreen forest and swamp. Much of the park is covered in miombo woodland. There are also significant areas of grassland dotted with acacia and baobab trees. The roads following the Ruaha River are said to be the best for game viewing.

Ruaha boasts the largest elephant population of any Tanzanian national park. Despite heavy losses due to poaching, there are still over 12,000 in the greater Ruaha ecosystem, which incorporates two neighbouring reserves.

Other common mammals include buffalo (over 30,000 in 1990), zebra (over 20,000), giraffe and warthog. Impala are the most numerous antelope; waterbuck, eland, roan, sable, bushbuck and both types of kudu are also likely to be seen. Predators include lion, leopard and cheetah. African hunting dogs are often seen in the Mwanyangi area. Over 400 bird species have been recorded.

A 64-page booklet, *Ruaha National Park*, is available from the National Park headquarters in Arusha and sometimes from the entrance gate of Ruaha. It contains maps, animal descriptions and checklists, and details of where to look for localised species.

Ruaha is best visited between July and November, when animals concentrate around the river. Internal roads may be impassable during the rainy season (December to May).

An entrance fee of $15 per 24-hour period must be paid in hard currency.

## Getting there and away

The park headquarters at Msembe are 120km from Iringa by road and can only be reached using a 4x4 vehicle. If organised in advance through Ruaha River Camp or the park authorities, you can charter a flight to Msembe and hire a vehicle to use in the park.

A number of Dar es Salaam-based companies run safaris to Ruaha. These are pricey, and unless you fly you will use up the best part of two days just getting there and back.

It is possible to arrange a safari in Iringa at a price comparable to that of a camping safari in the northern reserves. Only one company in

Iringa offers 4x4 hire: Iringa Safari Tours (PO Box 107, tel: (064) 2718/2291). Their office is on Uhuru Avenue between Benbella Street and Karume Road; the owner can also be contacted at the Iringa Hotel. The price will depend on how long you want the vehicle for. You will be looking at around $250 for up to four people for three days. This covers vehicle hire, a driver and fuel. Park entrance fees, food and accommodation costs must be added to this.

Hitching to Ruaha is for incurable optimists only.

## Where to stay

**Ruaha River Camp** (bookings through Coastal Travels, PO Box 3052, Dar es Salaam, tel: (051) 37479, fax: (051) 46045. This highly-regarded private camp is on a koppie above the rapids on the Ruaha River. Accommodation is in bandas or fixed tents. There is a restaurant and bar. $140/180 full board.

**Msembe Camp** This basic camp is near the headquarters and the river. There are nine double bandas and two family bandas. All are self-contained, with bedding, firewood and water provided. There is a basic campsite with pit toilets but no water. Campsites and bandas cost $20 HC per person.

## MIKUMI

This village on the southern border of Mikumi National Park has grown rapidly in the last few years. It is a service town to the national park and an important stopover along the Tanzam Highway. It is also on the junction with the B127 to Ifakara (and Udzungwa National Park). There are several guesthouses and you can get a reasonable meal at the *hoteli* with the covered verandah at the junction with the B127.

## UDZUNGWA NATIONAL PARK

Tanzania's newest national park opened to the public in October 1992. It protects the remote Udzungwa Mountains and an extensive montane forest community. Altitudes within the national park range from around 250m to over 2,500m. Facilities were limited when we visited in December 1992, but with publicity Udzungwa seems likely to become a major draw for hikers and nature lovers.

There are many similarities between the forests of west Africa, Madagascar and the eastern Tanzania mountains. Madagascar was once part of the African mainland, so these forests may once have been linked physically. The dispersal of seeds during cyclones may also be a factor. Madagascar split from the mainland about 165 million years ago and the eastern Tanzanian forests have been isolated from those in west Africa for over five million years. Forests such as those of the Udzungwa and Usambara are separated by large distances and thus have a high level of endemism. More than 25% of Udzungwa's plant species are not present elsewhere.

Two monkeys are endemic to the Udzungwa: Uhehe red colobus and Sanje crested mangabey. Blue, red-tailed, and black-and-white colobus monkeys are also present. Udzungwa is part of the Mikumi-Selous ecosystem, so it harbours large game species such as lion, elephant, leopard, buffalo and sable antelope.

Udzungwa is particularly alluring to birdwatchers, with a good range of forest birds present including a number of endemics such as the rufous-winged sunbird. The forests of Udzungwa are still relatively unexplored in scientific terms, as evidenced by the discovery in 1991 of a presumably endemic francolin which has been tentatively named the Udzungwa partridge and placed in an entirely new genus.

An entrance fee of $20 per person per 24-hour period must be paid in hard currency.

## Getting there and away

The entrance gate to Udzungwa is 100m from the main Ifakara road, at the village of Mangula 20km south of Kidatu. A few pick-ups do the Kidatu-Ifakara run every day and will drop you off there.

The best way to reach Ifakara is by rail. All trains on the Tazara line stop there; see *Rail* in *Chapter Three*. They arrive in the evening, so plan on a night at one of Ifakara's basic guesthouses.

Kidatu is reached by road. Any bus between Iringa and Morogoro can drop you at Mikumi. A daily bus from Morogoro passes through Mikumi at about 16.00 and reaches Kidatu at nightfall. The odd private vehicle goes through to Kidatu. There is accommodation in Kidatu; see *Where to stay* below.

If you visit Udzungwa as a round trip from Dar es Salaam, the ideal would be to come by rail and return by road. Slow trains to Ifakara pass through Selous Game Reserve in daylight. By road, you will pass through Mikumi National Park.

## Where to stay

There is no accommodation in the park. If you have a tent you might be allowed to camp at the entrance gate, but there are no facilities.

**Twiga Guest House**, in Mangula 200m from the entrance gate, is an attractive base for exploring the Udzungwa. The canteen serves cheap, filling meals, the bar has a fridge, and the grounds look across to the mountains. $10 s/c double.

You could also stay at **Kidatu**, a hot, mosquito-ridden town dominated by the Udzungwa's craggy peaks. Surrounded by sugar plantations and the site of a major hydro-electric plant, Kidatu is considerably larger and busier than maps suggest.

For a basic room in Kidatu, **Mkanga Guest House** and **Stop Over Lodge** are both adequate.

**Maryland Lodge**, 200m from the main road, has spotless rooms with mosquito nets and fans. A limited range of meals is served and there is a beer garden with a fridge.

## What to do
A short trail leads from the entrance gate to a small waterfall in the forest. We saw plenty of monkeys along this, including red colobus. If you sit quietly at the waterfall in the early morning or evening, you might see monkeys come to drink. The roads around Mangula are pleasant to walk on.

At the entrance gate, you can organise a four-hour guided walk to a waterfall deeper in the reserve, and several longer walks, one of which includes a night camping in the forest.

Two longer trails are planned: a seven-hour round trip to the nearest peak and an overnight hike to the 2,111m Mwanihana peak. Guides and porters will be available, but you should bring all food etc with you. Contact the National Parks office in Arusha for up-to-date information.

If any readers hike in the Udzungwa (or in the Mahenge range 80km south of Ifakara), I would like to hear about it so details can be included in the next edition.

## MIKUMI NATIONAL PARK

Mikumi is Tanzania's third-largest national park, covering 3,230km². It is relatively flat, but flanked by the Uluguru and Udzungwa mountains to the north and south respectively. Mikumi was gazetted in 1964, when the large herds which gathered on the Mkata flood plain were threatened by hunters after the area was opened up by the construction of the Morogoro-Iringa road. It was extended to share a border with the Selous in 1975.

Mikumi's main vegetation type is open grassland interspersed with patches of miombo and acacia woodland and the odd solitary baobab. The area becomes marshy after rain. A wide variety of mammal species is present; amongst the more commonly seen are elephant, buffalo, wildebeest, impala, warthog, zebra and giraffe. There are significant populations of three antelope species which are rare in the northern Tanzanian reserves: greater kudu, roan and sable antelope. Predators include lion, leopard, African hunting dog, and black-backed jackal.

A park entrance fee of $20 per person per 24-hour period must be paid in hard currency. A 44-page booklet, *Mikumi National Park*, available at the National Park headquarters in Arusha for $2.50, contains a wealth of background information, a good map, and details of the animals and birds found in the park.

## Getting there and away

Mikumi is bisected by the Tanzam Highway. It can be reached in an ordinary saloon car, but a 4x4 is needed to drive within the park. You can see plenty of game from a bus passing through the reserve; we saw 10 mammal species, including a herd of 20-odd eland and four herds of elephant.

Safaris to Mikumi run from Dar es Salaam, four hours away by road. A two-day, one-night trip is normal. It is the cheapest of the southern reserves to visit, but lacks the wild character which makes the others so attractive.

As it is only an hour from Mikumi by road, I expected people in Morogoro to organise safaris there. It seems not, but this could change. If you hired a vehicle in Morogoro, a day trip would be a feasible option. The Morogoro or Savoy Hotels or the New Green Restaurant would be the best places to enquire.

## Where to stay

Mikumi is a popular weekend trip for residents of Dar es Salaam. It is advisable to book over weekends and public holidays.

### Upper range

**Mikumi Wildlife Lodge** (PO Box 14 Mikumi, tel: Mikumi 27). This attractive TTC lodge, 3km from the main road, sits on a ridge above a waterhole. It has a swimming pool, a restaurant and a bar. $40pp HC (with a 25% discount for Tanzanians). Lunch and dinner cost $11 each.

**Mikumi Wildlife Camp** (Book through the Oyster Bay Hotel in Dar es Salaam). Accommodation here is in s/c bandas. It has a restaurant and bar. $40 HC per person, or $29 for residents on weekdays. Meals cost $11 each.

### Budget and camping

The three campsites near the main gate cost $20 per person. They have long drop toilets and firewood, but water is not available. Special campsites cost $40 per person. The cheapest option is to stay at one of the guesthouses in Mikumi village.

# MOROGORO

Morogoro is a likeable town, spacious and well-maintained. The Uluguru Mountains tower attractively 2,000m above it. Morogoro is the centre of a major agricultural region and its fruit market is known countrywide. There are few tourist attractions around Morogoro, but its healthy, lively feel – three hotels had live music playing when we visited – makes it worth a minor diversion.

## Getting there and away

Buses between Dar es Salaam and Morogoro leave every hour or so and take about four hours. There is regular transport between Morogoro and Iringa. A bus leaves Morogoro for Kidatu at around 2.00pm daily.

## Where to stay

### Upper range

The **Morogoro Hotel** (PO Box 1144, tel: (056) 3270), recently bought by the South African Protea group, lies on the slopes of the Uluguru 2km out of town. It has pleasant grounds and the usual facilities. $60/65 HC s/c single/ double.

### Moderate

Out towards the railway station, **Mama Pierina's** is a pleasant place to stay, and popular with expats. Bright, clean double rooms with fans, nets and hot showers cost $8/11 single/double. There's a good restaurant attached.

Nearby, the **New Savoy Hotel** (formerly the plain old Savoy) does little to live up to its recent name extension: the rooms are frightfully run-down, there's no running water, and the service is, well, a little on the hesitant side. Still, some respect is due for the sheer gall of asking $15 for a room.

About ten minutes' walk from the town centre, along Boma Road, the **Masuka Village Hotel** (PO Box 930, tel: (056) 4774/4430) lies in flowering gardens at the base of the Uluguru Mountains. It's an attractive retreat, and surprisingly inexpensive at $11 for a self-contained double with nets and hot showers – worth the walk out.

In the town centre, the **New Tegetero Hotel** seems exceptional value: large clean doubles with hot water, nets and fans for $9.

By contrast, the **Sofia Hotel** and **Roof Garden Hotel** both feel a touch overpriced at $16 and $11 respectively for an unexceptional self-contained double.

## Budget
There are a few basic guesthouses dotted around town. The main cluster, along Boma Road towards the Masuka Village Hotel, are mostly rather scruffy and overpriced. Far better is the **Lukumba Family Guest House** in the town centre and – arguably the best value in town – the **Luna Hotel**, which has spacious self-contained doubles with fan and net for $6.

# Where to eat
**Mama Pierina's** is universally acclaimed as the best restaurant in Morogoro. A diverse menu includes pizzas, curries and steaks for between $5 and $8 per main course. The verandah is a pleasant place for a cold beer.

The **New Green Restaurant** was also excellent when I last ate there, serving a variety of Indian and Portuguese dishes at reasonable prices. In February 1996, the restaurant was still in position but had been closed for a month – it wasn't clear whether this was a permanent or temporary thing.

# Excursions
## Rock Garden Resort
This is a sort of botanical garden on the lower slopes of the Uluguru Mountain. It is 1km past the Morogoro Hotel, and worth a look if you have an afternoon to spend.

### Uluguru Mountains
This range lies directly east of Morogoro. It rises to 2,646m. Like most eastern Tanzanian mountains, it contains extensive areas of forest. The Uluguru are less accessible than the Usambara or Udzungwa, but there is no reason why a determined hiker should be put off. Maps are available from the Department of Lands and Surveys in Dar es Salaam.

A possible base for hiking into the Uluguru is the disused **Morning View Camp** near a patch of natural forest halfway up the mountain. Though originally a research centre for Sokoine University, permission to camp there must now be obtained from the Department of Natural Resources, 2km out of town on Kingalu Road. Check the water situation before heading out. To get to Morning View, head out on Boma Road past Masuka Village Hotel for about 8km. You might get a lift some of the way, but don't bank on it.

Another possibility in the Uluguru area is the abandoned **Bunduki Fishing Camp** south of Morogoro. This ceased to function in the 1970s and the buildings are no longer habitable, but it remains a beautiful spot, on a river below an attractive waterfall enclosed by rain forest, and it would be of particular interest to birders. If you are self-sufficient and have the appropriate equipment, you could almost certainly camp at Bunduki (I recently spoke to somebody who did this in 1993). To get there, follow the Iringa road south of Morogoro for 20km until you reach Masomba College, then turn left towards Mgeta. Bunduki is reportedly about 10km past Mgeta. There is at least one bus daily to Mgeta.

## CHALINZE

Just over 100km west of Dar es Salaam, Chalinze is one of the most important junction towns in Tanzania, where the Tanzam and Northern Highways split. If you are travelling between the north and south of the country, and want to bypass Dar es Salaam, you will find a vehicle heading in your direction at Chalinze.

Its strategic position aside, Chalinze is enlivened only by the numerous vendors and stalls which sell food and curios to passing bus passengers. There are a couple of basic guesthouses.

## SELOUS GAME RESERVE

Because of its size and remoteness, a definite mystique surrounds the Selous. The reserve is difficult to describe without resorting to hyperbole: it is the largest in Africa (and the second largest in the world); 50,000 square kilometres of archetypal wilderness; home to 30,000 elephant, 200,000 buffalo, 80,000 wildebeest and significant populations of almost every other species of African mammal, including the rare African hunting dog and black rhinoceros.

Before you rush off and book a safari to the Selous, you should be aware of its drawbacks. The reserve is divided into two unequal sections by the mud-brown Rufiji River. The remote expanse of African bush described above lies south of the river; unless you have your own 4x4 and are thoroughly self-reliant, or are prepared to pay a fortune to make individual arrangements with a tour operator, this area is totally inaccessible.

The Selous most people see is the relatively small area north of the Rufiji. There is less tourism here than in the northern reserves, but it is nevertheless well-developed in tourist terms. The area is not as scenic as the northern reserves, nor are you likely to see as many animals or as much variety as you would in, for instance, the Serengeti. When we were there all the camps seemed intent on showing their visitors a particular pride of lions which had been resident in one area for a week. Spot-the-lion-along-with-three-other-vehicles is a game you can play in any large African reserve, and in theory is the type of thing people go to Selous to avoid.

That's not to say Selous isn't worth visiting. The walking and boat safaris offered by all the camps are a real bonus. The Rufiji teems with hippo and massive crocodiles which can be approached closely in a boat, and the bird and animal life along the shore is amazing. A variety of antelope is likely to be seen, as are buffalo and elephant. Of the birds, the African skimmer is often seen on the sand banks exposed during the dry season, fish eagles perch on the *borassus* palms which line the river, and waders, herons, kingfishers and weavers are all well-represented.

Game walks allow you to look at smaller animals and birds, and there is a real sense of excitement attached to wandering around in the bush, especially if the group is small. You will go with an armed ranger. The highlight of our trip was a family of elephant shrews feeding at dusk next to our tent.

The accessible part of the Selous is covered in miombo woodland and animals can be quite difficult to spot from a vehicle. Game drives consequently centre around a series of small lakes between the camps. Animals likely to be seen in this area include lion, elephant, impala, greater kudu, eland, giraffe, zebra, wildebeest and buffalo.

Not only does the Rufiji divide the reserve from a tourist's viewpoint, but it acts as a natural barrier between the ranges of two wildebeest subspecies (eastern white-bearded wildebeest north of the river and Nyasa wildebeest to the south). The Rufiji also forms the southern limit of the range of the Maasai giraffe, though this is in part due to the absence of acacia trees south of the river.

Roads within the Selous become impassable after heavy rain. As a consequence camps close towards the end of the wet season, in April, and re-open in July. An entrance fee of $15 per person per day is charged.

You'll hear a few different pronunciations of Selous; to the best of my knowledge *Selloo* is correct.

## History

Because of tsetse fly, much of the area that is now the Selous has never been densely populated. People who lived in the area suffered badly at the hands of the slave caravans in the 19th Century. Better-populated areas such as the Mutumbi Hills were virtually cleared of human habitation by the famine induced by the Germans after the Maji-Maji uprising.

The Selous is named after Frederick Courteney Selous, an English elephant hunter, explorer, naturalist and writer (his best-known book is *A Hunter's Wanderings in Africa*). Selous spent most of his life in East and southern Africa; amongst his many exploits, he was a white hunter for Theodore Roosevelt and the trailblazer for the troop of settlers sent by Rhodes to take over the area that became Rhodesia (now Zimbabwe). In World War I, Selous volunteered for service and was made a captain in the 25th Royal Fusiliers. He died in battle in 1917 at the age of 64, of wounds inflicted while advancing on a German encampment on the Beho river. His grave is on the north of the river near Selous Safari Camp.

The part of the reserve north of the Rufiji was proclaimed in 1905. Kaiser Wilhelm gave part of it to his wife as a present, which earned it the nickname of *Shamba la Bibi* (The Woman's Field). Selous received its current name in 1922 and reached its present size and shape in the 1940s, when the government moved the remaining tribes out of the area to combat a sleeping sickness epidemic. It has been declared a World Heritage Site, one of three in Tanzania.

## Getting there

The ideal way to visit the Selous is to organise your own safari starting in Dar es Salaam. This involves either hiring a vehicle and driver and making your own bookings, or getting one of the camps to put together a drive-down package. The advantage of doing it yourself is that it gives you the autonomy to explore away from the roads favoured by the camps. The drive from Dar es Salaam to Selous is along poor roads and takes about ten hours. All the camps have access to an air-strip and can charter a flight to take you down.

Four days is the minimum realistic length for a drive-down safari. Prices vary widely depending on the camp, your length of stay and the size of your group. Four people going for four days can expect to pay a minimum of $150 per person per day.

You can get to the Selous by train, but must make advance arrangements with the camp you plan to visit. Take the Tazara rail and disembark at either Fuga Halt or Kisaki, depending on the camp's instructions. Rail is the most practical way of getting to Selous Safari Camp or Stiegler's Gorge cheaply.

## Where to stay

There are five camps, all privately run, and all over $70 per person per night, inclusive of meals. All camps can organise game drives and boat safaris for around $25 per person and walking safaris for about $10 per person. The camps are all shown on the map of the South Coast (page 258).

**Impala Camp** (PO Box 4783 Dar es Salaam, tel: (051) 25779). The most basic and cheapest of the camps. Accommodation is in standing tents, with showers and long drops attached, overlooking the river. $90 per person full board, inclusive of park fees.

**Stiegler's Gorge Camp** (PO Box 348 Dar es Salaam, tel: (051) 32855). Built for a hydroelectric project in 1977, this camp is situated on a hill overlooking the sheer 100m-deep gorge after which it is named and into which the Rufiji bottlenecks in a spectacular fashion. Accommodation is in self-contained cabins. Stiegler's Gorge is some distance from the other camps, so it's a bit more exclusive.

**Rufiji River Camp** (PO Box 20058 Dar es Salaam, tel: (051) 63546). This is the oldest camp in the Selous, built on a bank overlooking the Rufiji. Accommodation is in standing tents with communal toilets. The owner is a German ex-hunter whose knowledge of the Selous is said to be unrivalled.

**Mbuyu Camp** (PO Box 1192 Dar es Salaam, tel: (051) 34535, fax: (051) 28486). This camp is built around a large baobab tree. Accommodation is in luxury self-contained tents on the banks of the Rufiji, near the lakes. Plenty of animals can be seen from the bar overlooking the river.

**Selous Safari Camp** (book through Oyster Bay Hotel in Dar es Salaam). Situated on a hill overlooking the plains around the lakes, accommodation here is in self-contained cabins. It is possible to swim in the nearby hot springs. Full board costs $160/240 per person. Park fees are not included.

## The SOUTH COAST & Selous Camps

Chapter Twelve

# The South Coast

## INTRODUCTION

This chapter covers the coast south of Dar es Salaam, which stretches for over 500km to the Ruvuma River on the Mozambique border. The only towns of any size on the south coast are Kilwa Masoko, Lindi and Mtwara. This chapter also includes coverage of the Makonde Plateau, the area immediately inland of Lindi and Mtwara. The major towns on the plateau are Masasi and Newala.

Lack of reliable transport and the long distances involved in getting there have left the south coast one of the most isolated parts of East Africa. The area offers little to those who value their creature comforts: only in Mtwara is there anything resembling a tourist hotel, few people anywhere speak even rudimentary English, there are no organised tourist attractions and buses are overcrowded, uncomfortable and painfully slow.

Despite all this, the south coast is a fascinating, thought-provoking and often enchanting area, endlessly rewarding to those with a sense of adventure and curiosity. The older towns are profoundly Swahili; crumbling German and Arab buildings create the air of being in a time-warp. The people, too, retain a gracious, slow pace of life into which it is easy to slip. Scenically the area is typical of the East African coast: palm-lined beaches, mangrove swamps and dense baobab-studded scrub.

The south coast's isolation can easily be romanticised, but there is a depressing reality behind the picturesque images. I was struck by the number of beggars, cripples and blind people in the towns, the malnourished children in roadside villages and the total lack of industry. This situation should be partly remedied when plans to extend the Mtwara-Lindi tar road to Dar es Salaam come into fruition.

If you visit the south coast, bear in mind the conservative nature of Swahili culture. Dress and behave accordingly.

# Climate

Like the rest of the Tanzanian coast, this region is hot and humid at all times. The ideal time to visit is in the drier, cooler months between April and October.

# Getting around

During the dry season there are daily buses between Dar es Salaam and all the large towns covered in this chapter. During the rainy season the road is often impassable. Buses to Lindi and Mtwara leave Dar es Salaam from Morogoro Road bus station. Buses to Kilwa leave from in front of Kariakoo Market. There are good local services on the tar roads connecting Lindi, Mtwara and Masasi. The south coast can be reached by road from the southern highlands; see *Songea* in Chapter Ten.

The ideal way to explore the south coast is to take a boat from Dar es Salaam to Mtwara and then work your way back overland. The boat that covers this route, the *Canadian Spirit*, runs to a rather whimsical schedule. In late 1992, it did the trip every other Thursday, stopping only at Mafia. Between 1992 and 1996, I heard all manner of odd rumours about its activities (the owners had gone bankrupt, the boat itself was no longer seaworthy, it was plying between Dar es Salaam, Kenya and Somalia). In 1996, it was back doing the Mtwara run every Wednesday, stopping at Mafia and Lindi en route. The only advice I can give is to ask around at the jetty in Dar es Salaam or Mtwara to ascertain what the current situation is – the one certainty is that the schedule will change from time to time.

Assuming the *Canadian Spirit* is running, it is a well maintained boat with an immaculate first class lounge (though, as the lounge is placed at the back of the boat and the weather can get very rough, second class may prove to be more comfortable). First class to Mtwara costs around $15 and second class $10, in addition to which you must pay the usual $5 port tax in hard currency.

# MAFIA ISLAND

This island opposite the Rufiji Delta has a near-legendary status amongst travellers, largely because so few ever get to it. It was an important Shirazi settlement between the 12th and 15th Centuries, with strong links to Kilwa. It is now mainly known for its excellent deep-sea fishing. I have not met anyone who has been to Mafia, but if what we saw from the *Canadian Spirit* is anything to go by, it is pretty much what you would expect a remote, densely vegetated and thinly populated Indian Ocean island to be. We were sorely tempted to get off the boat and, had we not had a schedule to stick to, we probably would have.

If you visit Mafia, it will probably be to fish or to laze around. There are, however, several sightseeing possibilities – Shirazi ruins at Ras Kisimani, Omani ruins on the nearby island of Juani and a turtle colony on another nearby island – but I have no idea how accessible they are. If any enterprising traveller does get to Mafia, it would be interesting to include more information in the next edition.

## Getting there and away

Mafia is relatively straightforward to get to, but getting away could involve a certain amount of improvisation. Budget travellers should only think about visiting Mafia if they are very flexible time-wise.

The weekly Air Tanzania flights between Dar es Salaam and Mafia are said to be unreliable. People do charter flights to the island. Presumably spare seats are sometimes available.

The only regular boat service is the *Canadian Spirit* (see *Getting around* earlier in the chapter). This always stops at Mafia on its way to Mtwara, but does not always stop on the return trip to Dar es Salaam. If you only want to spend a night on the island, speak to the captain in advance to clarify what the boat is doing. If you don't mind spending a week there (or two in the dry season), you can pick up the boat when it next goes to Mtwara. There may be other boats between mainland towns and Mafia, but I have not heard of any. There are certainly none on a regular basis.

## Where to stay

The TTC-run **Mafia Island Lodge** has air-conditioned rooms and costs $32/41 HC s/c single/double or $6.50 for residents. The only other option is to pitch a tent. It is said to be safe to camp anywhere on Mafia. You can buy basic foodstuffs such as fish locally, but it would be sensible to do some stocking up in Dar es Salaam.

## KILWA

There are three settlements called Kilwa. The oldest, Kilwa Kisiwani – Kilwa on the island – lies on a small island 2km offshore. It is the site of the most impressive ruins on the East African coast, those of the medieval city of Kilwa – the *Quiloa* of Milton's *Paradise Lost* and once thought to be the site of King Solomon's mythical mines.

The other settlements are both on the mainland. Kilwa Kivinje (Kilwa of the Casuarina Trees) was a major 19th century slave trading centre, only rivalled in importance on the mainland by Bagamoyo. Kilwa Masoko (Kilwa of the Market) is a more modern town, and is now the regional headquarters.

Although the Kilwa area is primarily of historical interest, the surrounding coast is lovely. The seas around Kilwa have the world's densest dugong population. Dugong are large, bizarre-looking marine mammals, believed to have been the origin of the mermaid myth. Common as they are, you would be lucky to see one.

## History

It is a reflection of the widespread ignorance regarding Africa's past that while tourists flock to Tanzania's game reserves only a handful pass through Kilwa every year. Even more disturbing is the fact we were told by a number of people in Kilwa (including the caretaker) that the Husuni Kubwa – the island's most impressive building and the apex of Swahili architectural aspirations – was Portuguese-built. With the above in mind, the following history is as detailed as space and the known facts will allow.

As with all African history, many details of Kilwa's past are open to conjecture. There have been extensive archaeological diggings on the site and some contemporary descriptions have survived. The primary historical source is the *Kilwa Chronicle*, written in 1520 under the supervision of the then-exiled Sultan of Kilwa. Two versions of this exist, one dating from 1565 and the other from the 19th century. Discrepancies exist, but the broad history of Kilwa is well-understood.

Kilwa was occupied by precursors of the Swahili in the 9th century. In about 1150 the island was bought by a trader called Ali bin Al-Hasan, generally regarded to be the founder of the Shirazi Dynasty which dominated coastal trade until the Portuguese invasion. His importance can be gauged by the fact that coins bearing his name – probably minted long after his death – have been found as far afield as Pemba and Mafia islands.

Although Kilwa's importance grew under Al-Hasan and his successors, its eventual dominance of the gold trade is linked to the arrival of Abu-al-Mawahib, a trader from Sofala in modern-day Mozambique, and is most plausibly explained by a simple accident of geography. Gold arrived at the coast from the interior at Sofala, but until the mid-13th Century it was sold to the Arabs at Mogadishu, in modern-day Somalia. The normal explanation for this is that Arab vessels could not reach Sofala within the annual monsoon cycle, and that the gold was transported up the coast by a succession of local middlemen.

As the volume of coastal trade increased, improvements in Arab navigation and ship design allowed them to penetrate steadily further south. Sofala would have been beyond their reach whatever they did – winds south of Kilwa are notoriously fickle – but it seems likely to have suited Sofalan traders to cut out the middlemen by bringing the centre of trade closer to home. In this scenario, Kilwa would have been the ideal compromise – by the mid-13th Century it was evidently within reach of Arab vessels, yet it was near enough to Sofala for traders there to control the trade from top to bottom.

The source of Kilwa's gold, shrouded in mystery for centuries, gave rise to such myths as Queen Sheba and King Solomon's Mines. It is now thought that the gold was mined in the Zimbabwean interior and arrived at Sofala via the Zambezi valley. There are strong parallels between the timing of the rise and fall of Kilwa and that of Great Zimbabwe. Furthermore, a coin minted at Kilwa was found at Great Zimbabwe in 1971. There are, however, no cultural parallels between the cities or their architecture. Assuming they were linked, it is uncertain what the mechanisms of trade were. No evidence suggests coastal traders ever visited Great Zimbabwe.

Kilwa prospered throughout the golden age of Swahili (1250 to 1450). It was the dominant town on the coast, considered by the medieval traveller, Ibn Battuta, who visited it in 1331, to be "among the finest and most substantially built in the world". It had a population exceeding 10,000, the first coin mint in sub-Saharan Africa, and an extensive system of wells which is still in use today. The Friday Mosque and *Husuni Kubwa*, the most impressive buildings on the island, if not the entire coast, date to this period. In addition to gold, Kilwa exported ivory and ebony, and it imported such fineries as eastern cloth and Chinese porcelain.

Kilwa's wealthy traders lived in houses of coral and had small private mosques. Ordinary townsmen lived in mud-and-wattle huts. Even though some Arab traders settled on Kilwa, the vast majority of its occupants were local Swahili. The island was too small to be self-sufficient in food, so had extensive agricultural interests on the mainland.

In 1498, the Portuguese explorer, Vasco Da Gama, rounded the Cape and sailed up the east coast on his way to establishing trade links with India. He described Kilwa in detail, but as he never visited the city, his oft-quoted report is probably pure fabrication. In fact, though it was still a trading centre of note, Kilwa was well past its peak by this time. For reasons that are unclear, Mombasa dominated coastal trade from about 1450 onwards. Da Gama met with a hostile reception in Mombasa; perhaps the Sultan there exaggerated Kilwa's strength in order to frighten the Portuguese away from the coast.

Da Gama's description of Kilwa might explain why it was so heavily targeted when the Portuguese took over the coast in 1505. Three-quarters of its residents were either killed or forced to flee. A Portuguese fort was built, the gold trade moved to Mozambique and the Sultan exiled to the mainland. By 1512 the town was virtually abandoned; even the Portuguese had moved on. In 1589, those residents who had remained were attacked and eaten by a tribe called the Zimba. The city was left to crumble.

to
KILWA
KIVINJE,
NANGURUKURU

Hoteli

MKT.

Guest House

Masoko
By Night

Mjana Enterprises
Guest House

Bar (Mickey Mouse on wall)

Salama Guest House

£$

to BEACH

to
CULTURAL
CENTRE,
HARBOUR

CCM Headquarters

KILWA MASOKO   (sketch map)

The island came briefly to life in the late 18th Century, after the Omani captured the coast from the Portuguese. Omani Arabs occupied Kilwa for a period, which is when they built the large fort which is visible from the mainland. They seem to have relocated to the mainland town of Kilwa Kivinje in the early 19th Century.

Kilwa Kivinje became the centre of the southern slave trade. By the mid-19th Century it was a very wealthy town, with up to 20,000 slaves passing through annually. In 1873, the Sultan of Zanzibar outlawed the slave trade. It survived at Kilwa longer than anywhere else, but had been stopped entirely by the end of the 1870s. Many of Kilwa's slave traders established rubber plantations and business continued to prosper. In 1886, Kilwa Kivinje become a German administrative centre.

Kilwa Kivinje remained a town of regional importance during the first half of this century, but since the end of the Second World War it has gradually been reduced to backwater status. The more modern town of Kilwa Masoko is now the regional headquarters.

## Getting there and away

A good tar road connects Kilwa Masoko to Nangurukuru on the main Dar es Salaam-Mtwara road. Vehicles from Nangurukuru to Kilwa Masoko run every hour or so and take 20 minutes. Nangurukuru has a guesthouse, should you get stuck there.

Daily buses between Dar es Salaam and Kilwa Masoko leave at 05.00 in either direction. In Dar es Salaam they leave from Kariakoo Market, not the best place to wander around in the dark. Instead, catch a bus to Mtwara or Lindi (from the Morogoro Road bus station), get off at Nangurukuru, and make your way to Kilwa from there. The road between Dar es Salaam and Nangurukuru is very rough; the journey takes about 12 hours.

There are no direct buses to Kilwa from other towns on the south coast. You will have to catch a bus to Dar es Salaam and get off at Nangurukuru.

## Kilwa Masoko

There is little of interest in Kilwa Masoko itself, but it is the best base for exploring the Kilwa area. It is a friendly place and sees few tourists; anyone who speaks English is likely to grab you for a chat. Kilwa Masoko's town centre – a small grid of dirt roads around a central market – is 1km inland of the harbour; a long tar road connects the two. All accommodation is in the town centre; government buildings and banks lie along the main tar road.

Kilwa Masoko's one attraction is the sandy baobab-lined beach east of the harbour. To get there from the town centre, walk down the main tar road for about 300m, then turn left at the CCM buildings (just past the bank – look out for a statue of a man running). The beach is 100m further.

## Where to stay/eat

There are three basic guesthouses in Kilwa Masoko, all clustered around the market and easy to find. A room costs around $2:

We stayed at **Mjaka Enterprises Guest House**, a friendly, clean place with single rooms only, all of which have a mosquito net and fan.

**Salama Guest House** seems similarly pleasant and it has double rooms. The third guesthouse, behind the market, is scruffier. It is popular with bus drivers, so a good place to stay if you want to be woken for the 05.00 bus to Dar es Salaam. Mjaka Enterprises has opened a grander guesthouse on the seaward side of the Masoka by Night bar. Rooms are self-contained with fans and cost $5/double. The restaurant does adequate breakfasts.

You can fill up for under $1 at the excellent *hoteli* opposite Mjana Enterprises. The **Masoko by Night** bar is a pleasant place to drink; it serves food grilled on a coal fire. A nicer place for a drink is a nameless bar, easily identified by the paintings of Mickey Mouse and friends on the wall, which is owned by the District Fisheries Officer.

## Kilwa Kisiwani

The modern settlement of Kilwa Kisiwani is little more than a mud and thatch village, unremarkable in itself, but surrounded by some of the most compelling ruins in East Africa. The island is separated from the mainland by a 2km channel; the only way to reach it is in one of the small fishing dhows moored in Kilwa Masoko's harbour.

Permission to visit the island must be obtained from the Kilwa Cultural Centre in Kilwa Masoko. This is a straightforward process and there is no charge attached, but expect it to take some time; you will probably be asked to complete several forms and have to spend a while making small talk with the rather bleak immigration officer (bring your passport). If possible, get the formalities over with the day before you plan to go.

The Cultural Centre can organise a fishing dhow to take you to the island. The price is negotiable and depends on how long you plan to spend there. Expect to pay around $10 per party for a half-day return trip. If you want to spend a night on the island, the Cultural Centre has restored a **small cottage** for the use of tourists. The Cultural Centre is opposite the post office, on the main tar road halfway between the town centre and the harbour.

There is a caretaker/guide on Kilwa Kisiwani. Although he is helpful, he speaks little English, has a minor obsession with medieval toilets (perhaps it's the only English word he knows) and is less than fully conversant with the island's history. He will expect a tip.

Before you visit Kilwa, don't miss the excellent display in the National Museum in Dar es Salaam.

## Around the island

The *Gereza* is the squarish, partially collapsed building which draws the eye as you sail across to the island. *Gereza* is a Swahili word meaning prison; it in turn is derived from a Portuguese word meaning church. The *Gereza* on Kilwa, however, is a fort. It was built by Omani Arabs in about 1800 and incorporates the walls of a smaller Portuguese fort built in 1505. It has thick coral walls and an impressive arched door.

Walking uphill from the *Gereza*, you pass first through the small modern village before coming to the main ruins. There are a number of interesting buildings here; an ornate *Domed Mosque* and the so-called *Great House* stand out. West of these is the triangular *Mukatini Palace*, parts of which are very well-preserved. The palace was built in the 15th century after the *Husuni Kubwa* fell into disuse (see below), and is enclosed by a crumbling 18th century wall built by the Omani. Also of interest are the remains of the ancient well system, still used by the villagers today.

The most impressive building in the main ruins is the *Great Mosque*, also known as the *Friday Mosque*. This multi-domed building is the largest mosque of its period on the coast, and was built during the 14th century gold boom as an extension of an earlier 11th century mosque. Most of its magnificent arches and domes are still intact, but many of the outbuildings are crumbling. In the 14th century the Great Mosque would have been the focal point of community life in Kilwa, where Friday prayers were held. A few hundred metres south of the mosque, a graveyard houses the tombs of many of Kilwa's sultans.

The most remarkable building on Kilwa lies about 1km east of the main ruins, on a low cliff overlooking the sea. Known locally as the *Husuni Kubwa*, it was described by the archaeologist Neville Chittick as "the only attempt to go beyond the merely practical and approach the grand" in pre-colonial Africa.

The word *Husuni* derives from an Arab word meaning fort, but there is no evidence to suggest the building ever was one. The name was probably acquired centuries after the building fell into disuse. The *Husuni Kubwa* was the Sultan of Kilwa's palace, used as both a dwelling place and a store house. The name *Husuni* has been attached to it by virtue of a nearby smaller, square building, the *Husuni Ndogo*, which superficially resembles a fort (*kubwa* and *ndogo* are KiSwahili for large and small). The purpose of the *Husuni Ndogo* is something of a mystery – there is no comparable building elsewhere in East Africa – but it may have been a fortified market place.

The *Husuni Kubwa* was built by al-Hasan ibn Talut, the first ruler of the Abu-al-Mawahib dynasty, in the early 14th Century, and was probably lived in for three generations. In some aspects – its geometrical design, for instance – it is a typical Swahili building, but its scale and complexity are unprecedented and many of its features are unique. The building includes domestic quarters, an audience court, a staircase leading down the cliff to the sea, large ornamental balconies and a swimming pool. The *Husuni Kubwa* is in poor condition, but the main features are clearly discernable.

Further ruins dating to the Shirazi era can be found on Songo Mnara Island. There is supposedly a daily boat between Kilwa Masoka and Songo Mnara via Pande, but it doesn't always go. You can also arrange private transport in a local fishing dhow – a fisherman called Juma Meli has been recommended by one reader as "a real gent". The ruins on Songo Mnara don't match those on Kilwa Kisiwani, but it's an enjoyable day out, and a good reason to stay on an extra day at Kilwa before braving the public transport again.

## Kilwa Kivinje

This small, run-down town is a living memorial to its more prosperous past. The overall impression is of a once important town gradually returning to its fishing village roots – much of the main street consists of boarded-up shops, while mud huts have been built using the walls of old Omani fortifications. I knew little about Kilwa Kivinje when I arrived there, but was able to piece together much of its history just by walking around.

The town came to prominence as an Omani slave-trading centre in the early 19th century. The crumbling remains of Omani dwellings and fortifications are dotted all around, and while none is habitable, many are in good enough condition to allow you to imagine what they must have looked like 150 years ago. There is an interesting mosque and, to the east of the town, an old Muslim graveyard.

The whitewashed German Boma overlooks the waterfront. It is the town's largest building, used as an administrative centre into the 1950s, but it serves no apparent purpose now. A cannon, presumably dating to World War I, stands on the common (complete with park benches) between the Boma and a stone sea wall. Behind the Boma a small monument commemorates two Germans who died in 1888.

Along the main street lie glimpses of Kilwa Kivinje in the 1940s and 1950s: double-storey buildings with ornate balconies, small homes with Zanzibar-style doors, and shops still carrying steel advertising boards which must date to the 1950s. The main covered market, still in use today, is said to have been built by the Germans.

As well as being historical, Kilwa Kivinje is a pretty town. It lies on an attractive stretch of coast surrounded by mangroves, and has a peaceful Muslim atmosphere. I could think of worse places to settle into for a few days. The **Savoy Guest House**, on the beachfront near the German Boma, may not live up to its name, but it is clean and cheap: double rooms with fans and mosquito nets cost $2. A couple of *hotelis* near the market serve cheap, basic meals.

## Lindi

Like Kilwa Kivinje, Lindi was a 19th century slave-caravan terminus. A chimney-like stone tower opposite the NBC club, said to have been used to hold prisoners, is the only obvious relic of this era.

There is every indication Lindi was a prosperous town at one time. The sprawling town centre contains numerous posh colonial-era buildings, many of which are now ruined or heading that way. On the beachfront, a building marked on a 1970 map as the Area Commissioner's Residence houses nothing but trees. A cyclone which hit the town in the 1950s may go some way to explaining this general state of disrepair.

With one eye closed you can imagine that Lindi's beachfront was a resort of sorts, possibly used by farmers living upcountry. Today, however, the benches are all broken, the Beach Hotel exudes squalor, and the town probably goes months at a stretch without seeing a tourist.

Whatever its history – and even that seems to have been lost or forgotten – Lindi is something of a backwater now. It is a pleasant and interesting place to visit, but ultimately a depressing reminder of what much of Tanzania was like in the mid-1980s. The only part of town which seems to escape the general air of torpor is the busy bus station, which – when the electricity is working – rings with the chimes of Zairean guitars and the pumping bass of reggae late into the night. Here the town's unemployed youth and orphaned children hang around all day, breaking into unselfconscious dances, while vendors scrape a living selling fried chicken and dried fish, melting sweets and single cigarettes to passing bus passengers.

Lindi lies on a glorious stretch of coast. Its sandy, palm-lined beach stretches for a couple of kilometres. The wooded hills on the opposite side of the bay provide a scenic backdrop. If you swim, dress modestly; this is a Muslim town.

Christopher Jerram, who lived in Lindi for 15 years from 1948, wrote to me saying that the main beach was never used much for swimming, but that there's a more attractive and secluded beach at Ras Bura, perhaps 30 minutes' walk from town along the Kilwa Road – it should be worth checking out if you're in Lindi a couple of days.

*to* KILWA

Coast
Guest House H

*Lindi*

*Bay*

OLD
COMMISSIONER'S
RESIDENCE

NBC
CLUB

STREET

MKT.

Paris
Restaurant

MARKET

ROAD

AVENUE

JAMHURI

SHEIKH

BADI

ST.

ST.

SABA SABA ST.

B

ASKARI

UHURU

AVENUE

MAKONGORO

ST.

KARUME

ST.

H City
G.H.

AMANI

MAZNDE

ST.

NZUNDA

H South Honour
G.H.

Town
G.H. H

EILAT

MSONOBARI

GHANA

BARAZA

ST.

ROAD

*to*
MTWARA

K's Cold Drinks

F

*Lindi* Beach Hotel
H

N

*LINDI*

0 　　100　　200

*metres*

Ferries run regularly from the pier next to the Beach Hotel to a small settlement on the opposite side of the bay. I didn't check them out, but if you want to explore further...

## Getting there and away

There are buses between Dar es Salaam and Lindi most days. They leave Dar es Salaam at the Morogoro Road bus station and should be booked in advance.

Lindi is connected to Mtwara and Masasi by good tar roads. A few buses run daily to and from Mtwara, leaving when they are full. There are no direct buses between Lindi and Masasi; buses to Masasi leave from Mtwara and bypass Lindi at Mingoyo.

A small, very crowded bus does a daily run between Lindi and Newala. It leaves Newala at 05.00, gets to Lindi at midday, and then turns back.

## Where to stay

There are guesthouses dotted all around the bus station. Two of the best are the **South Honour** and **Town Guest Houses**. Both are friendly and offer clean rooms with mosquito nets and fans for less than $3. The less central **Lindi Beach Hotel** is in a lovely position but, barring complete renovation, it is of interest to masochists and entomologists only (according to Christopher Jerram, the Beach Hotel has always been a bit of a tip – in the 1950s, it was known to locals as the Dysentery Arms). If you want a room on the beach, try the **Coast Guest House** instead. It is a bit scruffy and the rooms lack mosquito nets, but it's cheap, pleasant and has the beach on its doorstep.

## Where to eat

The most pleasant place for a cold beer is the **NBC Club** on the beachfront. Non-members are charged a nominal entrance fee ($0.50). Meals such as chicken and chips are served on request.

Otherwise try **K's Cold Drinks**, where you can get chicken or eggs and chips for less than $1. There are a few *hotelis* around the market and vendors sell snacks all day at the bus station.

# MINGOYO

This village is on the junction of the roads to Lindi, Mtwara and Masasi. If you are heading from Lindi to Masasi, you must head to Mingoyo to pick up a vehicle. Mingoyo apparently thrives on its position. The vendors here offer an array of roadside snacks second to none: fried and stewed chicken, fish, prawns, meat kebabs, cakes and fruit. There doesn't appear to be any accommodation in Mingoyo.

# GOOD INTENTIONS

In the first edition of *Guide to Tanzania*, I commented that Mtwara sprawled in a manner suggesting that somebody once intended greater things for it. And indeed they did, as became clear recently when I came across P H Johnston's gushing article about Mtwara Bay in an issue of the Tanganyika Notes and Records dating to the late 1940s.

Prior to World War II, Mtwara was a village of little note when compared to the nearby, more historical settlement of Mikindani. Its one pre-war claim to posterity was that it was used as a location for the original silent version of *The Blue Lagoon.* (According to Johnston, another film crew arrived in 1928 – is there *anybody* out there who can elaborate on his assertion that "strange but unfounded tales reached the home press as a result of this incursion into Mtwara"?).

In February 1947, Mtwara was chosen by the British administration as the port to be used by the infamous Groundnut Scheme of 1946-51. The idea behind this scheme was to turn southern Tanzania into a major groundnut producer; Britain pumped some 30 million pounds into creating the appropriate infrastructure before realising that the land was unsuitable and received insufficient rainfall to grow groundnuts. Not only was the scheme an expensive failure, but by coercing local farmers into replacing subsistence crops with groundnuts, its administrators caused more suffering than they ever alleviated. And an entirely new port was built at Mtwara, "to meet not only the needs of the Groundnut project but also such further requirements as future development beyond the groundnut areas might call for". If you've visited Mtwara, this isn't even funny, just grimly ironic.

In 1992, I met a Dutchman who was working for the fishery department at Mwanza on Lake Victoria. He had been baffled as to why so much of the fish exported from the lake was being sent to Mtwara. On a brief visit to this most remote of Tanzanian ports, situated on a stretch of coast abundantly rich in fish, he established that there was no deep-sea fishing equipment available to the residents of Mtwara. Just a large, modern and utterly useless port.

The surprising thing about Johnston's article, given that colonials are generally portrayed as a bunch of exploitative taskmasters, is its genuine idealism. Paternalistic it might be, culture-bound it most definitely is, but the tone is more than anything one of giddy optimism. The Groundnut project is "a great decision... one that will be, beyond doubt, the turning point in the history of at least one small part of Africa and its people... one that will advance the area and its people and provide opportunities of such progress in so short a time that none would ever have dreamed possible". He even goes so far as to talk of Mtwara as a "future Mombasa".

It is easy enough to sneer when you have hindsight on your side. To give Johnston his due, his otherwise elegiac piece of prose ends soberingly enough: "Let it be hoped," he asks, "that our planners will really plan soundly", a prophetic plea that might as well have been written twenty years ago – or for that matter yesterday.

Fifty years after the Groundnut Scheme was first mooted, I spent an evening with a Danish Aid worker who, after two months observing conditions in an African village, made the chilling observation that the West ought to implement a scheme which would "teach African women how to bring up children properly". She, and all the other culture-bound meddlers who would save Africa from itself, would do well to read Johnston's article, and then to visit Mtwara: a sprawling memorial to good intentions gone awry.

# MTWARA

The small town centre, about 1km inland, is surrounded by open fields. The harbour is 1.5km northeast of this, the market and bus station are about 1km south, the beach is about 2km north, and there is what appears to be a small industrial area east of the harbour.

If Mtwara is less than scintillating, the surrounding coast offers some consolation. A good swimming beach is within easy reach of the town, near the Beach Hotel. Local expats raved about the beach on the sandbar protecting the harbour entrance, but you need a boat to get there. Otherwise, much of the coastline immediately around Mtwara consists of coral flats; interesting for the rock pools that form on them and the wading birds that visit.

## Getting there and away

Buses between Dar es Salaam and Mtwara leave daily from the Morogoro Road bus station and should be booked in advance. A boat, the *Canadian Spirit*, runs between the towns at least once a fortnight; see *Getting around* at the beginning of the chapter.

There are several buses daily between Mtwara and Masasi, and Mtwara and Lindi. These leave when they are full.

## Where to stay

The most attractive places to stay are on the beach, 3km from the bus station. You can walk out or hire a taxi. The cheaper guesthouses are in and around the town centre.

### Moderate

**TCMB Club** This is run by the Cashew Marketing Board, which used to have another name, the initials of which were CATA. Everyone still calls it the CATA Club (pronounced like Carter). It is a pleasant place, not far from the beach, and has a bar and restaurant. Rooms have a fan and mosquito net. $4 double.

**Shangani Club** This overlooks the beach, but is rather dear and a bit disorganised. The food is excellent (worth trying if you are staying at the CATA club), and there is a well-stocked bar. A good second choice if the CATA club is full. $8 per person full board (negotiable if you eat elsewhere).

### Budget

**NBC Club** On the Lindi road about 500m from the town centre, this is the best of the guesthouses, and often full. Meals and drinks are served in the garden.

**Ngomeke Guest House** There are four guesthouses in the town centre, of which this is the most appealing. It's still no great shakes.

**Holiday Lodge** This is the closest guesthouse to the beach, but I thought it scruffy and unfriendly.

**Kisutu Guest House** Near the bus station, this is basic, but clean and friendly. Rooms have mosquito nets and fans. $3 single.

## Where to eat
There are reasonable *hotelis* in the town centre and around the market. The only proper restaurant in the town centre is the **Paradise Hotel**, where western-style meals cost around $1.50. The **Shangani Club** does excellent meals for around $2.50; these must be ordered in advance. The **Beach Hotel** should have a restaurant attached when it re-opens.

# Excursions
The village of Mikindani, 10km north of Mtwara, is far older than its larger neighbour and has considerably more character. Little more than a fishing village now, Mikindani was an important port in the 19th Century. It is where Livingstone set off for his last expedition into the interior, an event commemorated by the predictable plaque, and it has several dilapidated Zanzibar-style buildings, as well as ruins dating back to the slave trade and what appears to be a disused German fort alongside the main road. If you want to take photographs in Mikindani, it's advisable to get written permission from the Police Station in Mtwara – permission is free but bring along your passport.

Mikindani lies on the main Mtwara/Lindi road, on an attractive stretch of coast. It can be visited as a day trip from Mtwara, but could also be quite an interesting place to stay over. A small hotel was being built on a beach about 2km away when we visited; ask at the Paradise Hotel in Mtwara for details.

A canoe ferry runs regularly between Mtwara (leaving from behind the Catholic Church) to an attractive beach on the opposite side of the harbour.

# THE MAKONDE PLATEAU

The Makonde Plateau lies immediately inland of Mtwara and Lindi. It is the home of East Africa's most renowned craftsmen, the Makonde carvers. The Makonde originated in what is now northern Mozambique and have been practising their craft for at least 300 years. In its purest form, the intricate ebony carvings relate to the Makonde cult of womanhood; they are traditionally carried by the (male) carver as a good luck charm. This custom started when the first carver, who according to folklore was a person but not yet a man, carved a piece of wood into the shape of a woman and left it outside his home overnight. Overnight, the carving was transformed into a real woman. Twice the woman conceived, but both times the child died after three days. Each time, the pair moved higher onto the plateau, believing this would bring them luck. The third child lived and became the first true Makonde.

Typically, Makonde carvings consist of one or more people in a highly stylised and distorted form. Traditional carvings often depict a female figure surrounded by children. But, like any dynamic art form, Makonde is responsive to external influences and subject to changes in fashion; in recent years, carvings have become increasingly abstract and have incorporated wider moral and social themes. Recent innovations include *Ujamaa* sculptures, which relate to Tanzania's collective social policy, and *Sheteni*, grotesque but evocative figures modelled on Makonde ancestral spirits. Makonde carvings have become highly collectable in the West and are regarded as amongst the best and most imaginative produced anywhere in Africa.

Many of the carvings you see elsewhere in Tanzania come from the Makonde Plateau (many, too, are carved by Makonde who have settled in Arusha or Dar es Salaam), but you will need contacts to see any on the plateau itself. Most are bought by dealers for distribution in the more touristy parts of the country. In fact, the only carvings we saw in Mtwara were made not of ebony, but of ordinary wood covered in black boot polish. If you can buy directly from the carvers, however, you will get a far better price than you would in Arusha or Dar es Salaam. By cutting out the middleman, the carver will also get a fair price.

Another intriguing aspect of traditional Makonde culture is *sindimba* dancing, performed by men and women together using stilts and masks, but in the ordinary course of things, you are unlikely to come across this.

The two main towns on the plateau are Newala and Masasi. The road to Newala is interesting, climbing the plateau through dense *miombo* woodland and passing numerous Makonde villages. These villages are immaculately neat and orderly, and apparently rarely visited by tourists – every time the bus stopped a crowd of curious children gathered around us and stared in amazement.

There is a strong missionary presence in the area. Most schools and hospitals are run by missions. Some missions insist on importing western luxury goods for local distribution. As a consequence, all sorts of unlikely items are offered for sale at the roadside, ranging from lace petticoats to name-brand chocolates and toiletries.

## Getting there and away

There are regular buses between Mtwara and Masasi. The tar road between Mingoyo and Masasi is in a good state of repair.

There is a bus every other day in each direction between Masasi and Dar es Salaam. This leaves from in front of the Masasi Hotel, not from the regular bus station. Seats should be booked in advance at the Masasi Hotel.

A daily bus runs between Newala and Masasi, leaving Newala at 05.00 and arriving at Masasi at around 11.00. It then returns to Newala. See Lindi for details of buses from Newala to Lindi.

## Newala

Newala is mainly of interest for the drive there, described above. There are a few indifferent guesthouses if you need to spend the night.

## Masasi

The principal town on the Makonde Plateau is an attractive place, surrounded by large granite koppies which reminded me of parts of Zimbabwe. Masasi has a modern atmosphere – it feels remarkably healthy after the lazy degeneracy which characterises many of the coastal towns – but there is nothing much to do there. Unless you arrive late, you will probably want to move on.

If you do stay over, the **Masasi Hotel** is good value. Clean, spacious rooms with fans and mosquito nets cost $2.00/3.50 s/c single/double, and a bar and restaurant are attached. It is ten minutes' walk from the bus station along the main tar road to Lindi. There are also plenty of cheap **guesthouses** along the road between the bus station and the Masasi Hotel. You can eat at the hotel or the nearby **Top Spot Restaurant**, which serves cheap meals and cold beers and sodas in a garden.

Chapter Thirteen

# Zanzibar

*By David Else*

## INTRODUCTION

Zanzibar, a separate state within Tanzania, consists of two large islands, Unguja (Zanzibar Island) and Pemba, plus several smaller islets. Zanzibar Island is about 85km long and between 20km and 30km wide; Pemba is about 75km long and between 15km and 20km wide. Both are flat and low lying, surrounded by coasts of rocky inlets or sandy beaches, with lagoons and mangrove swamps, and coral reefs beyond the shoreline.

Zanzibar used to be hard to reach, and it had a reputation for being expensive and unfriendly. This has changed: the island now positively welcomes tourists. Most visitors come to see the fascinating buildings in the old Stone Town and the many ruined palaces dotted around the island. Other attractions are the clove and coconut plantations and the seemingly endless, palm-fringed tropical beaches.

Farming and fishing are the main occupations on Zanzibar. Most people live in small villages. Cloves are a major export, along with coconut products and other spices. The capital, and by far the largest settlement, is Zanzibar Town or City, on the island's west coast.

Like other coastal areas, Zanzibar is predominantly Muslim. Away from the beaches you should dress modestly.

Accommodation in Zanzibar *must* be paid for in hard currency, preferably US dollars. Public transport and food can normally be paid for in local currency.

## Climate

Zanzibar has a typical coastal climate, warm to hot all year round and often very humid. It receives more rainfall and is windier than the mainland.

## History

Zanzibar has been trading with ships from Persia, Arabia and India for about 2,000 years. From about the 10th century AD, groups of

immigrants from Shiraz (Persia) settled in Zanzibar and mingled with the local Swahili. The Portuguese established a trading station on the site of Zanzibar Town in the early 16th Century. At the end of the 17th Century they were ousted by Omani Arabs.

In 1840, Sultan Said moved his capital from Muscat to Zanzibar. Many Omani Arabs settled on Zanzibar as rulers and landowners, forming an elite group, while Indian settlers formed a merchant class. The island became an Arab state, an important centre of regional politics, and the focus of a booming slave trade. Britain had interests in Zanzibar throughout the 19th Century; explorers such as Livingstone, Speke and Burton began their expeditions into the African interior from there. In 1890 Zanzibar became a British protectorate.

Zanzibar gained independence from Britain in December 1963. In 1964, the Sultan was overthrown in a revolution. Nearly all Arabs and Indians were expelled. Later the same year, Zanzibar and Tanganyika combined to form the United Republic of Tanzania.

Today, the distinctions between Shirazi or Swahili are often blurred. The islanders fall into three groups: the Hadimu of southern and central Zanzibar, the Tumbatu of Tumbatu Island and northern Zanzibar, and the Pemba of Pemba Island. Many people of mainland origin live on Zanzibar; some the descendants of freed slaves, others more recent immigrants. Many of the Arab, Asian and Goan people expelled in 1964 have since returned.

# Getting there and away
## To/from Dar es Salaam
Air Tanzania flies between Dar es Salaam and Zanzibar every day. Tickets cost $43 one-way. The service is not very reliable, but is improving.

A more reliable option is to charter your own plane, at a cost of around US$180 for a six-seater. This can be organised through any travel agent in Dar es Salaam.

Most people prefer to cross to Zanzibar by boat. A number of hydrofoils and catamarans run between Dar es Salaam and Zanzibar daily. They normally take between one-and-a-half and three hours to do the crossing, and charge around US$30 one-way, payable in hard currency. Hydrofoil services include Sea Express and Condor, and catamarans include Kilimanjaro and Flying Horse. Tickets can be bought on the spot at the appropriate kiosk alongside the main jetty on Sokoine Drive; you will rarely have to wait much more than an hour for the next boat.

Much cheaper are the two boats owned by the Zanzibar Shipping Corporation (ZSC). These cost around $4 one-way, payable in local currency, but they only run once a week and the service is unpredictable and unreliable. It is now illegal for foreigners to travel across to Zanzibar by dhow.

It is possible to get from Arusha to Zanzibar in a day by catching the Dar Express coach which leaves Arusha at 06.30 and arrives in Dar es Salaam in time to connect with the 16.00 Sea Express ferry to Zanzibar.

All foreigners leaving Dar es Salaam by boat must pay a port tax of US$5, generally in hard currency.

## To/from Mombasa

Kenya Airways flies three times per week each way between Mombasa and Zanzibar. This service is reliable and costs around $40 one-way. Motorised dhows between Mombasa and Zanzibar cost about $15. They can take over two days and are uncomfortable and dangerously overloaded. Departure days vary; ask around at the old port. Bring your own food and water. Over the last few years, several companies have initiated boat services between Mombasa and Zanzibar, but invariably the service has been stopped within a few months. There is some talk of Sea Express and Flying Horse extending their services to include Mombasa in the near future – but then so was there a few years ago. You'll just have to ask around – if there are boats doing this run, you'll have no difficulty locating them.

## To/from Tanga

Unscheduled dhows run between Tanga, Pemba and Zanzibar about once a week. These take up to two days and are both uncomfortable and dangerous. We have heard stories of shipwrecks.

## Arrival and departure

As Zanzibar is a separate state, you must complete an immigration card and show your visa on arrival, even if you have come from mainland Tanzania. Customs officials may check your bag, but a detailed search is unlikely.

Non-Tanzanians must pay a departure tax of $20 in hard currency when flying out of Zanzibar Airport on international flights (eg to Mombasa). The tax for flights within Tanzania is $0.75.

# ZANZIBAR TOWN

Zanzibar's old quarter, usually called the Stone Town, is a fascinating maze of narrow streets and alleyways which lead the visitor past numerous old houses and mosques, ornate palaces, and shops and bazaars. Many buildings in the Stone Town date from the 19th century slave boom. Houses reflect their builder's wealth: Arab houses have plain outer walls and large front doors leading to an inner courtyard;

Indian houses have a more open facade and large balconies decorated with railings and balustrades. Most are still occupied.

A striking feature of many houses is the brass-studded doors and elaborately carved frames. The size of a door and intricacy of its design was an indication of the owner's wealth and status. The use of studs probably originated in Persia or India, where they helped prevent doors being knocked down by war-elephants. In Zanzibar, studs were purely decorative.

*studs*

The area outside the Stone Town used to be called Ng'ambo (*The Other Side*), and is now called Michenzani (*New City*). Attempts have been made to modernise it: at the centre of Michenzani are some ugly apartment blocks, built by East German engineers as part of an international aid scheme.

Walking is the easiest way to get around Zanzibar Town. Buses, pick-up vans (called *dala-dalas*) and taxis are available. You can also hire bikes and motor-scooters.

# Where to stay

In the last few years, many new hotels of all grades have opened in Zanzibar Town. A small selection is listed below. Hotel rooms must be paid for in hard currency. Most prices include breakfast.

## *Upper range*

One of the most attractive hotels in this range is **Emerson's House** (PO Box 4044, tel: 32153, fax: 33135), which lies in the old town near the market. Originally the home of Sultan Barghash's brother, Emerson's has been completely restored and furnished in traditional Zanzibari style, leading to it being listed by a British newspaper as "one of the great little hotels of the world". From $60-85 self-contained double.

**Mazson's Hotel** (PO Box 3367, tel: 33694, fax: 33695) is a newer place, even though the building itself dates to the early 18th Century. The lounge and lobby are furnished in Zanzibari style, but the rooms, though well-appointed and air-conditioned, are a little on the sterile side. Facilities include satellite television and a business centre. $60-80 self-contained double.

The **Tembo Hotel** (PO Box 3974, tel: 33005), a grand old house on Shangani Street, is the most upmarket place in the Stone Town, with rooms ranging from US$75-100.

Several other hotels offer self-contained doubles for around US$60-80; among the better are:

**Baghani House Hotel** (PO Box 609, tel: 20165, fax: 31816)

**Dhow Palace Hotel** (PO Box 3974, tel: 33012, fax: 33008)

ZANZIBAR STONE TOWN

1 Old Dhow Harbour
2 New Dock
3 Malindi Restaurant
4 Ciné Afrique
5 Warere Guesthouse
6 Malindi Guesthouse
7 Malindi Sports Club (Dhow Office)
8 Malindi Police Station
9 Bwawani Hotel
10 Sea View Indian Restaurant
11 Ijumaa Mosque
12 Pyramid Hotel
13 Narrow Street Hotel
14 People's Bank of Zanzibar
15 Zanzibar Tourist Corporation
16 People's Palace
17 Kiponda Hotel
18 Maharouky Bicycle Hire
19 Floating Restaurant
20 Jamituri Gardens
21 House of Wonders
22 Arab Fort
23 Sama Tours
24 Spice Inn
25 Emerson's House
26 Market
27 Le Pecheur Bar
28 Yoghurt Shop
29 Post Office
30 St. Joseph's Catholic Cathedral
31 Epicure Snack Bar
32 Dolphin Restaurant
33 UMCA Anglican Cathedral
34 Tippo Tip's House
35 Jasfa Tours
36 Africa House Hotel
37 Camlur's Restaurant
38 Flamingo Inn
39 Jamhuri Gardens
40 People's Gardens
41 National Museum

# ZANZIBAR STONE TOWN

**Kirwan Sarai** (PO Box 145, tel/fax: 33524).

There are a couple of very smart hotels south of the town centre.

The **Mbweni Ruins Hotel** (PO Box 2542, tel/fax: 31832/31942) is in the grounds of Mbweni Ruins near St John's Anglican Church. It has well maintained gardens and a small private beach. Rooms cost $85 per person.

The **Zanzibar Reef Hotel** (PO Box 2586, tel: 30208, fax: 30556) lies 7km out of town and 3km from the airport, in landscaped gardens overlooking the sea. There is a squash court, sauna, gym, swimming pool and conference room, as well as facilities for water sports and fishing. From $150 self-contained double.

About 20km north of town, near Chiuni, the **Mawimbini Club Village** (PO Box 4281, tel: 31163) is an international-style resort catering mainly for package tourists. Doubles cost from $100-200 per person.

**Zanzibar Serena Inn** (PO Box 2551, Arusha, tel: (057) 8175/6304, fax: (057) 8282) will open in November 1996.

## Moderate

The new **Shanghani Hotel** near the Post Office on Kenyatta Avenue has self-contained air-conditioned rooms with fridges for $55/double, and a beautiful roof-top dining room.

The **Spice Inn** (PO Box 1029, tel: 30278) is one of the oldest and most atmospheric hotels in the Stone Town, and good value with self-contained doubles starting at $40.

The **Hotel International** (PO Box 3784, tel: 33182) has modern, air-conditioned self-contained doubles starting at US$38.

The **Narrow Street Hotel** (PO Box 3784, tel: 32620) is a small hotel with clean, self-contained doubles, most of which contain traditional Zanzibar beds. Rooms in the main building cost $35, while those in the annexes are slightly cheaper.

The **Hotel Kiponda** is a small, quiet hotel which previously served as a Sultan's harem. Described by one traveller as a "budget Emersons", this place has plenty of character and is good value at $30-40/double.

The **Inn by the Sea Hotel**, a few kilometres off the airport road, has self-contained doubles for $40.

The **Island Guesthouse** lies about 5km offshore on Changuu Island. Doubles cost $25, and camping is permitted. Bookings can be made through the ZTC office on Creek Road.

## Budget

The **Malindi Guesthouse** (PO Box 609, tel: 30165) has been consistently popular with travellers for years. Clean rooms cost $16/24/36 single/double/triple. Another reliable bet is the **Riverman Hotel** (PO Box 1805, tel: 33188), which has good facilities and clean rooms for US$10 per person.

Near the People's Gardens, the **Victoria Guesthouse** and **Garden Lodge** are both unremarkable but adequately clean places with doubles for $16.

Similar in price, and popular with travellers, is the **Flamingo Guest House** on Mkunazini Street.

At the bottom of the price range, the **Pyramid Guesthouse**, behind the Ijumaa mosque near the sea-front, comes highly recommended. Single, double and triple rooms are available, all at $7 per person.

The **Bottoms Up Guest House** is rather more seedy, and difficult to find in the alleys between the Spice Inn and the House of Wonders, but it is popular with travellers, for its book-swap service, cheap and lively bar, and rooms costing only $6 per person.

If you prefer to stay outside of the Stone Town, the **Mtoni Sunset Beach Resort** in Mtoni, 4km north of the port, and the **Fuji Beach Guesthouse** in Bububu, 9km north of the port, both have rooms for $7 per person. Dala-dalas on Route B go right past the Mtoni Sunset Guesthouse and end up in Bububu.

If you come into Zanzibar by boat, expect to be met by a group of hotel touts. Some are quite aggressive, but others are friendly and will find you a suitable hotel if you tell them what you want. It won't cost anything (the tout gets a commission from the hotel) and may save a lot of walking.

## Where to eat

There are now dozens of restaurants catering specifically to tourists, and the following serves as an introduction only.

At the top end of the range, **Emerson's House** has been doing quality food for years, and no doubt the new restaurant in the hotel's annexe will live up to its billing as the "best on the island". Meals cost around $15. For sea-food, **The Fisherman** on Shangani Road is highly recommended, and similar in price to Emerson's.

For meals in the $3-6 range, recommendations include the **Hotel Kiponda** (Zanzibari dishes and sea food), the **Sea View Indian Restaurant** on the sea-front near the People's Palace (vegetarian and meat curries), **Camlur's** on Kenyatta Street (Goan dishes), the **Chit-Chat Restaurant** on Kenyatta Street (Zanzibari and Goan dishes), **Zee Pizza** between the market and Kiponda Street (Italian dishes) and

**Luna Mare Restaurant** on Gizenga Street (European, Indian and Chinese). The **Oman Bar and Restaurant** near the Africa House Hotel serves Swahili dishes on an attractive sea-facing terrace; the **Cave Restaurant** near the Africa House Hotel offers good value fish dishes and yoghurt.

You can eat cheaply in the evening in the Malindi area, near the Ciné Afrique Cinema, where stalls sell cakes, chapatis, samosas and mandazi. In the nearby streets several simple eating houses, including the **Malindi Restaurant** and the **Passing Show Hotel**, cater mainly for locals.

On the seafront, opposite the House of Wonders, is Jamituri Gardens, a gathering place for local people in the evenings, where stalls serve cheap snacks and drinks.

Most tourist restaurants serve beer and many of the larger hotels have separate bars. The roof-top bar at the **Africa House Hotel** is popular at sunset. **Le Pecheur Bar**, next to the Fisherman Restaurant, is the nearest thing in Zanzibar to a pub. It gets lively later in the evening.

# Excursions
## The Stone Town

You can spend many idle hours wandering through the fascinating labyrinth of narrow streets and alleyways of the old Stone Town. The following are some of the more interesting sights:

**The market** The market is worth a visit even if you don't want to buy anything. It's a vibrant place where you can buy anything from fish and bread to sewing machines and second hand car spares.

**The People's Palace** Overlooking the sea on the western edge of the Stone Town, this large white building with castellated battlements was built in the late 1890s. It was the official residence of the Sultan of Zanzibar from 1911 until the 1964 revolution, after which it was renamed the People's Palace. It is now a government office and closed to the public. Photos are not allowed.

**House of Wonders** This square multi-storey building next to the People's Palace is surrounded by tiers of impressive balconies and topped by a clock tower. It was built as a ceremonial palace in 1883, and was the first building on Zanzibar to have electric lights. Local people called it *Beit el Ajaib*, meaning the House of Wonders. Until recently it was the CCM party headquarters. It is now closed, but you can see the huge carved doors and two old bronze cannons with Portuguese inscriptions from the outside.

**The Arab Fort** Next to the House of Wonders, this large brown building with castellated battlements was built by the Omani in the early 18th Century. It is open to visitors. You can reach the top of the battlements and go into some of the towers.

**Tippu Tip's House** Tippu Tip was an influential 19th century slave trader. He knew the African interior well and helped explorers such as Livingstone and Stanley with supplies and route-planning. The house where he lived is near the Africa House Hotel, behind the offices of Jasfa Tours. It is privately owned and closed to visitors, but the huge carved front door can be seen from the street.

**Saint Joseph's Catholic Cathedral** This large cathedral with prominent twin spires is in the Baghani part of town. It was built between 1896 and 1898 by French missionaries and local converts. There are now few Catholics on Zanzibar. The cathedral is rarely used and it is closed to the public.

**The Anglican Cathedral** The Cathedral of the Universities' Mission in Central Africa (UMCA) is on the eastern side of the Stone Town. It was built over the slave market after it closed in 1873, and was completed in 1880. Tradition has it the altar stands on the site of the market's whipping block. Nothing of the slave market remains, though the cellar of the nearby St Monica's Guesthouse is reputed to be the remains of a pit where slaves were kept before being sold.

Sultan Barghash, who closed the slave market, is reputed to have asked Bishop Steere, leader of the mission, not to build the cathedral tower higher than the House of Wonders. When the Bishop agreed, the Sultan presented the cathedral with its clock.

The foundation of the UMCA was inspired by Livingstone: a window is dedicated to his memory and the church's crucifix is made from the tree under which his heart was buried in present-day Zambia. Several other missionaries are remembered on plaques around the cathedral wall, as are sailors who were killed fighting the slave trade and servicemen who died in action in East Africa during World War I.

The cathedral is open to visitors. You should show respect when inside and leave a donation if you can.

**The National Museum** The informative and well-organised museum, at the southern end of the Stone Town, has sections on archaeology, slavery, palaces, sultans, explorers, missionaries, traditional crafts, coins, and clove cultivation. In the annexe there is a library, and a natural history collection where dodo bones are exhibited. In the garden, a group of giant tortoises do their best to keep the grass short. The museum is open from 09.00 to 12.30 and 15.30 to 18.00 every day except Sunday. There is a small entrance charge. You may be asked to make an extra donation by the somewhat over-enthusiastic curator.

## Near Zanzibar Town

Many travellers go on organised tours to the spice plantations. Known as spice-tours, these often include a visit to one of the island's ruins. Tour companies can arrange trips to other parts of the island, such as Jozani Forest Reserve, and boat trips to Chunguu Island. They can also help you with hotel, ship and flight reservations, car hire, and so on. Recommended companies include Jasfa Tours, near the Africa House Hotel (PO Box 4203, tel: 30468), Dolphin Tours near the UMCA cathedral (PO Box 138, tel: 33386) and Sama Tours behind the fort, (PO Box 2276, tel: 33543).

Spice tours can be arranged through independent guides, known locally as *papasi* after a kind of insect. They are cheaper than tour companies, but their tours are often shorter and do not include a proper guide, which will detract greatly from your enjoyment and understanding of what you see. *Papasi* are worth using for boat trips, however, or to arrange transport to the east coast. Some taxi drivers also organise spice tours. Recommended guides include Mr Mitu, who can be found near the Ciné Afrique, and Saleh Mreh, who can also organise special environmental tours. Spice tours cost roughly $10.

Except for the islands, all the places listed below can be visited independently; by scooter or bike, or by a combination of foot and public transport. Maharouky Bicycle Hire (which is also a small grocery shop) between the market and the petrol station rents out bikes for $0.50 per hour or $4 per 24 hours. Nasor Aly Mussa's Scooter Service, near the UMCA cathedral, rents out motor scooters for around $20 per day.

*Dala-dalas* (pick-ups) carry passengers around town and to outlying suburbs. All routes start at the Darajani Bus Station on Creek Road. Route B goes past the Marahubi and Mtoni palaces to Bububu, from where you can walk to Fuji Beach, or the baths at Kidichi.

**Marahubi Palace** This palace, on the coast about 3km north of Zanzibar Town, was built in 1882 for the concubines of Sultan Barghash. At one time he kept around 100 women here. The palace was destroyed by fire in 1899; all that remains are the great pillars which supported the upper storey, and the Persian-style bath-house. You can also see the separate bathrooms for the women, the large bath used by the Sultan, and the original water tanks, now overgrown with lilies.

**Mtoni Palace** The ruins of Mtoni Palace lie a short way north of Marahubi. Mtoni is the oldest palace on Zanzibar, built for Sultan Said in the 1840s. A book written by his daughter Salme describes the palace in the 1850s. At one end of the house was a large bath-house, at the other the quarters where Said lived with his principal wife. Gazelles and peacocks wandered around the large courtyard. Mtoni was abandoned before 1885. Only the main walls and roof remain. It was used as a warehouse in World War I; evidence of this alteration can still be seen.

**Kidichi Persian Baths** These were built in 1850 for Said's wife, Binte Irich Mirza, the grand-daughter of the Shah of Persia, and are decorated with Persian-style stucco. You can enter the bath-house and see the bathing pool and toilets, but there is mould growing on much of the stucco. A colony of bats seems to have taken up residence. To get there from Bububu, a village on the main road north of Zanzibar Town, turn right into a dirt road and follow it for about 4km. The baths are the low white building on the right.

**Kizimbani Persian Baths** These baths near Kidichi were also built in the Persian style for Said. They are not decorated inside. The plantations surrounding Kizimbani originally belonged to Saleh bin Haramil, the Arab trader who imported the first cloves to Zanzibar.

**Mangapwani** Near this village, 20km north of Zanzibar Town, are a large natural cavern and a man-made slave cave. The natural coral cavern has a narrow entrance and a pool of fresh water at its lowest point. The Slave Cave, a square cell cut into the coral, was used to hold slaves after the trade was abolished in 1873. The natural cavern may also have been used to hide slaves, but this is not certain.

To get to Mangapwani village, take the main road to Chuini then follow the left fork towards Bumbwini for 7km. There are occasional buses to Mangapwani on Route 2.

At Mangapwani, a road forks left towards the coast. About 2km past the village this road ends and a small track branches off to the right. Follow this for 1km to reach the Slave Cave. About halfway between Mangapwani and the track to the Slave Cave, a narrow track to the left leads to the natural cavern.

**Fuji Beach** This is the nearest swimming beach to Zanzibar Town. Nearby is a small café where the staff will look after your gear while you swim. Fuji is just past Bububu village.

## Islands near Zanzibar Town

Several small islands lie near Zanzibar Town. Boat-trips arranged with a tour company or independent guide will cost from $20 to $60. To cut the individual cost, it is worth getting a group together.

**Changuu Island** Changuu was originally owned by a wealthy Arab who used it as a detention centre for disobedient slaves. It is also known as Prison Island; a prison was built on it in 1893, but was never used. A path circles the island (about an hour's easy stroll). There is a small beach, a restaurant and a guesthouse. Masks and flippers can be hired for snorkelling. The island is home to several giant tortoises, probably brought from the Seychelles in the 18th Century, which spend much of their time mating. This long and noisy process is apparently successful: the tortoise population is said to be growing. A fee of $1 per person must be paid in hard currency.

**Chapwani Island** Chapwani, also called Grave Island, has held a Christian cemetery since 1879. Most of the graves belong to British sailors who were killed fighting Arab slave ships; others date from World War I. There is a small beach.

## Useful information

**Zanzibar Tourist Corporation** ZTC is the state travel service. You can make bookings for all **ZTC bungalows** at the main office in Livingstone House (PO Box 216, tel: 32344) on the northeast side of town. The ZTC office on Creek Road, near Kenya Airways, sells good maps of Zanzibar.

**Banks and forex bureaux** The People's Bank of Zanzibar is near the Fort. There are several forex bureaux in Zanzibar Town.

**Post and telephones** The main post office in the new part of town has a post restante service. To make international phone calls, you can also use the old post office on Kenyatta Road, in the Shangani area.

**Hospitals and pharmacies** The main public hospital on Zanzibar Island is at Mnazi Moja, on the south side of the Stone Town. Private medical centres include Island Private Hospital, on Soko Muhogo Street, tel: 31837; Afya Medical Hospital, near the Zanzibar Hotel, tel: 31228; and Mkunazini Hospital, near the market, tel: 30076.

**Air companies** The Air Tanzania office is on Vuga Road, near its junction with Creek Road. The Kenya Airways office is at the northern end of Creek Road. Air Zanzibar Ltd (PO Box 1784, tel: 33098) charter flights throughout East Africa. If a plane is flying empty, spare seats are sold to the public. Seats on the newspaper-plane to Dar es Salaam are sold at Musoma Bookshop near the market and cost around $40.

**Dhows** The agent for dhows out of Zanzibar has an office in the Malindi Sports Club on Malawi Road, almost opposite the Police Station.

# THE EAST COAST

This is where you will find the idyllic tropical beaches you dreamed about during those interminable bus rides on the mainland: clean white sand, lined with palms and lapped by the warm blue water of the Indian Ocean. Some travellers come here for a couple of days, just to relax after seeing the sights of Zanzibar Town, and end up staying for a couple of weeks. Visitors on tighter time restrictions always wish they could stay for longer...

The most popular stretch of coast is in the south, between Bwejuu and Makunduchi. There is plenty of accommodation here, and most hotels have restaurants. You can usually buy fish and vegetables in the villages, but supplies are limited; if you are self-catering, stock up in Zanzibar Town.

## Getting there and away

The East Coast can be reached by rented car, scooter or bike. You can also go by bus: no 9 goes to Paje (and sometimes either Bwejuu or Jambiani) and no 10 goes to Makunduchi. Normally one bus leaves Zanzibar Town daily, in the market area. Buses are cheap but slow.

Several tour companies and some independent guides arrange minibuses to the popular East Coast beaches. There is normally at least one vehicle a day in each direction, costing between $3 and $5 per person each way. Unless you specify where you want to stay, minibus drivers prefer to take you to a hotel that gives them commission.

## Where to stay

Half a dozen ZTC bungalows are dotted around Zanzibar Island. These used to be the only out-of-town accommodation and are simple, somewhat delapidated buildings, costing around $20 for the whole building. This includes the services of a caretaker. For information and reservations go to the ZTC office in Livingstone House in Zanzibar Town.

### Paje

There are two guesthouses in this village: the **Ufukwe** and **Amani**. Double rooms cost $7 per person, including breakfast.

### Bwejuu

Bwejuu village is north of Paje. The clean and basic **ZTC bungalow** costs $20 if booked through the ZTC office, but you could try to make an arrangement with the caretaker if you only want one room.

Rooms in **Dere Guesthouse** cost $7 per person, including breakfast. Bungalows cost $20 for up to four people. Meals at the restaurant are good value.

Double rooms at the smarter **Palm Beach Hotel** cost $15 per person; beach bungalows $20 per person. The restaurant serves local meals for between $3 and $6. Advance orders are appreciated. The bar sells beer.

You can explore the offshore reef with snorkelling gear hired from the Dere Guesthouse (around $3 per day). You can also hire bikes (same price) from the hotel and cycle a few kilometres up the beach to a point where the reef can be more easily reached.

## Jambiani

Jambiani is south of Paje, and spreads for several kilometres down the coast. The **Horizontal Inn** and **Oasis Beach Inn** are both small family-run places where clean rooms cost $5 per person, including breakfast. Lunch and dinner cost $2 to $3, and must be ordered several hours in advance. The **ZTC bungalow**, in the usual style for the usual price, appears to be little-used.

The newly-opened **Sau Inn** is very smart and good value at $15 per person, and it also has the best restaurant in Jambiani.

About 2km further south, self-contained rooms at the smarter **Jambiani Beach Hotel** cost $10 per person. The restaurant serves local dishes for between $3 and $6. It has a bar.

A further 1km south, rooms at the friendly and clean **Shehe Guesthouse** cost $8-10 per person, including breakfast. A shop sells biscuits, sodas, and a few items of tinned food. The cafeteria serves fixed-menu lunch and dinner for around $3. Meals must be ordered several hours in advance.

## Makunduchi

Makunduchi New Town is at the southern end of the island. Despite the grand title, it is only a large village, though it does have a bank and a post office. Two **ZTC bungalows** offer the usual facilities for the usual price. Rooms at the **Kigaeni Reef Lodge** cost $7 per person, including breakfast. You can also camp in the garden for $3. It has a basic restaurant. Fishing and snorkelling trips can be arranged.

# Excursions

On the way to the East Coast beaches, you pass two places of interest: the Bi Khole Ruins and Jozani Forest. If you are in a group, you can arrange for a tourist minibus to stop on the way. Alternatively, these places can be reached as a day-trip from Zanzibar Town.

## Bi Khole Ruins

The Bi Khole Ruins are about 6km south of the village of Tunguu, to the west of the main Zanzibar Town-east coast road. Khole was a daughter of Sultan Said (Bi is a title meaning Lady). The house was used up to the 1920s, but only the main walls now stand. The main road there passes through a splendid boulevard of gnarled old mango trees, supposedly planted for Khole. The track to the ruins branches off about halfway down this.

## Jozani Forest Reserve

This remnant of the indigenous forest which once covered much of central Zanzibar is home to several rare mammals. Two endemic subspecies, Kirk's red colobus monkey and Zanzibar leopard, are found nowhere else; Ader's duiker is found only in Jozani and in one forest in Kenya. A red colobus monkey troop is habituated to tourists and close sightings can be almost guaranteed – a thrilling experience! The entrance to Jozani is off the main road, a few kilometres south of Pete.

## Kizimkazi Mosque

At the small settlement of Dimbani, near Kizimkazi village west of Makunduchi, are the remains of the oldest known mosque in East Africa. Kufic inscriptions date it to 1107AD. Kizimkazi was then a large walled city, traditionally founded by a king called Kizi. Little of the city remains, but the mosque has been rebuilt several times, most recently in about 1800.

The Kufic inscriptions, around the niche at the eastern end of the mosque (facing Mecca), are in the decorative floriate style. Similar inscriptions have been found in old buildings in Persia. The silver pillars on either side of the niche are decorated with pounded shells from Mafia Island. Two decorative clocks, which show Swahili time, were presented by local dignitaries. Recently-installed electrical sockets do not have a comparable degree of style or decoration.

To see inside the mosque, now protected by a corrugated iron roof, you must find the caretaker who lives nearby. It is respectful to cover any bare limbs and take off your shoes when you enter.

# PEMBA

Pemba Island lies northeast of Zanzibar, and directly east of Tanga. It is smaller than Zanzibar and has a more undulating landscape. It is also more densely vegetated, with both natural forest and plantation; it now produces more cloves than Zanzibar does. Few tourists visit Pemba and facilities are limited. For many people, this is its main attraction.

During holidays, traditional bull fights are sometimes held on Pemba. The origins of this sport are uncertain; it may have been a Portuguese introduction. Pemba is a centre for traditional medicine and witchcraft. People seeking cures for spiritual or physical afflictions come from Zanzibar Island and the mainland – even as far away as Uganda and Zaire – to see Pemba's doctors.

The island's largest town is Chake Chake, north of which lies the main port, Wete. Mkoani is a smaller port in the southwest. There are banks and post offices in Chake Chake, Wete and Mkoani, but only the Chake Chake bank can change travellers cheques. The main hospital in is Chake Chake. There is a ZTC office next to the ZTC Hotel in Chake Chake.

## Getting there and away

Air Tanzania flies between Zanzibar and Chake Chake a few times a week, but is notoriously unreliable. A charter company, Air Zanzibar, flies the same route. Spare seats cost around $35.

ZSC ships go between Zanzibar and Mkoani twice a week; they are cheap but unreliable. Dhows sometimes sail between Zanzibar and Mkoani, but there is no schedule; enquire at the Malindi Sports Club (see *Zanzibar Town*).

Dhows between Pemba and Tanga or Mombasa are irregular and less than idyllic. Mapicha Travelling Agency on the main street in Wete knows about dhows to Tanga.

## Where to stay/eat

There is a **ZTC hotel** in each of Chake Chake, Wete and Mkoani. Identical in style (angular concrete), they are all run down but clean and cost $10 per person, including breakfast.

**Sharook Guest House** in Wete is a simple family-run place near the bus station ($5 per person). The private guesthouse due to open in Mkoani in 1993 will cost about the same; contact Faizin Tours (see *Tour Companies* below) for details.

There are also two private guesthouses in Chake Chake. The **Star Inn** lies 3km north of town near the Gombani Stadium, and has rooms ranging from $7/single to $25/self-contained double. The staff is friendly and the food is good. The **Nassir Guesthouse** lies 2km north of town in Machomane. Rooms cost from $5-10 per person.

Meals at the ZTC hotels cost between $2 and $4. The **Standard Café** and **Naas Restaurant** in Chake Chake and the **Annuwar Restaurant** in Wete serve cheap, basic meals. There is a pleasant open-air café at the end of Wete's main street.

# Excursions

Chake Chake is linked to Wete by bus and dala-dala number 6, and to Mkoani by number 3. These normally run in the morning.

You can sometimes hire bicycles through the receptionist at the ZTC Hotel in Chake Chake, or through Faizin Tours in Mkoani. A Mr Nassour, contactable through the ZTC Hotel in Chake Chake, rents out a Suzuki 4x4 and driver for about $20 per day (petrol is extra). If you want to visit Mesali Island or the Ras Mkumbuu Ruins by boat, he also rents out a motor boat for about $35 per day (including petrol and captain).

Faizin Tours in Mkoani (PO Box 70, Mkoani, tel: 6028 or PO Box 702, Zanzibar Town, tel: 32501) is a cooperative encouraging small-scale environmentally sensitive tourism on Pemba. They can arrange trips to Mesali Island or the beach at Wambaa Bay.

**Ras Mkumbuu Ruins** These 11th century ruins on the end of the peninsula west of Chake Chake include the remains of a mosque and several pillar-tombs. The most enjoyable way to reach Ras Mkumbuu is by boat, combined with a visit to Mesali Island.

**Mesali Island** This small island west of Chake Chake is surrounded by a coral reef. Its idyllic beach is good for swimming, especially if you have a mask and snorkel. The notorious pirate Captain Kidd is reputed to have had a hideout here in the 17th century.

**Pujini Ruins** This is about 10km southeast of Chake Chake. You can walk there and back in a day, but it is easier to travel by hired bike or car. The ruins are the remains of a 13th century Swahili town, known locally as Mkame Ndume (milker of men) after a despotic king who forced the inhabitants to carry large stones for the town walls while shuffling on their buttocks. The overgrown remains of the walls and ditches can be seen, as can a walkway which joined the town to the shore, some wide stairways that presumably allowed access to the defensive ramparts, and the site of the town's well.

Appendix One

# Language

## INTRODUCTION

Swahili, the official language of Tanzania, is a Bantu language which developed on the East African coast about 1,000 years ago and has since adopted several words from Arabic, Portuguese, Indian, German and English. It spread into the Tanzanian interior along with the 19th century slave caravans and is now the *lingua franca* in Tanzania and Kenya, and is also spoken in parts of Uganda, Malawi, Rwanda, Burundi, Zaire, Zambia and Mozambique.

Even if you are sticking to tourist areas, it is polite and can be useful to know a bit of Swahili. In Dar es Salaam, Zanzibar, Arusha, Moshi and the northern game reserves, you can get by with English well enough. If you travel in other parts of the country, you will need to understand some Swahili.

There are numerous Swahili-English dictionaries on the market, as well as phrasebooks and grammars. The most useful dictionary is D V Perrot's *Concise Swahili and English Dictionary* (Hodder and Stoughton, 1965) as it has two sections – one translating each way – as well as a basic grammar. Peter Wilson's *Simplified Swahili* (Longmans) is regarded as the best book for teaching yourself Swahili. Of the phrasebooks, Lonely Planet's is probably the best. It is best to buy a Swahili book before you arrive in Tanzania; they are difficult to get hold of once you are there.

For short-stay visitors, all these books have practical limitations. Wading through a phrasebook to find the expression you want can take ages, while trying to piece together a sentence from a dictionary is virtually impossible. In addition, most books available are in Kenyan Swahili, which often differs greatly from the purer version spoken in Tanzania.

The following introduction is not a substitute for a dictionary or phrase-book. It is not so much an introduction to Swahili as an introduction to communicating with Swahili speakers. Before researching this guide, my East African travels had mainly been in Kenya, Uganda and parts of Tanzania where English is relatively widely spoken. We learnt the hard way how little English is spoken in most of Tanzania. I hope this section will help anyone in a similar position to get around a great deal more easily than we did at first.

## Pronunciation

Vowel sounds are pronounced as follows:

a   like the a in *father*
e   like the e in *wet*
i   like the ee in *free*, but less drawn-out
o   somewhere between the o in *no* and the word *awe*
u   similar to the oo in *food*

The double vowel in words like *choo* or *saa* is pronounced like the single vowel, but drawn out for longer.

Consonants are in general pronounced as they are in English. *L* and *r* are often interchangeable, so that *Kalema* is just as often spelt or pronounced *Karema*. The same is true of *b* and *v*.

You will be better understood if you speak slowly and thus avoid the common English-speaking habit of clipping vowel sounds – listen to how Swahili-speakers pronounce their vowels. In most Swahili words there is a slight emphasis on the second last syllable.

## Basic grammar

Swahili is a simple language in so far as most words are built from a root word using prefixes. To go into all of the prefixes here would probably confuse people new to Swahili – and it would certainly stretch my knowledge of the language. They are covered in depth in most Swahili grammars and dictionaries. The following are some of the most important:

### Pronouns

| | |
|---|---|
| *ni* | me |
| *u* | you |
| *tu* | us |
| *wa* | they |
| *a* | he or she |

### Tenses

| | |
|---|---|
| *na* | present |
| *ta* | future |
| *li* | past |
| *ku* | infinitive |

### Tenses (negative)

| | |
|---|---|
| *si* | present |
| *sita* | future |
| *siku* | past |
| *haku* | negative, infinitive |

From a root word such as *taka* (want) you might build the following phrases:

| | |
|---|---|
| *Unataka soda* | You want a soda |
| *Tutataka soda* | We will want a soda |
| *Alitaka soda* | He/she wanted a soda |

In practice, *ni* and *tu* are often dropped from simple statements. It would be more normal to say *nataka soda* than *ninataka soda*.

In many situations there is no interrogative mode in Swahili; the difference between a question and a statement lies in the intonation.

## Greetings

There are several common greetings in Swahili. Although allowances are made for tourists, it is rude to start talking to someone without first using one or other formal greeting. The first greeting you will hear is *Jambo*. This is reserved for tourists, and a perfectly adequate greeting, but it is never used between Tanzanians (the more correct *Hujambo*, to which the reply is *Sijambo*, is used in some areas).

The most widely-used greeting is *Habari*, which more-or-less means *What news*. The polite reply is *Mzuri* (good). *Habari* is rarely used by Tanzanians on its own; you might well be asked *Habari ya safari*, *Habari ako* or *Habari gani* (very loosely, *How is your journey, How are you* and *How are things* respectively). *Mzuri* is the polite reply to any such request.

When we were in Tanzania, *Mambo* was a fashionable greeting, especially on the coast. Few tourists recognise this greeting; reply *Safi* and you've made a friend.

In Tanzanian society it is polite to greet elders with the expression *Shikamu*. To the best of my knowledge this means *I hold your feet*. In many parts of rural Tanzania, children will greet you in this way, often with their heads bowed and so quietly it sounds like *Sh..oo*. Don't misinterpret this by European standards (or other parts of Africa where *Mzungu give me shilling* is the phrase most likely to be offered up by children); most Tanzanian children are far too polite to swear at you. The polite answer is *Marahaba* (I'm delighted).

Another word often used in greeting in *Salama*, which means peace. When you enter a shop or hotel reception, you will often be greeted by a friendly *Karibu*. This means *Welcome*. *Asante sana* (thank you very much) seems an appropriate response.

If you want to enter someone's house, shout *Hodi!*. It basically means *Can I come in?* but would be used in the same situation as *Anyone home?* would in English. The normal response will be *Karibu* or *Hodi*.

It is respectful to address an old man as *Mzee*. *Bwana*, which means *Mister*, might be used as a polite form of address to a male who is equal or senior to you in age or rank, but who is not a *Mzee*. Older women can be addressed as *Mama*.

The following phrases will come in handy for small talk:

| | |
|---|---|
| Where have you just come from? | *(U)natoka wapi?* |
| I have come from Moshi | *(Ni)natoka Moshi* |
| Where are you going? | *(U)nakwenda wapi?* |
| We are going to Arusha | *(Tu)nakwende Arusha* |
| What is your name? | *Jina lako nani?* |
| My name is Philip | *Jina langu ni Philip* |
| Do you speak English? | *Unasema KiEngereze?* |
| I speak a little Swahili | *Ninasema KiSwahili kidigo* |
| Sleep peacefully | *Kulala salama* |
| Bye for now | *Kwaheri sasa* |
| Have a safe journey | *Safari njema* |
| Come again (welcome again) | *Karibu tena* |
| I don't understand | *Sielewi* |
| Say that again | *Sema tena* |

# Numbers

| | | | |
|---|---|---|---|
| 1 | *moja* | 30 | *thelathini* |
| 2 | *mbili* | 40 | *arobaini* |
| 3 | *tatu* | 50 | *hamsini* |
| 4 | *nne* | 60 | *sitini* |
| 5 | *tano* | 70 | *sabani* |
| 6 | *sita* | 80 | *themanini* |
| 7 | *saba* | 90 | *tisini* |
| 8 | *nane* | 100 | *mia (moja)* |
| 9 | *tisa* | 150 | *mia moja hamsini* |
| 10 | *kumi* | 155 | *mia moja hamsini na tano* |
| 11 | *kumi na moja* | 200 | *mia mbili* |
| 20 | *ishirini* | 1,000 | *elfu (moja)* or *mia kumi* |

## Swahili time

Many travellers to Tanzania fail to come to grips with Swahili time. It is essential to be aware of it, especially if you are catching buses in remote areas. The Swahili clock starts at the equivalent of 06.00, so that *saa moja asubuhi* (hour one in the morning) is 07.00, *saa mbili jioni* (hour two in the evening) is 20.00 etc. To ask the time in Swahili, say *Saa ngape?*.

Always check whether times are standard or Swahili. If you are told a bus leaves at nine, ask whether the person means *saa tatu* or *saa tisa*. Some English speakers will convert to standard time, others won't. This does not apply so much where people are used to tourists, but it's advisable to get in the habit of checking.

# Day-to-day queries

The following covers such activities as shopping, finding a room etc. It's worth remembering most Swahili words for modern objects, or things for which there would not have been a pre-colonial word, are often similar to the English. Examples are *resiti* (receipt), *gari* (car), *polisi* (police), *posta* (post office) and – my favourite – *stesheni masta* (station master). In desperation, it's always worth trying the English word with an *ee* sound on the end.

## Shopping

The normal way of asking for something is *Ipo?*, which roughly means *Is there?*, so if you want a cold drink you would ask *Ipo soda baridi?*. The response will normally be *Ipo* or *Kuna* (there is) or *Hamna* or *Hakuna* (there isn't). Once you've established the shop has what you want, you might ask *Nataka koka mbili* (I want two cokes). To check the price, ask *Shillingi ngape?*. If your Swahili is limited, it is often simpler to ask for a brand name: *Omo* (washing powder) or *Blue Band* (margarine), for instance.

## Accommodation

The Swahili for guesthouse is *nyumba ya wageni*. In my experience *gesti* works as well, if not better. If you are looking for something a bit more upmarket, bear in mind *hoteli* means restaurant. We found self-contained (*self-contendi*) to be a good keyword in communicating this need. To find out whether there is a vacant room, ask *Ipo chumba?*

## Getting around

The following expressions are useful for getting around:

| | |
|---|---|
| Where is there a guesthouse? | *Ipo wapi gesti?* |
| Is there a bus to Moshi? | *Ipo basi kwenda Moshi?* |
| When does the bus depart? | *Basi ondoka saa ngapi?* |
| When will the vehicle arrive? | *Gari tafika saa ngapi?* |
| How far is it? | *Bale gani?* |
| I want to pay now | *Ninataka kulipa sasa* |

## Foodstuffs

| | |
|---|---|
| Avocado | *Parachichi* |
| Bananas | *Ndizi* |
| Bananas (cooked) | *Matoke/ batoke* |
| Beef | *(Nyama ya) ngombe* |
| Bread (loaf) | *Mkate* |
| Bread (slice) | *Tosti* |

| | |
|---|---|
| Coconuts | *Nazi* |
| Coffee | *Kahawa* |
| Chicken | *Kuku* |
| Egg(s) | *(Ma)yai* |
| Fish | *Samaki* |
| Food | *Chakula* |
| Fruit(s) | *(Ma)tunda* |
| Goat | *(Nyama ya) mbuzi* |
| Mango(es) | *(Ma)embe* |
| Maize porridge | *Ugali* |
| Meat | *Nyama* |
| Milk | *Maziwa* |
| Onions | *Vitungu* |
| Orange(s) | *(Ma)chungwa* |
| Pawpaw | *Papai* |
| Pineapple | *Nanasi* |
| Potatoes | *Viazi* |
| Rice (cooked plain) | *Wali* |
| Rice (uncooked) | *Mchele* |
| Rice | *Pilau* |
| Salt | *Chumvi* |
| Sauce | *Mchuzi/supu* |
| Sugar | *Sukari* |
| Tea (black/milky) | *Chai (ya rangi/maziwa)* |
| Vegetables | *Mbogo* |
| Water | *Maji* |

## Days of the week

| | |
|---|---|
| Monday | *Jumatatu* |
| Tuesday | *Jumanne* |
| Wednesday | *Jumatano* |
| Thursday | *Alhamisi* |
| Friday | *Ijumaa* |
| Saturday | *Jumamosi* |
| Sunday | *Jumapili* |

## Useful words and phrases

| | |
|---|---|
| Afternoon | *Alasiri* |
| Again | *Tena* |
| And | *Na* |
| Ask (I am asking for...) | *Omba (ninaomba ...)* |
| Big | *Kubwa* |
| Boat | *Meli* |
| Brother | *Kaka* |
| Bus | *Basi* |
| Car (or any vehicle) | *Gari* |
| Child (children) | *Mtoto (watoto)* |
| Cold | *Baridi* |

| | |
|---|---|
| Come here | *Njoo* |
| Excuse me | *Samahani* |
| European(s) | *Mzungu (wasungu)* |
| Evening | *Jioni* |
| Far away | *Mbale kubwa* |
| Friend | *Rafiki* |
| Good (very good) | *Mzuri (mzuri sana)* |
| Goodbye | *Kwaheri* |
| Here | *Hapa* |
| Hot | *Moto* |
| Later | *Bado* |
| Like (I would like...) | *Penda (ninapenda)* |
| Many | *Sana* |
| Me | *Mimi* |
| Money | *Pesa/shillingi* |
| More | *Ingine/tena* |
| Morning | *Asubuhia* |
| Nearby | *Karibu/mbale kidogo* |
| Night | *Usiku* |
| No | *Hapana* |
| No problem | *Hamna tatizo* |
| Now | *Sasa* |
| Only | *Tu* |
| OK or fine | *Sawa* |
| Passenger | *Abiria* |
| Pay | *Kulipa* |
| Please | *Tafadhali* |
| Person (people) | *Mtu (watu)* |
| Road/street | *Barabara/mtaa* |
| Shop | *Duka* |
| Sister | *Dada* |
| Sleep | *Kulala* |
| Slowly | *Polepole* |
| Small | *Kidogo* |
| Soon | *Bado kidogo* |
| Sorry | *Polepole* |
| Station | *Stesheni* |
| Stop | *Simama* |
| Straight or direct | *Moja kwa moja* |
| Thank you (very much) | *Asante (sana)* |
| There is | *Ipo/kuna* |
| There are | *Zipo* |
| There is not | *Hamna/hakuna* |
| Thief (thieves) | *Mwizi (wawizi)* |
| Time | *Saa* |
| Today | *Leo* |
| Toilet | *Choo* |

| Tomorrow | *Kesho* |
|---|---|
| Want (I want...) | *Taka (ninataka...)* |
| Where | *(Ipo) wapi* |
| Yes | *Ndiyo* |
| Yesterday | *Jana* |
| You | *Wewe* |

Useful conjunctions include *ya* (of) and *kwa* (to or by). Many expressions are created using these; for instance *stesheni ya basi* is a bus station and *barabara kwa Moshi* is the road to Moshi.

# African English

Although some Tanzanians speak a bit of English, few speak it fluently or grammatically. Africans who speak English tend to structure their sentences in a similar way to how they would in their own language: they speak English with Bantu grammar.

For a traveller, knowing how to communicate in African English is just as important as speaking a bit of Swahili, if not more so. It is noticeable that travellers who speak English as a second language often communicate with Africans more easily than first language English-speakers.

The following ground rules may help you to communicate with people who speak a limited amount of English:

• *Unasema KiEngereze?* (Do you speak English?). This small but important question may seem obvious. It isn't.

• Greet in Swahili then ask in English. It is advisable to go through the Swahili greetings (even *Jambo* will do) before you plough ahead and ask a question. Firstly, it is rude to do otherwise; secondly, most westerners feel uncomfortable asking a stranger a straight question. If you have already greeted the person, you'll feel less need to preface a question with phrases like *I'm terribly sorry* and *Would you mind telling me* which will confuse someone who speaks limited English.

• Speak slowly and clearly. There is no need, as some travellers do, to speak as if you are talking to a three-year old, just speak naturally.

• Phrase questions simply and with Swahili inflections. *This bus goes to Moshi?* is better than *Could you tell me whether this bus is going to Moshi?*; *You have a room?* is better than *Is there a vacant room?* If you are not understood, don't keep repeating the same question, find a different way of phrasing it.

• Listen to how people talk to you, and not only for their inflections. Some English words are in wide use; others are not. For instance *lodging* is more likely to be understood than *accommodation*.

• Make sure the person you are talking to understands you. Try to avoid asking questions that can be answered with a yes or no. People may well agree with you simply to be polite.

• Keep calm. No-one is at their best when they arrive at a crowded bus station after an all-day bus ride; it is easy to be short tempered when someone cannot understand you. Be patient and polite; it's you who doesn't speak the language.

## Appendix Two

# Further Reading

## History

The following are recommended as general introductions to African or East African history:

McEvedy, C. *Penguin Atlas of African History* (Penguin, 1980)
Oliver, R & Fage, J D *A Short History of Africa* (Penguin, 1988, 6th edition)
Oliver, R & Crowder, M (eds) *Cambridge History of Africa* (Cambridge, 1982)
Iliffe, J *A Modern History of Tanganyika* (Cambridge, 1979)
Maxon, R *East Africa: An Introductory History* (Heinemann, 1989)
Odhiambo, E & Ouso, T & Williams, J *A History of East Africa* (Longman, 1977)
Sutton, J *A Thousand Years of East Africa* (British Institute in East Africa, 1990)

Oliver and Fage's *Short History* has a thorough and useful further reading section. The following books cover the era of European exploration and colonisation:

Moorehead, A *The White Nile* (Hamish Hamilton; Penguin, 1960)
Hibbert, C *Africa Explored: Europeans in the Dark Continent* (Penguin, 1982)
Packenham, T *The Scramble for Africa* (Wiedenfield and Nicholson, 1991)

## National parks

For most visitors, the excellent series of booklets issued by Tanzania National Parks will be more than adequate. These are usually available from the National Parks Office in Arusha for $2.50, or from stalls in Arusha and Dar es Salaam for around $5. There are booklets for the Ngorongoro Conservation Area and Arusha, Tarangire, Kilimanjaro, Serengeti, Lake Manyara, Ruaha, Mikumi and Gombe Stream National Parks. The Gombe Stream booklet is also useful if you are visiting Mahale Mountains.

If you are interested in the poaching problem in Tanzania, Nicholas Gordon's *Ivory Knights* (Chapman, 1991) makes compelling reading.

A number of field studies and photographic books cover individual national parks:

**Gombe Stream**
Goodall, J *In the Shadow of Man* (Collins, 1971)
Goodall, J *Through a Window* (Wiedenfield and Nicholson, 1990)

**Kilimanjaro**
Reader, J *Kilimanjaro* (Elm Tree Books, 1982)
Savage, M *The Walker's Guide and Map to Kilimanjaro*

**Mahale Mountains**
Nishida, T *The Chimpanzees of Mahale* (University of Tokyo, 1990)

**Lake Manyara**
Douglas-Hamilton, I *Amongst the Elephants* (Penguin, 1978)
Matthiessen, P and van Lawick, H *Sand Rivers* (Aurum, 1981)

**The Rift Valley**
Willock, C *Africa's Rift Valley* (Time-Life Internationa,l 1974)
Smith, A *The Great Rift: Africa's Changing Valley* (BBC, 1988)

Both of these are coffee-table in style, but have informative text. The latter is based on an excellent BBC three-part documentary.

**Serengeti**
Grzimek, B *Serengeti Shall Not Die* (Collins, 1959)
Goodall, J & Van Lawick, H *Innocent killers* (Houghton Mifflin, 1971)
Hanby, J & Bygott, D *Lions Share* (Collins, 1981)
Schaller, G *Serengeti: A Kingdom of Predators* (Collins, 1973)
Iwago, M *Serengeti* (Thames and Hudson, 1987)
Van Lawick, H *Savage Paradise* (Collins, 1977)
Van Lawick, H *Among Predators and Prey* (Elm Tree, 1986)

# Field guides

The following will be adequate for most visitors' needs:

Dorst, J and Dandelot, P *A Field Guide to the Larger Mammals of Africa* (Collins, 1970)
Blundell, M *A Field Guide to the Wild Flowers of East Africa* (Collins, 1987)
Carcassan, R *Handguide to the Butterflies of Africa* (Collins, 1971)
Van Perlo, B *Birds of Eastern Africa* (Collins, 1995)
Ber van Perlo's *Birds of Eastern Africa* is the first comprehensive one-volume field guide to the birds found in Tanzania, Kenya, Uganda, Ethiopia and Eritrea, making it an essential purchase for anybody with more than a passing interest in Tanzania's abundant bird life. All 1488 birds recorded in this region are described and all but one are illustrated. There are useful distribution maps. Don't confuse it with John Williams' *Field Guide to the Birds of East Africa*, also published by Collins. This older book only illustrates around half the species present in the region, and it is practically useless when it comes to the identification of migrants, localised species, and more difficult bird groups such as small birds of prey, larks and warblers.

Almost without exception, the best African mammal field guides come from South Africa, but until recently none of these has covered species which are only found north of the Zambezi. The appearance of Chris and Tilde Stuart's *Southern, Central and East African mammals: A Photographic Guide* (Struik, 1993) is therefore highly welcome. It's remarkably lightweight but very thorough, with photographs, distribution maps and text covering 152 mammal species; definitely the book I'll take with me next time I visit East Africa. Rather less compact, but highly absorbing if you are interested in animal behaviour, is Richard Estes' *The Safari Companion* (Russel Friedman Books, South Africa; Chelsea Green, USA; Green Books, UK, 1992), which contains detailed behavioural studies of virtually all the large mammal species found in East and southern Africa.

When I was last there, a good range of South African-published field guides was available at most large bookshops in central London.

## Travel guides

Two other travel guides are available to Tanzania, both published in Africa. Neither has much practical information, but they are strong on background. I enjoyed Gratian Luhikula's *Tourist Guide to Tanzania* (Travel Promotion Services, Dar es Salaam, 1991 edition) for its historical information, and would recommend it highly as a companion to this guide. *Spectrum Guide to Tanzania* (Camerapix, 1992) is lavishly illustrated and informative, but not really practical for backpackers. It would make a good memento.

David Else's *Guide to Zanzibar*, also published by Bradt Publications, expands greatly on the information about Zanzibar and Pemba he supplied for this book.

## Fiction

Very little fiction has been written about Tanzania. William Boyd's *The Ice-cream War*, set in Tanzania during World War I, is a notable exception, and well worth reading before you go to Tanzania, especially if you plan to visit the Rufiji and Makonde regions. Although it has a fictional setting in West Africa, there are links between the same author's bestselling *Brazzaville Beach* and chimp behaviour first noted at Gombe Stream (I should add these similarities are limited to the chimps; the human characters are fictional).

Even less fiction has been written by Tanzanians: no-one I know (including people who have studied African literature) can name any Tanzanian writers. There are, however, a number of well-known Kenyan authors who write in English: try Ngugi wa Thiongo or Meja Mwenge.

## Maps

A number of maps covering East Africa are available. The best is the Austrian-published Freytag-Berndt 1:2,000,000 map. Most European maps seem to get their accommodation information from the same source, and they show plenty of hotels which either never existed or closed years ago. The best map of Tanzania that I have seen is the 1:1,250,000 map produced by BP. This is generally available in Dar es Salaam and Nairobi, but don't bank on it. One major inaccuracy on this map is that Mlalo in the Usambara Mountains is shown in the wrong place (it should be where Mbangala is).

Town plans and 1:50,000 maps of most parts of the country can be bought from the Department of Lands and Surveys on Kivukoni Front in Dar es Salaam.

## Bibliography of Tanzania

Darch, C *Tanzania* (World Bibliographical Series; Clio Press, 1988).

This series lists and describes every book of importance on a given country. Invaluable to those with special interests or insatiable curiosity.

# Bradt Publications

## Travel Guides

41 Nortoft Road • Chalfont St Peter • Bucks • SL9 0LA • England
Fax/Telephone: 01494 873478

August 1996

Dear Reader

Do write to tell me about your trip to Tanzania.
Every visitor experiences a country differently, and
the readers of this guide will collectively stay in
more hotels, eat in more restaurants, and experience
many more aspects of the country than I could ever
hope to as an individual. Every letter will help to
make for a second edition which is as current as the
first and which reflects the widest possible spectrum
of experiences and opinions and, not least, it is
always a pleasure to hear from other travellers and
to be kept in touch with countries I have come to
know well.

Happy travels,

Phillip Briggs

# INDEX